SS 3

£1·50

1983

THE SCOTTISH CHURCH
1688–1843

THE
SCOTTISH CHURCH
1688–1843

The Age of the Moderates

ANDREW L. DRUMMOND

and

JAMES BULLOCH

EDINBURGH

THE SAINT ANDREW PRESS

© A. L. DRUMMOND & J. BULLOCH 1973
First published 1973 by
The Saint Andrew Press
121 George Street, Edinburgh EH2 4YN

PRINTED IN GREAT BRITAIN
BY R. & R. CLARK, LTD, EDINBURGH

CONTENTS

FOREWORD

Born at Jedburgh on 4 February 1902, a son of the manse, Andrew Landale Drummond studied for the Scottish ministry at Edinburgh University and afterwards, as a post-graduate student, at Montpellier, Marburg, and Hartford. After a spell in charge of the Scottish Mission Church at Tiberias in Palestine he returned to Scotland and became minister of the Eadie Church in Alva from 1932 until his death on 7 May 1966. All his life he was both pastor and scholar. In 1930 he received the degree of Ph.D. from Edinburgh University and in 1965 that of D.D. from St Andrews. His interests in Church History were wide. In 1934 he published *The Church Architecture of Protestantism*, and this was followed by *Edward Irving and his Circle* in 1937, *The History of American Protestantism* in 1949, *The Churches in English Fiction* in 1950, *German Protestantism since Luther* in 1951, and *The Kirk and the Continent* in 1957, as well as many articles and papers.

At his death he left behind him a manuscript on the history of the Scottish Church since 1688. The first half of this, covering the years from 1688 to 1843, has been considerably rewritten and it is therefore now issued as a joint work. At every stage in the book the present writer owes a great obligation to Dr Drummond, but he must also acknowledge indebtedness to the Rev. Henry Sefton, Ph.D., the Rev. Arthur Fawcett, Ph.D., for permission to consult unpublished theses, to the Rev. Ian Muirhead, B.D., and the Rev. T. R. Robertson, B.D., for counsel and assistance, and to Mr T. B. Honeyman of the Saint Andrew Press.

JAMES BULLOCH

ABBREVIATIONS

AGA *Acts of the General Assembly.* Edinburgh 1688–1843.
APS *Acts of the Parliament of Scotland.* Records Commission.
    Edinburgh 1824–75.
Fasti Hew Scott, *Fasti Ecclesiae Scoticanae.* 1st edition. Edin-
    burgh 1866–71.
SCHS *Scottish Church History Society.*
SHR *Scottish Historical Review.*
SHS *Scottish History Society.*

The Decay of Intolerance

A Protestant wind carried the transports of William of Orange down the English Channel while it kept King James's navy at anchor and, on 5 November 1688, the anniversary of the Gunpowder Plot, brought the Prince of Orange to land at Torbay. Among the returning exiles aboard the Dutch ships were Gilbert Burnet and William Carstares. Burnet had been minister of the country kirk of Saltoun in East Lothian under the Second Episcopate, and before him lay a splendid future as Bishop of Salisbury. Carstares had been brought up in the opposite camp. His father had been a Covenanting minister from the west country who had been captured by Cromwell at the battle of Dunbar in 1650 but who afterwards, as one of the Protesters, had been a member of the minority group of Presbyterian extremists who had been the most zealous Scottish supporters of the Commonwealth. The Protester's son, who had endured the thumbscrew to make him betray King James's opponents, was now to return to Scotland to become minister, first of Greyfriars and then of the High Kirk of Edinburgh, Principal of Edinburgh University, and Moderator of the General Assembly. A practical man, he was prepared to leave the trappings of power to others so long as he had the reality. Though he lacked the scholastic attainments with which Macaulay[1] credited him, he was a remarkable man, shrewd, courageous, reasonable, upright, and determined. "An honest and pious man in essentials, he had his full share of the wisdom of the serpent." He might have been — and in fact was regarded by many as being — a representative of that uncompromising Presbyterianism which had opposed the Crown since 1638 and now appeared to be triumphant. Appearances were deceptive. There were men among his colleagues whose mind was still that of the men who fought

[1] Lord Macaulay, *History of England*, ii, p. 440.

at Dunbar, but Carstares was no longer of their outlook. There can have been few points where he differed seriously from Burnet, but loyalty to the Church of his fathers drew him back to accommodate himself, up to a point, to men whose prejudices he did not share.

No more than token resistance was offered to William. On 20 December King James VII of Scotland and II of England secretly sent his wife and child out of the kingdom. Following them in the darkness of the next morning he was captured by some fishermen and sent back to Whitehall; but his presence was an embarrassment and his absence no menace, so he was allowed to sail for France. The fury and passion of the seventeenth century had spent themselves and it was only in the Celtic lands of Scotland and Ireland, out of touch with the general mood of European civilization, that a stand was made for the Jacobite cause. The Lowlands did not lift a finger for Scotland's rightful king, but in the Highlands John Graham of Claverhouse, Viscount Dundee, raised the clans in the summer of 1689 as Lieutenant-General for his absent king. Just before sunset on 27 July his Highlanders scattered General McKay's army with a single charge at Killie-crankie, but Claverhouse himself lay dead, killed — it was said — by a silver bullet. When Steenie Steenson saw the ghosts of the enemies of the Covenanters in Wandering Willie's Tale[1] he saw "Claverhouse, as beautiful as when he lived, with his long, dark, curled locks, streaming down his laced buff-coat, and his left hand always on his right spule-blade, to hide the wound that the silver bullet had made. He sat apart from them all, and looked at them with a melancholy, haughty countenance." Claverhouse had always been something of a man apart; he left no successor; without him the rising was doomed; and at Dunkeld his Highlanders were defeated by the newly raised regiment of Cameronians, scarcely a quarter of their number.

In Ireland James's concessions to his co-religionists in the latter part of his brief reign had given him greater expectations of support. On 22 March 1689 he landed at Kinsale in County Cork, supported by French soldiers and diplomats, the native population, the Anglo-Irish aristocracy, and Tyrconnel, the viceroy. Had it not been for the Scottish colonists settled in the north the whole of the country would have been his without a blow. In the first decade of the century an attempt had been made to colonize Ulster,

[1] Sir Walter Scott, *Redgauntlet*, xi.

and such limited success as it had had was due to discontented Scots of Presbyterian outlook. These Ulster Scots secured their first Presbyterian minister when Edward Bruce,[1] formerly of Bothkennar near Falkirk, was admitted to Broadisland in County Antrim in 1613, and their numbers were greatly augmented when a Scottish army under General Robert Munro arrived in April 1642 to quell the rebellion. Its chaplains and officers, ministers and elders of the Church of Scotland, formed a Presbytery which met for the first time at Carrickfergus on 10 July 1642. From the descendants of these men came the only body of Irish opponents of King James. They proclaimed William and Mary, drew their people in from the outlying and undefended farms, and concentrated on a few strong towns until relief should come from across the channel. At Enniskillen, where the town blocked the crossing between the two lakes which separated Connaught from Ulster, a combination of courage and initiative held their opponents at a distance. At Derry the gates of the walled town were closed against King James and Tyrconnel in the great siege which was to become a legend in Ulster. On 24 June 1690 King William landed at Carrickfergus. In one of the critical battles of Irish history he forced the passage of the Boyne Water. King James despaired too quickly and abandoned his Irish followers whose courage had deserved a more heroic leader. In 1691 they made their last stands at Aughrim and Limerick. Provision was made in the terms of surrender for toleration, but on the Sunday after the signing the Bishop of Meath,[2] preaching in Christ Church in Dublin, argued in his sermon that with such faithless people no faith need be kept. King William removed him from the Privy Council, but it was the Bishop's spirit that prevailed and any opportunity of peace in Ireland was lost. Meantime the safety of Presbyterianism in Ulster had been assured. What was virtually a Scottish colony had been created, and through the eighteenth century there was to be a steady movement between Ulster and Scotland and a continuous influence upon the church life of both.

In December 1688, as the news of William's advance on London reached Edinburgh, rioters sacked the chapel of Holyroodhouse and assaulted prominent Roman Catholics such as the Earl of Perth. Alarmed at the course of events the Scottish bishops sent

[1] John M. Barkley, *A Short History of the Presbyterian Church in Ireland*, p. 3.
[2] Sir George Clark, *The Later Stuarts*, p. 310.

Dr Rose, the Bishop of Edinburgh, to look after their interests in the south. By this time, as William frankly told Rose in the brief and unsatisfactory conversation which they had, he had learned that the strength of Presbyterianism in Scotland had been greatly overstated, but any chance that he might support the episcopal cause was forfeited by the decision of the Scottish bishops to stand by their oath to King James.[1]

The Estates of Scotland met on 14 March 1689. After some characteristic disputes over the precedence of the commissioners, they declared the throne vacant on 4 April, and on 11 April they offered it to William and Mary and ordered them to be proclaimed at the Mercat Cross of Edinburgh. All ministers were commanded to pray publicly and by name for their new sovereigns, those in Edinburgh on Sunday 14 April, others south of the Tay on 21 April, and those north of it on 28 April. At intervals the Estates interrupted their other business to change the constitution of the National Church. On 25 April they repealed the Act of Charles II which declared the royal supremacy, and ordered all Presbyterian ministers who had been deposed since 1661 to be reinstated. On 26 May the Westminster Confession — but not the National Covenant — was approved and engrossed in the record; and on 7 June Episcopacy was abolished, not on grounds of high principle but of expediency. It was "contrary to the inclinations of the generality of the people". Untested at the time, this is a highly doubtful statement. In the summer of 1689 Lord Tarbet,[2] an Episcopalian, wrote, "The matter of church government hath been made a pretence for the troubles of Scotland now for a hundred years. Episcopacy appears insufferable to a great party, and Presbytery is as odious to another. The Presbyterians are the more zealous and hotter; the other more numerous and powerful. The present parliament is more numerous of Presbyterians by the new method of election of burghs; but the major part of the nobility and barons are not for Presbytery", and General McKay, writing from a Presbyterian standpoint, substantially agreed with his judgment. Even had the means been available, no one had sufficient confidence in the outcome to put the matter to the test. While parliament was considering what action to take the commissioners of the Diocesan Synod of Aberdeen arrived with a

---

[1] George Grub, *Ecclesiastical History of Scotland*, iii, pp. 295-8.
[2] Ibid. iii, p. 317.

petition that the Estates would convene a free General Assembly for the rectifying of disorders, the healing of divisions, and the settlement of the polity of the Church.[1] But the wary leadership of the Estates decided to take no risks and placed the government of the Church in a minority group, those ministers expelled since 1661 and the ministers and elders whom they should admit, and it authorized them to hold a General Assembly.[2]

William could not afford to be intolerant. When the coronation oath was put to him he hesitated at the clause which obliged him to "root out all heretics and enemies to the true worship of God", and accepted it only on the understanding that it did not require him to persecute.[3] The uncertainty of his position forbade his becoming the instrument of a mere party, even had he been so inclined. But the command that ministers should pray for the sovereigns provided for the deposition of any who refused, and throughout the Lowlands the riot at Holyrood had set the pattern for the rabbling of all ministers who had conformed to Episcopacy. Wodrow, who chronicled the sufferings of the Covenanters, brought his work to a sudden halt at this point when fortunes were reversed and it was the turn of others to be victimized. Half a century of civil war and intolerance had left bitter memories too strong to be forgotten overnight. Between the Covenant in 1638 and the Restoration in 1660 some 210 royalist or Episcopalian ministers had been deprived of their charges. Under Charles II it was the turn of the Presbyterians of whom, by 1684, 312 had been deposed, apart from 63 who lost their parishes under the Test Act of 1681. Many of these last were Episcopalians, penalized by a badly drafted act, but among the Presbyterians was John Veitch of Westruther, who had already been deprived in 1662 and then reinstated under the Indulgence. Leaving the manse for the second time in 1682 he philosophically pointed out the peat stack to his successor and asked him to leave as good a one when his turn came. That day had now come, perhaps not so quickly as Veitch anticipated, for a good peat stack took four years to build, but still in good time.

[1] F. Goldie, *Short History of the Episcopal Church in Scotland*, p. 29.
[2] *APS*, ix, pp. 133–4.
[3] A. Ian Dunlop, *William Carstares and the Kirk by Law Established*, p. 66. Thomas Maxwell, "William III and the Scots Presbyterians", *SCHS*, xv, p. 175.

Of thirty charges in the Presbytery of Edinburgh one, Camp-vere, can be ignored, for it was in Holland and already had a Presbyterian minister. Three charges were vacant. Twenty-five ministers were deprived in one way or another. Only Thomas Wilkie of the Tolbooth Kirk, who had been nominated as a Presbyterian by the Town Council in 1687, remained. This is representative of what happened over all Scotland south of the Tay. At Spott in East Lothian Archibald Buchan, the minister, was roused from his bed about 3 a.m. on the morning of 27 January 1689 by three armed men who led him in his nightshirt through the chill night air into the kirk. There, by candlelight, in a parody of the act of institution as practised under the Episcopate, he was formally deposed by depriving him of the pulpit bible and the kirk keys.[1] Such things went on everywhere except where ministers had already fled their parishes.

In East Lothian[2] and Berwickshire,[3] later to be strongholds of the Moderates, there were exceptions. John Gibson of Oldhamstocks was got rid of in 1690 on a charge of drunkenness, an offence of which presbyteries took no note except in times of political stress. At Humbie, an Episcopalian remained until 1695, and another at Morham until 1697. At Garvald, Archibald Muir survived until deposed by the Synod on 5 November 1719 for drunkenness and swearing and the even more heinous offence of saying that "the king had no more right to the crown than had the muircock". At Saltoun, another East Lothian parish, the Presbytery was refused access to the church at a vacancy in 1696; Archibald Lundie was then ordained and held his charge as Father of the Kirk till his death in 1759. "He had been bred an old Scotch Episcopalian," wrote Alexander Carlyle,[4] "and was averse to the Confession of Faith. The Presbytery showed lenity towards him, so he did not sign it to his dying day, for which reason he never could be a member of Assembly." At Tranent an Episcopalian was removed in 1689, but the deprived minister of Cromarty was installed in his place by the Earl of Winton with the support of the parishioners. An Act of Parliament on 9 June 1695 was

[1] *Fasti*, i, p. 381.
[2] James Bulloch, "Conformists and Nonconformists", *Transactions of the East Lothian Antiquarian and Field Naturalists' Society*, VIII, pp. 70–84.
[3] James Bulloch, "Ecclesiastical Intolerence", *Berwickshire Naturalists' Club*, XXXVI, pp. 148–58.   [4] Alexander Carlyle, *Autobiography*, p. 105.

needed to expel him, but he continued to conduct worship in a house in the town which had similarly been used by the Presbyterians until then, and it was not until 1740 that a reliable Presbyterian held the parish. Outside this area there were a few other exceptions, two in Peeblesshire, five in the Presbytery of Duns, and two in the Presbytery of Chirnside. In the west of Scotland there were five uncertain cases, but otherwise every minister south of Forth and Clyde was deprived. In Ireland, William had been ready to show some generosity to his opponents, but their defeat had been so conclusive that the Irish Protestants could afford to disregard the King's intention. But in Scotland, Episcopalianism was strong and the Presbyterian ascendancy anything but sure. Until the death of Queen Anne there was always a fair chance that Episcopacy might regain its former position, and it was largely due to the shrewdness and restraint of Carstares that Presbyterianism survived and emerged in control.

William and his advisers had been anxious that the treatment of Episcopalian ministers would be wise and generous and that as many as abstained from support of the Jacobite cause should be retained in their parishes, but popular violence and the actions of the Estates led to deprivations more arbitrary and widespread than any previously known in Scotland. This led to what had, until then, hardly been acknowledged, a complete separation between Presbytery and Episcopacy in Scotland.[1] Presbyterian and Episcopalian ministers, as Principal Rule had said,[2] had been indistinguishable in doctrine and even in liturgy, but "we disagree in government, and therefore we cannot rule together". On this plausible pretext Episcopalian ministers could thus be excluded from the courts of the Church, most of which they would otherwise have controlled. "The Assembly of 1694," said a partisan historian,[3] "set itself deliberately to make arrangements in the most liberal way for the reception into the Church of ministers who conformed to Prelacy. . . . It redounds to the credit of this Assembly, that it looked at the question of the needs of Scotland in no narrow, fanatical spirit, but was willing, if it could be honourably managed, to include in the service of the Church

[1] Grub, op. cit. iii, p. 309.
[2] John Warrick, *The Moderators of the Church of Scotland from 1690–1740*, p. 41.　　　　　　　　　　[3] Ibid. p. 68.

those ministers whose sympathies were evangelical, even though their views on ecclesiastical government were not in harmony with the prevailing opinion. The fact is that if this had not been done, wide districts in the north of Scotland would have been deprived of the ordinary public means of grace."

The facts, however, are contrary. The intolerance of the victorious Presbyterians exceeded any previous instance in this one respect. Only to the north of Tay where general support for Episcopalian ministers frustrated their opponents did the Presbyterians fail to eject them, until the Rising of 1715 brought government help. In Perthshire ten ministers survived 1689. In Argyll all but three were at least interrupted in their tenure, but some recovered their position. Archibald McLaine was displaced in Lochgoilhead by a Presbyterian, John Monro, but he was received back into communion in 1691 and was minister at Kilbride until removed again in 1698.[1] These men were needed, but in any case it was often hard to get rid of them. Colin Campbell[2] of Ardchattan defeated his bishop's attempts to depose him for immorality, survived the Revolution Settlement, and in 1694 wrote to the Synod to state that prolonged biblical study had convinced him of the Presbyterian case. No such conversion is related of Dugald Lindsay[3] of Glenorchy, but his people, armed with drawn swords and with two pipers playing the Dead March, escorted to the parish boundary the minister sent to read his deposition. Archibald McLauchlan[4] of Arrochar equalled the feat of the Vicar of Bray. Inducted as a Presbyterian under the Protesters in 1658, he accepted first the Restoration Episcopate and then the Presbyterianism of 1690 to die as senior minister of his parish in 1731. In Episcopalian Aberdeenshire ministers remained in their charges until death or the disaster of 1715. A characteristic instance is that of Andrew Jeffrey[5] of Alford, inducted in 1679, whose prayers for the success of the Rising led to his deposition, together with that of three neighbouring ministers, each of them settled in their parishes for more than thirty years. The records are complicated, for plain necessity was often disguised as generosity, but the survival of these ministers is a tribute, not to any forgiving spirit

---

[1] *Fasti*, III, pp. 27, 42. William Ferguson, "Problems of the Established Church in the West Highlands", *SCHS*, XVII, pp. 18–19.

[2] *Fasti*, III, pp. 62–4.   [3] *Fasti*, III, p. 67.

[4] *Fasti*, II, p. 340.   [5] J. Warrick, op. cit. pp. 315–16.

among the Presbyterians, but to their impotence in the north. In 1688 the Church of Scotland had 926 parishes. Between then and 1716 the ministers of 664 were deprived. Of the rest, many had died; few who served under the Episcopate escaped.

"The Antediluvians" — those ministers who had survived since the depositions of 1661 and 1662 — had not the slightest intention of trying to include within the bounds of the Revolution Settlement the parish ministers, now nicknamed "the Curates", who had served under the Episcopate. As we have seen, they were highly successful in dealing with them. But in another respect King William's intention was fulfilled. The old intemperate passions were out of favour. Neither the new generation of students for the ministry, nor the laity as a whole, were prepared, for the most part, to associate themselves with Covenanter or Episcopalian; they chose the Church of their country, and as they came to influence in it they were to obliterate much of the older Presbyterianism. The form remained, but the spirit had changed. Episcopalians had increasingly accepted the outlook of the Eastern Church by which the Church was rightly subject to the Crown;[1] Presbyterians had followed the Hildebrandine tradition of the Western Church, but their demand for a theocracy had equally been one for popular rights. Theirs was a tradition which went back, not only to George Buchanan, but to John Major.[2]

For a few years after the Covenant the General Assembly had threatened to be the governing body not merely of the Church but of the country, and it had in the lower courts of the Church, which were closely integrated with the structure of a landed society, what the Crown had not, a potential system of local administration. Neither William nor his advisers relished the reappearance of this body in Scotland, but once he had committed himself to the Presbyterians there was no alternative. It had therefore to be made innocuous, and so all possible precautions were taken beforehand. The Act of Parliament had so restricted its membership that it contained only sixty "Antediluvians", ordained before 1662, 56 who had been received into the ministry by them during the years of strife, and 47 elders, or 163 in all.[3]

[1] D. H. Whiteford, "Jacobitism as a Factor in Presbyterian and Episcopalian Relationships", *SCHS*, xvi, pp. 138-9.
[2] John Major, *A History of Greater Britain*, SHS, pp. 213-15.
[3] J. Warrick, op. cit. p. 40.

The vast majority of Scottish parishes were thus unrepresented.

A more pertinacious body of men it would have been hard to find, so the leading members were flattered by letters from high quarters urging them to restrain the zealots. Lord Crauford, an enthusiast who might have expected to be Lord High Commissioner, was diplomatically passed over and the more responsible Lord Carmichael appointed instead. When the King's letter[1] was read at the second sitting on 17 October 1690 it demanded restraint. "We expect that your management shall be such as we shall have no reason to repent of what we have done. A calm and peaceable procedure will be no less pleasing to us than it becometh you. We never could be of the mind that violence was suited to the advancing of true religion; nor do we intend that our authority shall ever be a tool to the irregular passions of any party. Moderation is what religion enjoins, neighbouring churches expect from you, and we recommend to you." "Great revolutions of this nature," said the Assembly in reply to this straight warning, "must be attended with occasions of complaint, and even the worst of men are ready to cry out of wrong for their justest deservings; but as your Majesty knows these things too well . . . so we assure your Majesty that we shall study that moderation which your Majesty recommends."

The Assembly could afford to write thus as most of its opponents in the ministry south of Tay had already received what was called "their justest deservings". On the other hand King William's counsel, a new voice in seventeenth-century Scotland and one that could not be ignored, was backed by a large body of national opinion. Those who had been admitted to sit in the Assembly were in no way representative of the country as a whole or of its church life, and their position was not so strong that they could afford to presume upon it. Events were to prove that although they had been given formal control of the Assembly they were unable to shape the outlook of more than a minority of the membership of the Church.

Certain consequences had followed from the divisions of the Western Church in the sixteenth century and the association of its branches with national states. First of these had been the religious wars of the seventeenth century, but the failure of the Covenanting Rising of 1679 and Argyll's fiasco in 1685 showed that, so far as

[1] *AGA*, 1690, ii.

Scotland was concerned, these days were ended. A second had been the confusion of the respective spheres of Church and State. Here matters were not so plain. From the year of the Covenant until 1652 the records of the General Assembly are full of business which would normally fall to civil government, but from 1690, though the popular character of Presbyterianism and its relationship with the national life remained intact, they are almost entirely concerned with what might be reckoned the proper business of a church court. A third and persistent consequence was religious intolerance. This was still far from dead. The Cameronians of the west country complained bitterly against what they called "a sinful toleration". Wodrow[1] complained that had the Act of 1663 against the Quakers "been prosecuted with the same vigour as those against the Presbyterians were, we might in this land have been freed from that dangerous sect". But the times were changing. The temper of the new age can be seen in the fact that whereas in Covenanting times ecclesiastical issues had been uppermost in the public mind no one can read through the parliamentary proceedings of 1689 and 1690 without being aware that they now took second place, and by a long way. Presbyterians had reasons of their own for hating bishops, but Parliament had got rid of them because, among other reasons, their position among the Lords of the Articles had ensured crown control of the Estates of Scotland. With their departure the Scottish Parliament was to display initiative and independence unknown before.

Having gained so much, the Assembly was cautious. It appeased the enthusiasts by an emotional Act proclaiming a national fast and humiliation, lamented "the great decay of piety under the late prelacy", and appointed two commissions to visit north and south of the Tay respectively "for purging and planting of churches". In any case, by this time almost all Episcopalian ministers who were vulnerable had already been removed, so a promise to obey the King's instructions cost little.

The new generation of churchmen had lost the old theological passion. Despite an enormous flood of pamphlets no theological writings of any quality were produced by either side for many years.[2] A list of Carstares' books in 1685 consists almost entirely of what he must have bought in college days. John Calvin was

---

[1] Robert Wodrow, *History of the Church of Scotland*, i, p. 377.
[2] J. Hill Burton, *History of Scotland*, vii, p. 466.

missing from the list of authors and theology was represented, not by any of the great names, but by students' textbooks. His taste had been sufficiently catholic for him to buy a copy of the Poems of George Herbert.[1] Unexpectedly, he also had a volume from the pen of Robert Leighton. The Covenanting remnants in the west might still treasure Samuel Rutherford and George Gillespie, but if the men who now formed public opinion in Scotland had read any theology at all they had been influenced, more than they knew, by the devotional writings of Leighton and Henry Scoughal, perhaps even by those of John Forbes of Corse and Robert Barclay of Urie, the Quaker. Scholastic Calvinism, arid in tone when compared with the writings of Calvin himself, was coming to be confined to the classroom and the followers of Covenanting tradition. In the north the Episcopalian clergy had been supported by their people. Many laymen in the south had little or no active hostility, but the reason behind their failure to lift a finger in defence of their ministers was that they were uninterested in theological quarrels, tired of disputes, and prepared to worship under a minister of any party. The Barrier Act[2] of 1697, while apparently conservative, in fact insured against hasty action by extremists of either party by requiring that any innovations should be sent down to the presbyteries and only enacted when their assent had been secured.

But intolerance, even if declining, was far from dead, and the terrible record of Scottish persecutions of witchcraft, which had been somewhat restrained under the second Episcopate, was not yet closed. Of many cases, the most famous is that associated with the name of Christian Shaw,[3] the daughter of the laird of Bargarran in Renfrewshire. At the age of eleven she was cursed by a woman servant whom she had detected in some petty theft and commenced a succession of fits during which she denounced various persons as having caused the fits through the intervention of Satan. Seven of them were brought before the court at Paisley. On 13 April 1697 before the hearings began, the Reverend James Hutcheson of Killallan preached before the judges on Exodus 22:18, "Thou shalt not suffer a witch to live". "We have here,"

[1] A. I. Dunlop, op. cit. p. 31.
[2] *AGA*, 1697, ix.
[3] Hugo Arnot, *Criminal Trials in Scotland*, pp. 361–6. Robert Chambers, *Domestic Annals of Scotland*, ii, pp. 167–74.

he said,[1] "a precept of the law of God in reference to a certain sort of malefactors to be found within the visible church, even among the Israelites. These malefactors are called witches. The person to whom this direction is given is not expressed . . . but may be easily understood by the nature of the precept itself. It is a precept of the Judicial Law given to the judges of the children of Israel that was a national church as having the power of the sword committed to them." He then went on to define a witch, to tell of the compact with Satan, the nature of the black art, and the mark of Satan. Witches could forecast the future and practised infanticide. Those who let such wicked persons escape must expect the vengeance of God as befell Ahab when he released Benhadad. On 10 June on the Gallow Green of Paisley a gibbet and a fire were prepared together. Five of the accused were hung for a few minutes on the one, then cut down, and burned in the other. A sixth would have died, but he had anticipated his persecutors by committing suicide in his cell. The story of the supposed witches of Pittenweem, the victims of unspeakable barbarity connived at by local ministers and magistrates, is best left untold.[2] The earliest case in which the central authorities showed some inclination to let the accused escape is that of a dozen witches before the Privy Council in January 1700. In 1727 two poor women of Loth in Sutherland, mother and daughter, were condemned to death at Dornoch. The girl made her escape. Part of the charge had been that her mother had transformed her into a pony for the devil to ride upon, and the girl was said to have been crippled in her hands and feet as a result. Not till 1736 was the death penalty for witchcraft abolished. Scotland was not alone in this. A witch was burned near Angers in France as late as 1780.

A second field of intolerance has more contact with the modern world. "It cannot be denied," said the Assembly[3] of 1690, "that there hath been in some a dreadful atheistical boldness against God, some have disputed the being of God, and His providence, the divine authority of the Scriptures, the life to come, and immortality of the soul." When the Assembly met in January 1696 it complained that there were those who, under the name of Deists, in fact taught atheism.[4] In the following December a boy

[1] SHR, VII, pp. 390ff.   [2] R. Chambers, op. cit. ii, p. 298.
[3] AGA, 1690, xii.   [4] AGA, 1696, xxi.

of eighteen named Thomas Aitkenhead,[1] the son of an Edinburgh surgeon, was charged with having said that theology was "a rhapsody of feigned and ill-invented nonsense". He had called the Old Testament "Ezra's Fables",[2] and the New Testament "The History of the Impostor Christ". The charges against him were based on a variety of incidental remarks made over the course of a year. Passing by the Tron Kirk one winter night he had said to a companion that he would like to warm himself in "the place Ezra called Hell". But behind these remarks there lay a fairly consistent rejection of the Christian faith drawn from reading of a type new to Scotland. Aitkenhead had accepted pantheism in an elementary form. God and nature were one, he had said, and had existed from all eternity. He dismissed the concepts of creation and redemption, laughed at the doctrine of the Trinity as "not worth any man's refutation", and at the doctrine of the Incarnation as a contradiction in terms. Christianity, he was confident, "would be utterly extirpated by the year 1800". Aitkenhead did not deny the charges, but pleaded that he had read these things in the books of some atheist writers which had been lent to him by a witness. "May it therefore please your lordships to have compassion on my young and tender years, not being yet a major, and that I have been so innocently betrayed . . . that I do truly own the Protestant religion . . . and am resolved, by the assistance of Almighty God, to make my abhorrence of what is contained in this libel appear to the world in my subsequent life and conversation." Strong prejudices must have been aroused, for serious flaws in the prosecution and judgment were ignored at the time, and the court lacked the elementary humanity to appoint counsel for the prisoner. Aitkenhead may have been rash and outspoken, but his opinions were not his alone. Despite all this he was found guilty — on Christmas Eve — and sentenced "to be taken to the Gallow-lee on the eighth of January, between the hours of two and four in the afternoon, and to be hanged; his body to be buried at the foot of the gallows, and his moveable estate to be forfeited".[3] Even among those who did not share his outlook there was sympathy for the boy. Five persons refused to sit on the jury that heard his case and were fined 100 merks each. And there

[1] R. Chambers, op. cit. ii, pp. 160–6.
[2] cf. Richard Simon, *Histoire critique du Vieux Testament*, 1678.
[3] H. Arnot, op. cit. pp. 324–7.

was some resentment against the city clergy, who had pursued an ambiguous course, and cannot be held innocent of his death.[1] The evils of the seventeenth century had made contact with the scepticism which they had done so much to create and provided a strange prelude to the century of the Enlightenment.

In a third field steady intolerance, though unequal to the ferocity of these terrible instances, was meted out to Episcopalian ministers so far as circumstances made possible. A minority, largely confined to the south-west, hated Episcopacy on doctrinal and historical grounds, but north of Tay, where half the country's population lived,[2] the Episcopalians had general support and were the Church of the people; while south of Tay there were many, especially among the landed classes, who shared their outlook, or at least were indifferent to the dispute. In their eyes, Presbyterianism was a revolutionary cause. But the refusal of the Scottish bishops to acknowledge William as king had thrust him into the acceptance of the Presbyterians, with whom otherwise he might not have had much in common. Up to a point, therefore, the enemies of the Episcopalians could harass them to their heart's content. Expelled from their charges and deprived of their stipends, the Episcopalian ministers were constantly harried. Typical of their experience is the fate of two such deprived clergy who were known to have held services in Dumfries according to the rites of the Book of Common Prayer. One Sunday in February 1692 about sixteen "mean country persons living about four or five miles from Dumfries, who disowned both Presbyterian and Episcopal ministers, and acknowledged none but Mr Houston",[3] dragged both of them out of town, took away their prayer books, thrashed them, and then released them. Early next morning one of the prayer books was burned at the Mercat Cross. The Privy Council censured the Provost, warning him not to permit the excuse for such happenings again. In other words, he was to prevent the use of the Prayer Book.

One party to such troubles had cause to hope, and the other to fear, that the Revolution Settlement might be no more than temporary, and each had good grounds. William had been anxious

---

[1] J. Warrick, op. cit. pp. 100–2.

[2] T. C. Smout, *A History of the Scottish People, 1560–1830*, p. 119.

[3] M. Hutchison, *The Reformed Presbyterian Church in Scotland*, pp. 76, 129, 398–9.

to include the Episcopalians in the new establishment and had retained contact with them as long as possible. He kept a careful eye on the General Assembly. As the Assembly of 1690 drew to a close there was discussion about the date of the next until the Lord High Commissioner rose, declared it dissolved, and appointed another to meet on 1 November 1691. But no such meeting took place. A royal proclamation adjourned it till January 1692, for William was exerting his authority.[1] In the spring of the year when he was in Holland he received representatives of the Episcopalian clergy and took some well-meaning but rather ineffective steps on their behalf. Provided they acknowledged his title to the throne and signed the Westminster Confession they were to keep their benefices and share in the government of the Church. A number applied to the Assembly of 1692 for admission on these terms, but the Assembly first kept them waiting and then, to the fury of the Lord High Commissioner, shelved the matter by referring it to a committee. Without naming another date, he dismissed the Assembly, but the Moderator[2] protested and the members agreed to meet again on the third Wednesday of August 1693. A clash between the Crown and the Church was thus in the offing. On 19 May 1693 Parliament[3] imposed an oath that all should acknowledge William and Mary as sovereigns, *de jure* as well as *de facto*. Until this had been done, no one could be a member of the Assembly. On royal instructions the Privy Council postponed the Assembly arranged for August 1693 until 16 December, and again until 29 March 1694. Similarly William changed the date of the next meeting from April to July, then to November, and finally to December 1695. To Presbyterians who held it to be the right of the Church to hold Assemblies at will, this was as Erastian as anything that James VI had done, and the Lord High Commissioner[4] emphasised the point when he said, "You are now met in the Assembly conform to the King's appointment".

If this tension raised the hopes of Episcopalians, the accession of Queen Anne in 1702 did so further, and there was always the prospect that the exiled Stewart King might succeed her, if not on the throne of England, at least on that of Scotland. To prevent this, negotiations for a union began in 1705, and part of the price

[1] T. Maxwell, op. cit. p. 186.   [2] Ibid. p. 189.
[3] *APS*, ix, p. 264.   [4] T. Maxwell, op. cit. pp. 186–90.

for the union of 1707 was the security provided for the Church of Scotland in the Treaty. Until this time the distinguishing marks of the Scottish Episcopalians had been their Jacobitism and episcopal orders. A third factor now appeared, and one much against the wishes of many of their laity; a growing liturgical outlook among their clergy which had been stimulated by association with English Nonjurors who had used their freedom to revert to the First Prayer Book of Edward VI. It is hard for a modern reader to realize that the Assembly so construed its position as to legislate, not merely for its own congregations, but for those outside its membership; but for the older school of Scottish Presbyterianism the Assembly was as much a part of the government as was Parliament, its decisions as binding on the nation and, at times, even more so. In 1707 the Assembly[1] revealed how far its members had failed to understand the changed times by legislating against the use of the liturgy by Episcopalians and seeking government support. There had been widespread, if ineffective, hostility to the Union of 1707 and had the Church taken over the leadership of the opposition the negotiations would, at the very least, have faced great obstacles but, whether or not the restraining influence was that of Carstares, the Assembly refrained from stimulating patriotic feeling. If the legislation of the Estates of Scotland since 1688 had failed to show the Church that any return to the partnership of Covenanting times was out of the question, the surrender of Scotland's independence to an English majority at Westminster might have done so. That lesson was now to be learned by experience.

In 1709 the Reverend James Greenshields, an Episcopalian who had taken the oath to Queen Anne and prayed for her and so was indulged, opened a meeting-house opposite St Giles for the conduct of worship according to the Book of Common Prayer. His landlord raised a case against him and the Dean of Guild ejected him. When other premises were found the Presbytery instructed him to desist, but Greenshields replied that as he was not one of their clergy it was none of their business. The magistrates then had him arrested and sent to the Tolbooth. In November 1709 the Court of Session more or less agreed with the magistrates' contention that "there needs no law condemning the English service, for the introducing the Presbyterian worship

[1] *AGA*, 1707, xv.

explodes it as inconsistent", and they left Greenshields in jail until he should give an undertaking to stop. To the great surprise of the magistrates, who had scarcely realized that the Treaty of Union now made this possible, he next appealed to the House of Lords. His appeal was upheld. After a year in jail he was released and was free to conduct worship as he and his congregation wished.[1] The magistrates had to pay damages.

So the hopes of Episcopalians grew stronger while a succession of Acts of Parliament, passed by the Tory ministry which had replaced the Whigs, gave great offence to the nominally dominant Presbyterians. On 3 March 1712 the royal assent was given to an Act of Toleration which gave freedom to the Episcopalian clergy of Scotland to conduct worship according to the Prayer Book upon condition that they took the oath of allegiance, renounced the Jacobite cause, and prayed for Queen Anne and the Princess Sophia of Hanover. There was an immediate outcry in Scotland. The General Assembly confirmed the protests which had been made by its Commission when the first tidings of the Bill had reached Scotland.[2] What made the blow more painful was the requirement that, not only Episcopalians, but also Presbyterians were obliged to swear this Erastian oath. Once again the Commission and the Assembly protested,[3] asserting that the new legislation was explicitly contrary to the Treaty of Union. "We cannot possibly be silent," they wrote, but they were in a cleft stick, for this Erastian legislation was laid upon them by a Protestant Succession which they were not free to repudiate. A clause in the Act had drawn the fangs from the Church's ancient weapon of excommunication by restricting it to spiritual penalties and applying it only to her own people. But this was not the worst. Patronage had been abolished in 1690, and the choice of a minister had been given to the elders and heritors, subject to the consent of the congregation; but to the dismay of Presbyterians the right of nomination was restored to the patrons by an Act passed in April 1712. This, too, was a primary object of protest. A letter to the Queen argued that the legislation of 1690 had been "ingrossed as an essential condition of the ratifications of the Treaty of Union" and therefore "must be understood to be

[1] G. Grub, op. cit. iii, pp. 361-2. R. Chambers, op. cit. ii, pp. 350-62. D. H. Whiteford, op. cit. p. 196.
[2] *AGA*, 1712, x.   [3] *AGA*, 1712, xvi, xvii, xviii.

a part of our Presbyterian Constitution, secured to us by the Treaty of Union, for ever".[1]

It has been said that in opposing the Act of Toleration the Assembly displayed an equal want of wisdom and charity.[2] To a twentieth-century reader it must appear so, but until now the Assembly had supposed that when Parliament ratified the Westminster Confession it knew the meaning of the statement in chapter xxiii that it was the duty of the civil magistrate to preserve unity and peace in the Church and that, accordingly, God had armed him with the power of the sword for this purpose. The resistance to the Act restoring patronage was of a different character since it struck at the roots of Presbyterianism, but there was no response from the government. When the Queen's letter was read to the following Assembly it contained no explicit reply or acknowledgment but instead recommended the Fathers and Brethren to observe moderation and unanimity among themselves.

This was an event of grave import for the Church and nothing can be more surprising than the small stir it produced. Contrary to the spirit,[3] if not to the letter of the Treaty of Union as the Assembly contended, the Act ensured the gradual decay of popular control of the Church. Those who had been instrumental in passing it were known to be hostile to the Presbyterian Establishment.[4] Nothing could have exposed more remorselessly the impotence of the Assembly even in the internal affairs of the Church as compared with the hopes of the militants. "Father Kennedie" and his colleagues of 1690 would scarcely have recognized as an Assembly a gathering prepared to stomach this humiliation with no more than an annual protest to an indifferent government. The reintroduction of patronage flouted the deepest convictions of nascent Scottish democracy; it revealed that an English parliament, where Scotland had only one member more than Cornwall,[5] knew little and cared less for Scottish opinion; and it laid up a legacy of trouble for the Scottish Church which was not to be dealt with for a couple of centuries.

But any real prospect of a Jacobite restoration ended with the death of Queen Anne and the accession of George I in 1714; and with this went any chance of a return to Episcopacy. By this

[1] *AGA*, 1712, p. 29.   [2] G. Grub, op. cit. iii, p. 365.
[3] *APS*, xi, p. 413.   [4] G. Grub, op. cit. iii, p. 366.
[5] David Daiches, *The Paradox of Scottish Culture*, p. 4.

time a slow change had begun in the leadership of the Scottish Church as the veterans of Covenanting strife passed away. Perhaps the first sign of change was the election in 1702 of David Williamson[1] of St Cuthbert's as Moderator. Williamson had an impeccable background in one respect, for he had been "outed" in 1662, but a stricter generation would have thought twice before electing as Moderator a man who had been married seven times and under suspicion, whether unjustly or not, on another occasion. One who saw his portrait described[2] him as "a handsome, sly looking, pawky priest, with a large wig, a curious leering expression in his eye, and a book in his hand". John Currie[3] had only been fourteen years in the ministry when elected Moderator of the Assembly in 1709. Principal Stirling, his predecessor, though not ordained until 1691, had at least experienced the effects of persecution in his father's manse, but from now on the Moderators were men who had had no personal connection with the fight for Presbyterianism under the Stewart kings. They were men of a different temper. Yet if they were losing animosity against the Episcopalians, the government, after 1715, had strong political reasons.

On 12 May 1716 a letter in the king's name[4] required the Lords of Justiciary in Scotland to close the meeting-houses in Edinburgh and elsewhere in which divine service was said without prayer for the king and his family. Of those prosecuted only one, Greenshields, could produce letters of Order in terms of the Act. The others were debarred from the conduct of worship until they could do so, and fined £20 each, half of which was paid to the poor of the parish and the balance to the Lord Advocate as informer. The victims, who numbered twenty-one, then obtained their letters of Order and so became entitled in Scotland to that toleration which Dissenters received in England. The Magistrates in turn asked for the guidance of the court and "their Lordships returned an answer, dark and equivocal as the Sybilline Oracles, imputing that the process was ended". Both parties thus avoided further action. An Act of April 1719[5] at last relaxed the oath of abjuration so far as the Presbyterians were concerned, but heavy burdens were now laid on Episcopalians who did not take the oath. Under penalty of six months' imprisonment and the closing

---

[1] J. Warrick, op. cit. pp. 140–57.   [2] Ibid. p. 157.   [3] Ibid. p. 213.
[4] H. Arnot, op. cit. pp. 343–6.   [5] G. Grub, op. cit. iii, p. 378.

of the meeting-house for the same period they were forbidden to officiate to any congregation where nine or more persons were present. This legislation was not always enforced but Nonjuring Episcopalians constantly lived under the threat of it. As late as 30 January 1755 John Connochar, "a nonjuring clergyman of the Episcopal Church of Scotland", was arrested in the Highlands and taken to Inveraray, a place of ill repute in such matters, for trial. It was observed from the Bench "that nonjuring Episcopal clergymen of the prisoner's activity, were dangerous to the present happy establishment". The jury found him guilty, but recommended mercy, and so he was only sentenced to banishment, never to return under pain of death.[1]

Meantime a settlement which had once been precarious gradually became permanent. The support of the laity steadily drifted away from the Episcopalian clergy because of their liturgical practices, their disputes among themselves, and their Jacobitism. They became reconciled with the national Church, in which they now had considerable power. The cause of Episcopacy which once had held, it may be, the majority of the nation, dwindled to tiny numbers. Settled within the national Church the laity gave it their own outlook to a large degree, and as new clergy were ordained the outlook of the sixty veterans found itself in a hopeless minority.

From time to time the Acts of Assembly[2] show traces of anxiety about the orthodoxy of schoolmasters and probationers. In 1703 George Turnbull,[3] the minister of Tynninghame, lost a son of seven years old. Meditating sadly in his diary the bereaved father wrote, "I observed that for a long time I had been secure, formal, yea, and carnal in my frame; this security had introduced a strange withering and universal decay in all my graces." Turnbull was probably correct in noting a change in his outlook. In the comparative calm after 1690 many had begun to mellow, and the temper of the Church was not what it had been in the years of strife. Carstares, the spokesman of the Assembly at court and the King's instrument for restraining the Assembly, was one of the few men who had learned the lesson of tolerance in the school of persecution. Whether or not he had been responsible

[1] H. Arnot, op. cit. pp. 339–43.
[2] AGA, 1694, x; 1699, xiii; 1700, x.
[3] "The Diary of George Turnbull", SHS, I, p. 428.

for drafting the royal letter to the Assembly of 1690, he exemplified its principles and consistently furthered them. He was
the first of the Moderates. This rather colourless word, which
became the mark of those ministers who dominated the Assembly
in the eighteenth century, began as one of praise and ended as
one of condemnation. Its origin, so far as it was attached to a
party, seems to be found in an Indulgence issued by James VII
on 12 February 1687.[1] In England, if the Vicar of Bray is to be
credited, the age of the Moderates did not begin until Queen
Anne was dead, "when George in pudding time came o'er, and
moderate men looked big, sir". It referred to the opponents of
the High Church party, the future Nonjurors, within the English
Church. In Scotland its use became prominent with the advice
of King William to the Assembly, and it referred to the toleration
of ecclesiastical opponents. At the first, therefore, it did not have
the associations which it later had under Principal Robertson, in
the full reign of the Moderates, and still less that which it had in
its declining days when it became little more than a word of
abuse. Its original application to the treatment of defeated opponents gradually changed to the description of a temper, a
mood of tolerance, an absence of dogmatism.

From 1690 the men of this type began, first to control, and
then to displace those who inherited the strong convictions of
Covenanting days. The election of David Williamson as Moderator
in 1702, and the restricted opposition to the Patronage Act of
1712, are signs of the change. In 1709 John Currie was Moderator.[2]
He had been in the ministry only fourteen years and had no direct
personal experience of the years of conflict. From his time on,
the Moderators belong to the new generation. William Hamilton,
who was Moderator no less than five times from 1712 onwards,
is the outstanding instance of this. He was related to Sir Robert
Hamilton of Preston who led the Covenanters at Bothwell Bridge
in 1679 and among those who fought was his elder brother, a
lad of nineteen,[3] but he had totally changed his outlook. Hamilton,
who had been minister of Cramond, became Professor of Divinity
at Edinburgh in 1709.[4] At one time his students numbered two
hundred, and among them was the future Professor Leechman as
well as most of those who later were counted Moderates. Hamil-

---

[1] Robert Wodrow, op. cit. iv, p. 418.   [2] J. Warrick, op. cit. p. 213.
[3] Ibid. pp. 240-57.   [4] H. R. Sefton, The Early Moderates.

ton had a Covenanting background and had actually been baptized at a conventicle, but his teaching, while guarded and orthodox, left a different impression. "By severalls who knew him well," said Wodrow,[1] "it's thought he is departed from the Calvinistic doctrine taught in the Church, though he hath the wisdom to keep himself in the clouds." He was unwilling to press matters to a conclusion against Simson or Glass, and Wodrow, picking up the term "New Light" from his Irish friends, applied it to Hamilton's students.[2] Francis Hutcheson of Glasgow has been regarded as the teacher of the Moderates, but Hamilton has the better claim; but this is more than a personal matter, for the whole mind of the age was changing.

As the formerly Episcopalian laity came to accept the Church of the Revolution Settlement they did not see as much change as might have been expected. There had been kirk sessions and presbyteries under the Second Episcopate. The synods, which had been the bishops' courts,[3] survived under the new régime, partly because the Presbyterians found them useful where their own presbyteries were not functioning as they wished. Kirk sessions were responsible for discipline, poor relief, and schools under the one régime as under the other. Heritors paid the same teinds for ministers' stipends. Despite signs of liturgical changes in the last years of the Episcopate the ordinary worshippers would see only trifling alterations in the conduct of worship.[4] Most of the country churches survived from pre-Reformation days, if much patched, and bore no resemblance to the great churches of rural England but were simple oblongs, unadorned and barely furnished, like the ruined Alloway Kirk where Tam o' Shanter had his grim experience. Those built under the Episcopate or under Presbyterianism after 1690 were much alike. Glencorse, Lauder, Yester, Carrington, and Durrisdeer are all of the same type.[5] They were simple buildings, though not without their merits. Cross-shaped or T-shaped, they centred round a long communion table with a pulpit behind and a laird's loft in front. In one respect the church at Durrisdeer is the most

---

[1] R. Wodrow, *Analecta*, iii, p. 139.   [2] Ibid. ii, p. 360.
[3] W. R. Foster, *Bishop and Presbytery, 1661–1688*, pp. 42–3.
[4] Ibid. pp. 125–37.
[5] George Hay, *The Architecture of Scottish Post-Reformation Churches 1560–1843*, pp. 36–69. Ian G. Lindsay, *The Scottish Parish Church*, pp. 50–60.

informative. Seen from outside it is surprisingly massive, but the great block at the west end is a school such as few villages can have possessed. Internally the church is of the familiar T plan with a central pulpit. Behind this, in the north aisle, is the great surprise, the splendid black and white marble monument of the second Duke of Queensberry and his Duchess. Something similar can be seen at Kilbirnie where the loft of the laird of Garnock, which would make the dress circle of most theatres seem plain, looks down upon a homely kirk. The contrast between baroque magnificence and plain interiors tells of a community where social and cultural differences ran very deep. Those to whom the right to nominate a minister had been given, and those who were to receive his ministrations, belonged to different worlds of thought, and out of this were to come the divisions of the Scottish Church in the eighteenth century.

CHAPTER TWO

The Coming of Division

Until the Revolution of 1688 the Scottish Church had been in-
clusive, if not always united. Whatever the bitterness, she had
never accepted sectarianism. "There is nothing," James Durham[1]
wrote, "that doth more tend to the reproach of the blessed name
of our Lord Jesus, that maketh Christianity more hateful, that
rendereth the Gospel more unfruitful, and more marreth the
progress and interest of the Kingdom of our Lord Jesus; and,
in a word, doth more shut out all good, and let in by an open
door everything that is evil into the Church, than the woeful
evil of division doth." This was now largely forgotten.

In the years before 1688 there had grown up among the hunted
survivors of the Covenanters groups of uncompromising, fanatical men, who withdrew their allegiance from an uncovenanted
King and refused to have communion with fellow Presbyterians
who did not share their stand. Sometimes known as the Hillmen,
and sometimes as the Societies, they are best remembered as
Cameronians from their leader, Richard Cameron, who died at
Airsmoss in Auchinleck in 1680. Among the first important acts
of the Assembly of 1690 was the reception into the Church of
the three Cameronian ministers, Thomas Lining, Alexander
Shields, and William Boyd. These men had presented two documents to the Assembly: the first a characteristically long and
detailed account of the failings of the National Church which was
more or less ignored, despite "its uncharitable and injurious reflections"; and the second a shorter request for admission. Indignant at being abandoned by their ministers, their people
disowned William and Mary and the Assembly as uncovenanted,
and worshipped apart, no longer persecuted by the state, in conventicles in the hill country of Ayrshire and Galloway. Being

[1] James Durham, *Treatise Concerning Scandal*, Part, 4 vi.

strongly Presbyterian, they were distressed by their lack of a properly ordained minister until John Macmillan of Balmaghie came to join them. He had long sympathized with them until his Presbytery declined to receive a statement from the Cameronians. Macmillan then announced that he would cease to attend the Presbytery, and that he was withdrawing from the National Church as then established.[1] Some months later the Presbytery, not unnaturally, removed him from his charge but, like the Episcopalians in the north, Macmillan continued in his church, manse, and glebe until 1727. His successor was obliged to conduct worship in the open air and, after a time, in a cottage locally known as "the house of Rimmon".[2] But Macmillan was now travelling widely across the south-west of Scotland, ministering to the scattered groups of Cameronians and baptizing their children. Over some years his baptisms averaged 38 annually and this indicates that his followers numbered about 1,200, some as far away as East Lothian, but most in the south-west.[3] In 1743 the Cameronians were able to form a Presbytery and in time became known as the Reformed Presbyterian Church. By the close of the century they had a dozen Scottish congregations, but emigration had taken many of their people to Northern Ireland and America. Their first Irish congregation was founded at Rasharkin in County Antrim in 1757. Six years later they founded an Irish Presbytery. This lapsed for a time, but was refounded in 1792, and since 1811 the Irish Reformed Presbyterians have formed an autonomous synod.[4] There are now more Reformed Presbyterians in America than on this side of the Atlantic. Intensely conservative, they have lived, so far as possible, a distinct life of their own. Few people have been so ill served by their literature. From the start it was controversial and argumentative, but those who knew them found them to be the kindliest and most devout of men. They were the first American Church to refuse to admit any slave-owner to their membership.[5]

It is an odd fact that the Cameronians, who were the survivors

[1] H. M. B. Reid, *A Cameronian Apostle, being some account of John Macmillan of Balmaghie*, p. 105.   [2] Ibid. p. 168.

[3] W. MacMillan, "The Baptismal Register of John MacMillan", *SCHS*, x, p. 27.

[4] J. M. Barkley, *A Short History of the Presbyterian Church in Ireland*, p. 30. W. D. Killen, *Ecclesiastical History of Ireland*, II, p. 335n.

[5] M. Hutchison, *The Reformed Presbyterian Church in Scotland*, p. 406.

of seventeenth-century disputes, grew in numbers, if on a small scale, while the Episcopalians, who had opened their minds to new currents of thought, steadily declined. The position of the Episcopalian Church after 1690 was highly ambiguous, for in the north they were virtually a part of the national Church, though indifferent to the General Assembly, while in the south they had assumed much more the character of a separate and ill-used denomination. Apart from the unremitting pressure against them from the dominant Presbyterians, there were several reasons for their decline. One such was their growing interest in liturgy.[1] In 1712 the Earl of Winton, who maintained episcopal chaplains at the medieval church of Seton and the meeting-house at the foot of New Row in Tranent, arranged for the reprinting by James Watson of Edinburgh of the Prayer Book of 1637, mistakenly known as "Laud's Liturgy". His part in the rising of 1715 put an end to it in these two congregations, but its use spread elsewhere. These experiments were anything but popular with many of the conservative laity who found themselves more at home with Presbyterians who still conducted worship much as it had been before 1688. Increasingly the National Church displayed the temperament, as distinct from the polity, of the Church under the Second Episcopate, but the Episcopal Church moved further and further away from national traditions. In 1710 Bishop Rose[2] was asked at Oxford whether he and his fellow bishops in Scotland were in communion with the Church of England. He replied that without consultation with them he could give no adequate reply. Already the sympathies of the Scottish bishops were not with the Church of England but with the Nonjurors, and had the question been put a few decades later the reply would hardly have been sincere. In August 1716 the Nonjurors in England and the Episcopal Church in Scotland opened negotiations for "a Concordate betwixt the Orthodox and Catholic remnant of the British Churches, and the Catholic and Apostolic Oriental Church".[3] We do not know the opinion of the Scottish laity about these negotiations but they are unlikely to have been favourable.

Losses were increased by the interminable quarrels and divisions into which the displaced clergy lapsed. For the most

---

[1] G. Grub, *Ecclesiastical History of Scotland*, iii, pp. 368–9.
[2] Ibid. iii, p. 370.   [3] Ibid. iii, pp. 400–4.

part the Scottish bishops continued to exercise most of their functions, but without reference to their former dioceses. Bishop Archibald Campbell, a grand-nephew of the Covenanting Argyll, resided in London and there, with the aid of Bishop Falconer and Bishop Hickes, an English Nonjuror, consecrated Dr James Gadderar,[1] the former minister of Kilmacolm, to the Episcopate. When Campbell was invited to become Bishop of Aberdeen in 1721 he declined, but Gadderar went in his place, and gave a fresh impulse to those in favour of liturgical change. Four main innovations were made, the use of the mixed chalice in the eucharist, the commemoration of the faithful departed, the epiclesis — or invocation of the Holy Spirit at the consecration — and the prayer of oblation.[2] The three last are now authorized by the Book of Common Order of the Church of Scotland, but their introduction split the Episcopalians into two factions, the Usagers and the Non-Usagers.

In 1724 a settlement of sorts was reached in the disputes over the Usages by allowing the use of either Prayer Book, the English or the Scottish, but the unhappy atmosphere was further complicated by the element of control exercised by the absent Stewarts through their Scottish representatives, the Trustees. They were opposed both to the Usages and to the use of a diocesan system in the King's absence, and proposed to maintain continuity by creating a college of bishops, headed by a primus. Against this there was a characteristically Scottish rebellion among the Episcopalian clergy who demanded the right to elect their own bishops for their own dioceses. A minority Church was thus deeply divided. On 4 June 1727 the college bishops numbered four, headed by Gadderar, but on that day the Usagers independently consecrated a fourth to their number. A week later the college bishops retaliated by consecrating two others. The college bishops now reversed their tactics; they suspended two of the original Usagers, and declared the others to be invalidly consecrated. Ultimately the college scheme was abandoned in 1732, but by that time the harm had been done.

After the Risings of 1715 and 1745 the Scottish Episcopalians suffered very heavily, but it is only necessary to recapitulate these disputes to know that the repressive acts of the government

---

[1] G. Grub, *Ecclesiastical History of Scotland*, iii, pp. 357, 386.

[2] Ibid. iii, pp. 387–95.

against the Church of the Jacobites were not the only reason for its decline. Trivial as the grounds of dispute appear today, in their time these quarrels were suicidal. Apart from this, Scottish Episcopalianism was rooted in a part of the country and in classes of the community which were steadily counting for less. The 'Fifteen was followed by the notorious Act of 1719 and the 'Forty-five reduced the Episcopalian cause to ruin. Their clergy had now dwindled from over 800 to about 130 aged men. In 1746 an Act of Parliament[1] required that all Scottish Episcopalian clergy should take the oath before 1 September and pray explicitly for the King and the royal family. Failing this, their meeting-houses were to be closed, for a first offence the clergy were to be imprisoned for six months, and for a second offence transported to the planta-tions of America for life, with life imprisonment should they return to Britain. A meeting-house was defined as a place where five or more persons met for worship, or where five persons in addition to the household met. Those attending were liable for a fine of £5 for the first offence and two years' imprisonment for a second. From now on no ordination by Scottish bishops would be recognized by the law, but only those by English or Irish bishops. Five clergy complied with the statute and continued to officiate in their meeting-houses, but the public ministrations of the remainder ceased. Despite the opposition of the English bishops it was enacted that after 29 September 1748 all orders conferred by Scottish bishops should be void. Thus Jacobitism came near to crushing a cause which dissension had already broken, and it is significant that from the passing of the penal laws until their repeal in 1792 the ablest historian of the Scottish Episcopal Church has little to tell.

In 1764 a new edition of the Scottish Communion Office was published, based largely on the First Prayer Book of Edward VI and the Book of 1637, but with those alterations which have given the rite in the Scottish Episcopal Church its distinctive form.[2] In 1788 Prince Charles Edward died and, ignoring the Cardinal York, the majority of Scottish Episcopalians abandoned the Stewart cause by publicly praying for King George. When the penal laws were rescinded in 1792 the Scottish bishops, who

[1] Ibid. iv, pp. 35–6.
[2] John Dowden, *The Scottish Communion Office*. W. Perry, *The Scottish Prayer Book; Its Value and History.*

had given the episcopal succession to America by the consecration of Bishop Seabury for the state of Connecticut,[1] found themselves presiding over the last fragments of what had once been a
great cause. In the words of Counsellor Pleydell in Scott's *Guy
Mannering*, the "suffering and Episcopal Church of Scotland was
but the shadow of a shade". Few can have supposed that it would
rise again.

The Covenanting cause had left behind, not merely the
Cameronians, but a strong tradition. In cottages and farmhouses
Peden's *Prophecies*, volumes such as *Naphtali* and *The Cloud of
Witnesses*, and the writings of Wodrow and Howie of Lochgoin
kept the flame alight. The graves of the martyrs were tended by
Old Mortality and others like him. Church History became a form
of propaganda. There was also an Episcopalian literature, such
as Calder's ironically entitled *Scotch Presbyterian Eloquence Display'd*,
but Calder was concerned with abuse, often scurrilous, of opponents who preached to the working class in a language they
understood. One may find in his pages eccentricities like the
prayer of William Erskine[2] of the Tron Kirk, "Lord, have mercy
upon all fools and idiots, and particularly on the magistrates of
Edinburgh", but the heroic character, the emotive force, and the
popular appeal of the Covenanting story is absent. The Covenanting tradition and literature, on the other hand, made an effective
appeal to a strong section of the membership of the Church, and
one which was by no means at home with its rather uninspiring
leadership which lacked, it seemed, enthusiasm for Calvinist
doctrine.

"Reviewing Scottish history from the Reformation," writes
Professor Gordon Donaldson,[3] "it is a little difficult to avoid the
conclusion that the principal mark of 'the Church of Scotland' is
establishment." It might be more accurate to say that it is identity
with the common people of Scotland, or continuity at the grass
roots, rather than recognition by the State or association with
any closely defined system of theology, for through all the changes
the congregations in the parish churches varied little. The West-

---

[1] G. Grub, op. cit. iv, pp. 91–8. J. B. Craven, *Journals of Bishop Forbes*,
pp. 20–2. William Walker, *John Skinner*, pp. 18–43.

[2] *Scotch Presbyterian Eloquence Display'd*, p. 99.

[3] Gordon Donaldson, *Scotland: Church and Nation through Sixteen Centuries*,
p. 112.

minster Confession and its related documents had been drafted in the vain hope that they would be the basis for union between the churches of England, Scotland, and Ireland. Despite the opinion of Professor James Cooper[1] that the wording of the Assembly's acceptance was limited to the substance of the Confession as distinct from "every form of expression in it", complete adherence to it was speedily demanded, and gave rise to a conviction that the unity and continuity of the Church depended upon a uniform acceptance of its doctrine. From the day when John Forbes of Corse dissented from the Confession this was an illusion, for the Confession was accepted from the heart and in detail by no more than a section of the Church, but it was an illusion which was long in dying. In mid-Victorian times Professor Cunningham[2] wrote that there were wide divergencies in doctrine within the Church of England. "But not so with the Church of Scotland. Down to the middle of the present century all her ministers spoke precisely the same things. The mind of each one reproduced with wonderful distinctness all the theological conclusions of the Westminster divines." This supposed uniformity of doctrine was to do for continuity and unity in the Church of Scotland what the Book of Common Prayer did in the Church of England.

Shortly before the failure of the rising of 1715 signalled the decline of the Episcopalians the orthodox adherents of the Westminster Confession began to have serious questionings about the teachings of John Simson, Professor of Divinity at Glasgow. Wrapped in its own disputes the Scottish Church of the seventeenth century had shown little awareness that beyond Tweed the world of thought was changing. It was not merely such Christian minds as those of John Bunyan and George Fox that were almost unknown in Scotland, but those, such as Robert Boyle, Sir Isaac Newton, and John Ray who worked on the border-line between theology and science. Gershom Carmichael, Hutcheson's predecessor in Glasgow for a couple of years, had lectured on Descartes but, taken on the whole, it was not merely the name of Descartes, but those of Hobbes, Pascal, Spinoza, and Locke that counted for nothing in Scotland. This could not last. Simson is an obscure, enigmatic, but significant figure, who

[1] James Cooper, *Confessions of Faith and Formulas*, p. 36.
[2] John Cunningham, *The Church History of Scotland*, ii, p. 246.

appears for a moment on the Scottish scene to tell of great changes at hand and then, having made the intimation, vanishes without trace. Undoubtedly he had been reading where other Scottish ministers did not venture, but he seems to have been an academic of little courage or manliness, who did not commit himself to writing or even to bold statement in his lectures or conversation.

At the Assembly of 1714 there was some disquiet about the outlook of theological students,[1] and James Webster of the Tron Kirk, a stalwart of the Covenant who had drawn the suspicion of Archbishop Sharp in his own student days, brought a charge against Simson. Almost simultaneously the pugnacious Webster was in trouble with the courts for calling Dr Alexander Pitcairn a Deist. Pitcairn turned on his accuser and it would seem that an action for libel was settled out of court for some payment, but in Simson Webster had an inoffensive, if elusive, quarry. After long delay a conclusion — for the time being — was reached in 1717.[2] Simson had been reading John Locke, though the name was not mentioned. He had "adopted some hypotheses different from what are commonly found among orthodox divines, that are not evidently founded on Scripture, and tend to attribute too much to natural reason, and the power of corrupt nature, which undue advancement of reason and nature is always to the disparagement of revelation and efficaceous free grace". Simson declared his full adherence to the Confession and disowned the errors attributed to him. His language, he claimed, had been misunderstood.[3] Principal Stirling[4] of Glasgow University defended Simson, and there were others who criticized his pursuers; so the Assembly, anxious to preserve "purity of doctrine and peace of this Church, and to prevent strife and contentious debates, which are prejudicial to truth, brotherly love, and the life of serious religion", let Simson off, telling him to be more cautious in future.

But this was not the end of his troubles, for in 1726 commissioners from several presbyteries arrived at the Assembly instructed to press for an enquiry into his teaching on the doctrine of the Trinity.[5] This time there was more general alarm. A com-

---

[1] *AGA*, 1714, vii.   [2] *AGA*, 1717, ix.

[3] H. M. B. Reid, *The Divinity Professors in the University of Glasgow*, pp. 207ff.

[4] John Warrick, *The Moderators of the Church of Scotland from 1690–1740*, pp. 208–9.   [5] *AGA*, 1727, x.

mittee was appointed. No less than five of its seven lay members were Law Lords, Senators of the College of Justice, and the ministers chosen were men of standing. If need be, they were empowered to suspend Simson from teaching, but a final decision was reserved to the Assembly. Once again Simson hedged. He stated his full adherence to orthodox Trinitarian teaching, but the committee found that he had "expressed himself in such terms as are subversive of these blessed truths", and that he had been lacking in frankness.[1] The evidence against him was shaky, depending largely on the evidence of his students. As was usual at the time, he had lectured in Latin; his Latin was weak and that of his students was weaker for, in Wodrow's[2] words, they were "young, raw lads, that, I believe, do not really understand what Mr Simson has taught", but the prejudice against him was strong. He had lacked the candour to tell men whose minds were those of an older day that he was dealing with a world of contemporary thought of which they knew little more than rumours and fears. He had been reading Samuel Clarke's *Scripture Doctrine of the Trinity*, and his opponents saw in him a tendency to Arianism concealed by formal acceptance of the Confession. He had used accepted words to hide divergent thought, and to their minds was guilty of what Communist thought today would call revisionism. Had Simson been bolder and franker he might have fared better. As it was, the Assembly of 1729[3] was almost as equivocal, for it condemned and suspended but did not depose him. He was relieved of his duties but left with his salary, a compromise which did credit to neither party, but which is explained by the fact that he had more prominent sympathizers than cared to speak openly for him. Some did. Three university principals and Mr Dundas of Arniston, a prominent elder, did so, and George Logan, who was to be Moderator in the year when final action was taken against the Seceders, spoke for him in a sermon preached before the Lord High Commissioner.

> George Logan held forth with an insolent air,
> In the pulpit, the House, and the Press;
> In pleading for Simson no pains he did spare,
> He's so like him, he could do no less.

[1] *AGA*, 1728, ix.   [2] Robert Wodrow, *Correspondence*, iii, 279.
[3] *AGA*, 1729, vi.

He thought to run down by a forehead of brass,
Each man who did Simson oppose,
While he did but the part of a Fop or an Ass,
And his impotent folly disclose.[1]

The intensity of the prejudice against Simson and the evasive-
ness of his defence make it difficult to assess his true position,
but the stifling of theological debate by the demand for apparent
conformity led to the concealment, for well nigh a century, of the
thought of many men in the Scottish ministry. At the same time
it would be unjust to suggest that his prosecution was due to
obscurantism. Central issues of the Christian faith were involved,
as was to be seen in contemporary and later developments in
Ireland.[2] Ulster had strong connections with Scotland and with
Glasgow in particular since it was there that most Irish students
of theology were trained. In 1705 a number of Irish Presbyterian
ministers founded the "Belfast Society",[3] whose members claimed
to adhere to the Westminster Confession but avoided subscribing
it. From 1720 there was a growing conviction that their refusal to
subscribe was not on the grounds stated, but because they had
abandoned Trinitarian doctrine and the belief in the divinity of
our Lord. In their case, as in Simson's, it is not easy to say where
criticism of the Confession ended and divergence from the
Christian faith began. In June 1726 they were excluded from the
Presbyterian Church in Ireland to form the Presbytery of Antrim,
Non-Subscribing in name but Unitarian in fact. John Abernethy,[4]
the founder of the Belfast Society, had been a fellow student of
Simson and remained a friend, while the younger members had
been students under Simson. Simson's opponents were aware of
this and had good cause to be disturbed. Such success as they
achieved was limited. Led by men who later became prominent
among the Seceders, they had been meeting at an Edinburgh inn
called the "Spread Eagle", and as the verdict of the Assembly was

[1] J. Warrick, op. cit. pp. 275-6, 291-4, 382-3.
[2] Robert Allen, *The Principle of Non-Subscription to Creeds and Confessions of Faith as exemplified in Irish Presbyterian History.*
[3] T. Witherow, *Historical and Literary Memorials of Presbyterianism in Ireland,* pp. 158-68, 192-204, 221-5, 310-16. *Records of the General Synod of Ulster,* II, pp. 104-9. J. C. Beckett, *Protestant Dissent in Ireland, 1687-1780,* pp. 75, 83.
[4] T. Witherow, op. cit. pp. 192-204. David Stewart, *The Seceders in Ireland,* p. 35.

announced one of them, Thomas Boston[1] of Ettrick, rose and dissented. It was, he said, "no just testimony to this Church's indignation against the dishonour done by the said Mr Simson to our glorious Redeemer . . . saddening to the hearts of the generality of the ministers and the godly through the land, and not sufficient to dash the hopes of the proud condemners of revealed religion." Simson, he was convinced, had been disseminating that rationalistic theology which was to issue as Unitarianism among the Irish and English Presbyterians.

While Simson's first case was disturbing the Church, the members of the Presbytery of Auchterarder, suspicious that formal acceptance of the Confession concealed heretical thoughts, took it upon themselves to cross-examine a student on trials for licence as a probationer for the ministry. They put it to him that "it is not sound and orthodox to teach that we must forsake sin, in order to our coming to Christ, and instating us in covenant with God".[2] By this they meant no more than the evangelical faith that Christ died to save sinful men, but the young man, pardonably, failed to see it in that light. Even the friends of the Presbytery realized that this was one of those things which might have been better expressed. The student appealed to the Assembly,[3] which supported him and condemned the Presbytery for what came to be called "the Auchterarder Creed". Listening to the debate, Boston of Ettrick "believed the proposition to be true, howbeit not well worded". Sitting next to him was John Drummond, the minister of Crieff. Boston observed that what the Presbytery had sought to say was enshrined in the words, "Come unto Me, all ye that labour and are heavy laden, and I will give you rest,"[4] and he recommended to Drummond an obscure book, *The Marrow of Modern Divinity*, which he had found in a cottage at Simprin where the master of the house, an old soldier, had brought it home from England in the time of the civil war.[5] Drummond read the book, was deeply impressed, and passed it on, first to one kindred spirit, and then to another.

First published at London in 1646, *The Marrow of Modern Divinity*[6] was the work of Edward Fisher. It takes the form of a

[1] Thomas Boston, *Memoirs*, p. 416.   [2] Ibid. p. 317.   [3] *AGA*, 1717, x.
[4] St Matthew 11:28.   [5] T. Boston, op. cit. p. 169.
[6] Donald Beaton, "The Marrow of Modern Divinity", *SCHS*, 1, pp. 112–134.

discussion between Evangelista, a minister, and three of his people, Nomista, a legalist who holds that the essence of the Christian life lies in obedience to God's law, Antinomista, who relies on grace and stands lightly to moral obligations, and Neophyta, a young Christian. Antinomista bids this youngster "to believe in Christ, to rejoice in the Lord, and live merrily", whatever corruptions he feels in his heart. Nomista tells his pastor, "Sir, I have been born and brought up in a country where there was very little preaching, the Lord He knoweth, I lived a great while in ignorance and blindness; and yet because I did often repeat the Lord's Prayer, the Apostles Creed, and the Ten Commandments, and in that I came sometimes to divine service — as they call it — and at Easter received the communion, I thought my condition to be good." At that point he had met with preachers of the Gospel who told him how much more was required, so that he became very strict in his manner of life. When this proved insufficient he turned to continual prayer, but this only confirmed his sense of inadequacy. Evangelista informs him that he has still been seeking to live under the covenant of works. Antinomista, on the other hand, as Neophyta observes, is confident of his faith in Christ and yet somewhat indifferent to the keeping of Christ's commands. Evangelista, who has never lost control of the discussion, sets forth the central place of faith in the Christian life. "When a man once comes to believe that all his sins, both past, present, and to come, are freely and fully pardoned, and God in Christ graciously reconciled unto him; the Lord doth hereupon so reveal His fatherly face unto him in Christ, and so make known that incredible union betwixt Him and the believing soul; that his heart becomes quietly contented in God, Who is the proper element of its being . . . when a man's heart is at peace in God . . . then the devil hath not that hope to prevail against his soul as he had before."

As a result of this conversation at the Assembly a new Scottish edition of "The Marrow" was published in 1718 with a preface by James Hog of Carnock and at once drew attention, not only for its contents, but because it was the manifesto of a discontented party within the Church. Controversy arose; Hog[1] and three colleagues — "all of them noted preachers of the doctrine of free grace" — were questioned before the Commission of

[1] T. Boston, op. cit. pp. 347–8.

Assembly, and on 20 May 1720 the Assembly[1] condemned the book. It had taught that assurance was of the nature of faith, that the atonement was universal, that holiness was not essential for salvation, that fear of eternal punishment and hope of reward were not Christian motives, and that the believer was not under the law. Part of the reason for this condemnation lay in the paradoxical style often used by its writer rather than in the substance of the book, and part of the reason must also be found in the personalities of the men who republished it; but a deeper reason is that the Westminster Confession, whatever men said of it, was again proving inadequate to express the mind of a new generation. Simson's case revealed the rise of rationalism; and the dispute over "The Marrow" was the first sign of the rise of an evangelical party.

For very different reasons the party in control of the Assembly, soon to be known as the Moderates, had little sympathy with either. Explicit rationalism, whatever their private estimate of it, was an open assault on the traditional pattern of doctrine which was bound to stir unwanted controversy, and the evangelical movement had a popular character with which the Moderates were ill at ease. They were men who held that the disputes and divisions of the seventeenth century had much less to do with the Christian Gospel than their participants had supposed, and should be forgotten, that the minds of congregations should be turned, not to theological debate and doctrine, but to the practical duties of the Christian life, that the Church should not permit herself to be carried away by the prejudices of the illiterate, and that it was necessary to make a deliberate attempt to secure the allegiance of the educated and thoughtful. In England the uniformity of worship secured by the Prayer Book had been accepted as the mark of a unity within which wide variations of doctrinal teaching could be permitted; but in Scotland the Westminster Confession created the conviction that uniformity of theological teaching was essential to unity. The Moderates were largely prepared to work for this by keeping silent on many doctrinal matters, but others were not, and the framework was to prove inadequate to maintain the unity of the Church.

After the Revolution Settlement the Church had long nursed three grievances against the government, the toleration of Episcopalians who took the oath of allegiance, the imposition of the

[1] *AGA*, 1720, v.

oath upon all ministers, and the reintroduction of patronage. The first two of these soon ceased to rankle greatly with those who controlled the Assembly. While theoretically an instrument of ecclesiastical democracy, the General Assembly, up to a point, proved capable of manipulation through the simple economic fact that beyond a certain distance impoverished ministers and elders could ill afford to travel to it. It could be controlled, more or less, by those within a convenient day's journey on horseback to Edinburgh. The Moderator of the Assembly of 1690 was Hew Kennedy, a Covenanting veteran who had unjustly been charged with receiving 6,000 merks of the ransom price paid by the English parliament to the Scottish army for the delivery of the royal martyr.[1] "For some mysterious reason," says his bio-grapher,[2] "his opponents called him 'Bitter Beard', but his friends lovingly spoke of him as 'Father Kennedie'." The nomination as Moderator was virtually a preserve of the clergy of Edinburgh and the Lothians. Between 1690 and 1731 only four were not from this district, and the general temper of these men soon came to be quite different from that of "Father Kennedie". In Covenanting times this simple fact had worked out to the advantage of the Covenanters whose Episcopalian opponents had to travel down from the north, but after 1688 it worked in favour of the Moderates, and this had not been foreseen. Much depended on the numbers attending from Dumfries, Galloway, and the West. "This year," says Alexander Carlyle[3] in 1766, "there was the last grand effort of our opponents to carry through their Schism overture. . . . Jardine told me that he had examined the list of the Assembly with care and that we should carry the question — that it would be nearly at par till we came as far on the roll as Loch-maben, but that after that we should have it hollow. . . . The calling of the roll began, and when it had passed the presbytery of Lochmaben, he gave a significant look with his eye to me, as much as to say, 'Now the day's our own.'[5]"

If this enabled the Lothian ministers to have a grip on the Assembly it was doubly true of the Commission of Assembly so that in time it became the chief instrument of the Moderates for controlling recalcitrant presbyteries which refused to induct un-popular nominees of patrons. While the Church had never ceased

[1] *Fasti*, I, p. 175. J. Warrick, op. cit. p. 26.
[2] Ibid. p. 46.   [3] A. Carlyle, *Autobiography*, p. 490.

to protest annually[1] against the reintroduction of patronage, in 1712 the Moderates had come to accept it, at first as inevitable since the State would not alter it, but later as a benefit since it placed the choice of ministers in the hands of those most likely to select educated men of their own outlook. Among their opponents it was seen as a restriction, not merely of popular rights, but of the Church as a spiritual fellowship, and as an instrument for imposing legalist ministers upon unwilling evangelical congregations. Those who opposed the Moderates were thus in a permanent minority whatever their popular support. It became clear that the hopes of 1688 were not to be realized. The leniency shown to Simson and the harshness shown to the advocates of *The Marrow of Modern Divinity* convinced them that the control of the Church was in the hands of men who, though Presbyterian in name, were not so in spirit.

Controversy about "The Marrow" continued in the Assembly until 1722 when a defence of it by twelve ministers, led by Ebenezer Erskine, which even their own historian[2] describes as "long and elaborate and somewhat tedious", was bluntly dismissed. But the argument was carried on outside the Assembly and tended to polarize the opposing parties. "A line of separation . . . began at this time to be drawn betwixt the ministers themselves . . . according to the side which they espoused in the ecclesiastical courts. Many of the ministers acquired clearer and more enlarged views of the system of revealed truth; the doctrine of free grace was better understood, and more faithfully preached."[3] Many of the laity were ill at ease; they missed the fire and passion associated with Covenanting days and the ethical piety of the new generation of clergy seemed an inadequate substitute for the warmth of the Gospel. As the evangelical party received increasing popular support and virtually none among the landowners who held the rights of patronage, there came a flood of disputes about unpopular presentations to parishes. Much of the patronage had been in the hands of the Crown and with the confiscations after 1715 the number was increased. For a time the crown patronage was exercised with considerable respect for popular opinion, as indeed patronage was in general, but with

[1] *AGA*, 1715, ix, etc.
[2] John McKerrow, *History of the Secession Church*, p. 16.
[3] Ibid. p. 17.

the coming to power of Argyll and his brother, Lord Islay, in 1725 this ceased. Disgruntled congregations appealed to the presbyteries as was their legal right. Here they were commonly successful, for the first generation of Moderates, as distinct from those who followed them, were hostile to patronage and sympathetic to popular demands, but when the appeals reached the Assembly, congregations almost invariably found their cases dismissed. When presbyteries refused to act against popular feeling the Assembly or its Commission appointed what were called "riding committees" to induct unwanted ministers. This was first done in 1729, a year in which there were no less than twelve disputed presentations, at New Machar, where the nominee was thrown into the horse-pond by his congregation, and it marks a change in the mind of the Moderates. They were no longer inclined to defer to congregations. The opponents of the nominee at New Machar were probably Episcopalians, for they resisted the induction of several Presbyterians that year in the county, but in the south they were Presbyterians, the natural allies of the ministers, so the change in policy foreshadows the coming of division.

The demand that congregations should chooose their own ministers had a long history in Scotland, but it was particularly strong in those parts of the country such as Ayrshire and Fife where there were classes of the community sufficiently independent of the landed gentry to express a will of their own. Tension was obviously growing and presbyteries, not unsympathetic to the claim for congregational rights, found a loophole in the law through the provision that if a patron failed to exercise his rights within six months the presbytery could fill the vacancy. When doing so they frequently consulted local wishes. But in 1731 the Assembly[1] sent down to presbyteries under the Barrier Act a proposal that in such cases the choice should be made by the elders and heritors in country parishes, and by the elders and town council in burghs. Thirty-one presbyteries rejected this proposal; six accepted it; and twelve did so only with modifications. Nevertheless the Assembly of 1732 interpreted this as acceptance on the grounds that eighteen presbyteries which had failed to reply were presumed to have been favourable.[2]

When the Synod of Perth and Stirling met in Perth that autumn

[1] *AGA*, 1731, iv.   [2] *AGA*, 1732, viii. J. McKerrow, op. cit. p. 39.

Ebenezer Erskine, one of the ministers of Stirling and an outspoken member of the Evangelical party, seized upon the fact that he was obliged, as moderator, to open the Synod with a sermon, to make a full blooded attack upon the Assembly's decision. He compared its members to the Jewish priests who had rejected Christ. Called to account for the outburst, he launched out into a defence of the right of a congregation to choose its own minister. "It is a natural privilege of every house or society of men to have the choice of their own servants or officers . . . and shall we suppose that ever God granted a power to any set of men, patrons, heritors, or whatever they be, — a power to impose servants on His Family?" Erskine's case was good, and it was a restatement of the claim of the medieval Church for spiritual independence, but his conduct at the Synod amounted to an open defiance. One can only presume that it was calculated and that the consequences were foreseen.

When the Synod met again in April, Erskine refused to retract. In May he was called to the bar of the Assembly to be rebuked by the Moderator. He refused to listen in silence and handed in a written protest, asking that its contents be minuted. For the moment the document was thrown aside, but later when someone picked it up and read it such indignation was roused that next morning the Assembly decided that, failing an apology to the Commission, Erskine and the three ministers who had supported him should be suspended from the ministry. All four appeared to state the case before the Commission. Here they received unexpected sympathy and so strong was their support that a motion to delay their suspension divided the house in exactly equal numbers until the casting vote of the Moderator carried the decision for suspension.[1] Despite this, further negotiations took place, but when these broke down it was decided, this time by a very large majority, to remove the four from their parishes and declare them no longer ministers of the Church. Only seven ministers dissented. The four victims retaliated in a document dated 16 November 1733 in which they claimed that they adhered to the true Presbyterian principles and that they were seceding, not from the Church, but from "the prevailing party in this established Church . . . who are carrying on a course of defection from our reformed and covenanted principles".

[1] J. McKerrow, op. cit. p. 61.

On 5 December they met at Gairney Bridge near Kinross, along with Ralph Erskine and Thomas Mair, and together they formed what was called "The Associate Presbytery" with Ebenezer Erskine as Moderator, thus making the best of both worlds by claiming an association with the national Church while constituting themselves as a rival Church. To vindicate themselves they issued a lengthy "Testimony". In this they asserted that the ruling party in the Church was enforcing policies contrary to Presbyterian principles, that they were tolerating heresy, that they were depriving ministers of their right to testify against this, and that they were tyrannical. By contrast, their own position was stated in terms of Presbyterian and Covenanting orthodoxy, but with certain additions. These were, firstly, that when the majority within the Church defected it was lawful for the minority to assume "to manage the keys of the Kingdom of Heaven", secondly, that it was the right of congregations to elect their own ministers, and, thirdly, that it was the duty of faithful ministers to protest and, if suspended, to continue in their ministry. With time, even the Seceders became aware that the word "Testimony" came to mean self-righteous abuse of others and that the ordinary man was "filled with nausea at the very sight of it".[1]

Whether or not Erskine had foreseen the results of his Synod sermon, the Assembly had certainly not foreseen the results of its action. There was a widespread regret, and the Church hastened to do everything possible to bring the lost shepherds back to the fold. In 1734 the Assembly repealed the objectionable Acts of 1730 and 1732, suspended forcible action in disputed settlements, and instructed the Synod of Perth and Stirling to receive the four ministers back. So strong was the confidence that they would return that the Presbytery of Stirling anticipated events by electing Ebenezer Erskine as its moderator. But if the four had gone out into the wilderness, they had found it not unpleasant, for they had suffered no material loss and their hearts had been warmed by the crowds that flocked to hear them preach. Whatever the Church did, they did not mean to return, and they replied with tedious arguments on obscure points.[2] Further concessions by the Assembly of 1735 were equally unsuccessful while all over the Lowlands there were manifestations of popular sympathy with the Seceders. Elders attended the courts of the national

[1] J. McKerrow, op. cit. p. 73.   [2] Ibid. pp. 87-92.

Church, not in proportion to their zeal, but to social status, those sitting in Presbytery and Assembly being higher in rank than those on Sessions. The Seceders drew from the unprivileged as did the Protesters in the previous century. In 1736 the Seceding Presbytery commenced a policy of proselytizing; and they revealed the root of the trouble by a corporate act of penance for failure to bear proper testimony against Simson. By 1736 it was plain to all that the breach was to last and that a new denomination had been created.

Perhaps the unwillingness of the Assembly to press home the case against the Seceders was partly rooted in a genuine spirit of tolerance, a mood new to Scotland, but quite certainly it was also due to the fact that the Assembly was aghast at the prospect of another Presbyterian Church in Scotland. Until now the essential unity of the Church had been rooted in Scottish minds. John Macmillan of Balmaghie could be overlooked as an eccentric and a solitary, but the leaders of the Secession were men of ability and standing who could not be ignored. The Episcopalians of the north could also be discounted, for every year that passed saw their numbers steadily decline until it seemed that they must die away within a foreseeable period. In contrast to this, the Secession had a strong popular base; it appealed to a wide and growing circle and especially to those of the strongest conviction and greatest responsibility. It made no appeal to the landed and titled. Those of their number whom the Seceders rather pathetically described as lairds were only the proprietors of a few acres; but they drew their support from a class which was growing in numbers and wealth, the small tradesmen, the farmers, and the craftsmen. It may be that the leaders of the Secession miscalculated on the number of ministers who would follow them, but they made no mistake about the strength of their support among the laity. Only delay in providing ministers kept the Secession cause from rapid increase.

Had no action been taken against Erskine, the malcontents would sooner or later have found some other excuse for going their own way. As it was, the Assembly showed extraordinary tolerance. For eight years, while they denounced the national Church, gathered adherents and drew sympathy as martyrs, they were left undisturbed in their churches, manses, and stipends. When at last they were deposed[1] in 1740 the sentence was delayed

[1] *AGA*, 1740, iv.

to the afternoon of the term day so that they might be entitled to receive the stipend for the previous half year. Far from being grateful for this consideration, the Seceders were indignant. "What idea are we to form . . . of the morality and justice of the General Assembly of the Church of Scotland at that period?" wrote their historian. "The sentence of deposition which, in the frenzy of party spirit, they pronounced against the founders of the Secession . . . will stand to future generations as a blot upon their annals which no sophistry will ever be able to wipe out."[1]

[1] J. McKerrow, op. cit. p. 136. Nathaniel Morren, *Annals of the General Assembly of the Church of Scotland*, i, p. 18.

CHAPTER THREE

Evangelicals and Moderates

Under the last two Stewart kings the theory and practice of Scots Law had made steady progress, and until the Union of 1707 put an end to it the Estates of Scotland had been assuming a new constitutional stature. A third factor in the life of the time, similarly concealed by the interminable disputes of Church and State, had been the development of Scottish education.[1] Schools in every burgh and virtually every parish — Knox's long unfulfilled dream — provided the mass of the population with a basic education surpassing that available in most European countries. Books were scarce and newspapers almost unknown but catechizing and continual sermonizing, free from competition, produced in every rank of society a capacity for abstract thought and reasoning. Village theologians split hairs over Calvinist doctrine much as groups from industry did over Marxist-Leninist doctrine in the nineteen-thirties. Little attention was paid, for a long time after 1707, to the remote and slightly irrelevant group of Scottish members at Westminster, but the General Assembly was nearer and more representative and its debates were more to the mind of contemporary Scots. Issues of principle were debated and beneath the strange and new tranquillity of Scottish life there was a ferment of thought.

While the Church was disturbed about "The Marrow" and Professor Simson, John Glass, the minister of Tealing in Angus, was reading his Bible with an independent mind. In Israel, he concluded, Church and State had been no more than two aspects of one divine community in which prophet, priest, and king alike had served. By contrast, the Church of Christ was a spiritual community, with no national associations, since she was called out of all nations. The National Covenant of 1638 and the Solemn

[1] William Ferguson, *Scotland: 1689 to the Present*, pp. 96–8.

League and Covenant of 1643, far from being Scotland's crowning glory, were unrelated to the New Testament Church. Glass therefore refused to sign the Westminster Confession on the grounds that civil magistrates had no authority to reform religion or to suppress false worship. "The National Covenants were without warrant of God's Word, and those who suffered in late times for adhering thereunto were so far unenlightened."[1] Formed out of independent congregations, the Church should have no bond with the state. In 1728 Glass published his outlook in *King of Martyrs*; on 15 October of that year he was deposed by the Synod and on 12 March 1730 the sentence was confirmed by the Commission of Assembly. Glass was a kindly and pleasant man, unambitious and deeply devout. Neither he nor his wife showed the slightest anxiety about the problem of bringing up a family of fifteen without a guaranteed income, or uttered any reproach. At Perth, where he went to live, a small meeting-house was built for his tiny congregation. Glass took an unprejudiced look at the New Testament and followed as literally as he could the example of the Church as he saw it there. His congregations had no professional ministry, but were led by groups of elders or bishops. His people had dietary laws. They abstained from blood and from things strangled. They regarded their property as subject to the demands of the Church and the poor. In worship they practised the kiss of peace and washed one another's feet in literal obedience to the Gospel command. In especial, Glass saw that the central act of worship of the early Church had been the weekly Eucharist at which all were present. The worship of his congregations — the "Eucharist" — therefore took place after a common meal—the "Agape"—in which the common food of Scotland in his time had been shared. The Assembly took second thoughts about Glass and restored him to the status of a minister, though holding him ineligible for a charge until he changed his opinions. But Glass had no intention of changing. He had no interest in making converts and the number of his followers was always small, but they survived and still receive an occasional addition to their numbers, usually from the ranks of the educated. Sometimes known as Glassites, and sometimes as the "Kail Kirk", they are better known as Sandemanians from his son-in-law, who succeeded to the leadership and whose family, well known as

[1] *Fasti*, III, p. 731.

importers of port, still lead this little Church. Michael Faraday,[1] the Victorian scientist, was one of their number.

At the other extreme there were those in Scotland who were reading the writings of the English Deists. Francis Hutcheson, the son of an Irish Presbyterian minister, arrived in Glasgow in 1710 as a boy of sixteen to study for the ministry, but after a period of teaching and writing in Ireland he came back to Glasgow in 1729, not as a minister, but as Professor of Moral Philosophy. Hutcheson followed Lord Shaftesbury in seeing the law of God in the order of the universe and in defining virtue as an agreement with this universal harmony. His ethics were utilitarian. "That action is best which procures the greatest happiness for the greatest numbers, and that worst which, in like manner, occasions misery."[2] A whole generation of students for the ministry from Ireland and Scotland sat at his feet and absorbed his dispassionate ethics.

But a more destructive spokesman of Deism than Shaftesbury was Matthew Tindal, whose *Christianity as Old as the Creation; or The Gospel a Republication of the Religion of Nature* was published in 1730. Whereas others had argued that the order of nature gave grounds for believing the Christian faith, Tindal turned this upside down by arguing that the faith must contain nothing which is not justified by nature and reason. Morality, the end for which all religions existed, was, he contended, the same in all, and accordingly whatever depended on revelation alone might be jettisoned. No more was necessary than nature and unassisted reason taught. Distinctively Christian doctrines such as those of the fall, original sin, and the atonement, could be dismissed. This characteristic Deist standpoint was not unfairly parodied by an opponent[3] when he wrote, "The Scriptures are the word of God; in His word no propositions contradictory to reason can have a place; these propositions are contrary to reason, and therefore they are not there. . . ."

The Assembly of 1735 showed itself aware that Deist teachings were making an impression when it urged ministers to

[1] James F. Riley, *The Hammer and the Anvil*, p. 3. "I am of a small and despised set of Christians known, if known at all, as Sandemanians, and our hope is founded in the faith that is in Christ."

[2] Francis Hutcheson, *Inquiry Concerning Moral Good and Evil*, p. 3.

[3] Soame Jenyns, *A View of the Internal Evidence of the Christian Religion*, p. 31.

recommend moral duties in their preaching "not from principles of reasons only but also, and more especially, of revelation . . . and in order to attain to it, it is necessary to show men the corruption and depravity of human nature by their fall in Adam . . . and to lead them to the true fountain and source of all grace and holiness, viz. union with Christ by the Spirit, faith, and the renewing of the Holy Ghost".[1]

Along with this went an enquiry into the teaching of Professor Campbell of the chair of Ecclesiastical History at St Andrews. It was reported at the next Assembly that he had been criticized on four points: firstly, in teaching that man was unable, by his own nature, to find out God; secondly, in teaching that the law of nature was sufficient to guide rational minds to happiness; thirdly, that self love was the principle and motive of all virtuous and religious actions; and fourthly, that between Christ's death and Pentecost the apostles had regarded Him as an impostor. Campbell was a more straightforward man than Simson. He soon satisfied the committee of enquiry that the apparent implications of the first three points were not what had been supposed. As regards the fourth, he had taught that until Christ's death the disciples had expected only a worldly kingdom, and that between His death and resurrection they had considered Him an impostor, learning His divinity only at His resurrection. Plainly, he was orthodox; the committee[2] advised him to avoid shocking the simple, and dropped the matter. Campbell, it can be seen, had been reading contemporary philosophy and had used its language against Deism, but the party of the Seceders[3] saw his case as yet another instance of the Assembly's failure to denounce incipient heresy.

There was a vocal minority within the Church, most of them soon to find their way into the Secession, which saw itself as the legitimate heir of the Covenanters, and saw scholastic Calvinism of the seventeenth century as the only permissible teaching within the Scottish Church. Despite this, they were to prove no more immune to the spirit of the age than those they denounced. Elements of rationalistic theology were to appear among them in time, but in the early years a more important factor was the rise

---

[1] *AGA*, 1735, Overtures, i.
[2] *AGA*, 1736, x.
[3] J. McKerrow, *History of the Secession Church*, p. 98.

of a new Evangelicalism. Outside the ranks of Lutherans and Calvinists in sixteenth-century Protestant Europe there had been scattered groups who repudiated the connection between Church and State, were more or less indifferent to the clergy, and gathered in the company of their fellows for prayer and Bible study. They thought much of conversion, assurance of salvation, and the guidance of the Holy Spirit. America gave them shelter from an unfriendly Europe. Today one can find in the States and Canada bodies such as the Mennonites and the Amish who are almost forgotten in the lands which gave them birth, and while they have often remained as enclaves within the general population they have spread a wide influence through American Protestantism. Both in their theology, which was inconsistent with strict Calvinism, and in their pattern of Church life with its emphasis on conversion and the gathered congregation, they differed from the traditional way of the Reformed Church in Scotland. How their influence spread into Scotland is unknown.

Communion was celebrated in the average congregation of Scotland only at long intervals, but early in the seventeenth century the pattern of the great Communion season already existed. Crowds of the faithful travelled in from other parishes, relays of preachers preached in the open air to listening crowds, and in the church itself the worshippers went in by turns to take their seats at the long tables to receive the sacrament. When John Livingstone was assisting at a Communion season at Kirk of Shotts on the windswept moorland halfway between Glasgow and Edinburgh in 1630, his preaching produced the response of mass conversion which later became known as a Revival. Similar events followed his subsequent ministry when he was driven to Ireland, and take an early place in the history of evangelical revivals. Those who emigrated from Scotland to Ireland did not always remain there, but left for America, where they are still known as "the Scotch Irish". Through them these movements obscurely spread to America. Archibald Alexander of Princeton and Charles Hodge came from ancestors of this stock, but while they were strict Calvinists, others brought the evangelistic outlook and found a greater response than at home. Periodically they have recrossed the Atlantic under such leaders as Moody and Sankey or, more recently, Dr Billy Graham.

Personal contact, rather than anything written, was the agent of communication, and so the early stages can scarcely be observed. In the time of Charles II a young man of Clydesdale named Walter Ker[1] had joined one of the eccentric groups of the time, but when staying at the home of two of the surviving converts of the Shotts gathering, he was deeply influenced by them. He carried their outlook with him to New Jersey in North America, where he took an active part in "the Great Awakening" of 1734. In this way, handfuls of the devout, known as Praying Societies, carried on the tradition of the Shotts Revival within Scottish congregations, and as early as 1640 the General Assembly, somewhat coldly, took note of them when it passed an Act seeking to restrict their activities.[2] Frequently discontented with their own ministers, these Praying Societies welcomed the Seceders[3] and were ready to form the nuclei of new congregations.

In the summer of 1736 two of the Secession ministers went on a preaching tour to show the flag in the west of Scotland; everywhere they went they found a welcome from these Societies and requests for sympathetic ministers. A similar request came from eighty Presbyterian families at Lisburn in Northern Ireland, but to these, as yet, the Seceders could return no more than friendly words.[4] The field was ready for harvest so in November they turned their attention to increasing their numbers by securing recruits to their ministry, and one of their number was entrusted with the training of theological students. A few ministers joined them and in 1737 their original four congregations increased to fifteen. Every year as students became available new congregations were formed. One instance, typical of many, may be given. East Lothian had given strong support to the Episcopalians and was to be the county of the Moderates, but on 3 March 1737 several Praying Societies in the county applied to the Seceders for "a day of fasting". This was not granted, as it was doubted whether they had a grasp of Secession principles and as the leaders of the Seceders had had trouble with one or two Societies of Covenanting principle and did not wish more. However, late in September, two Seceding ministers preached in Haddington[5] and

[1] John MacLeod, *Scottish Theology*, p. 98.

[2] William McKelvie, *Annals and Statistics of the United Presbyterian Church*, p. 1.

[3] J. McKerrow, op. cit. pp. 94, 100.

[4] David Stewart, *The Seceders in Ireland*, p. 57.

[5] Robert Small, *Congregations of the United Presbyterian Church from 1753 to 1900*, i, p. 513. Robert MacKenzie, *John Brown of Haddington*, p. 75.

agreed to give help, but owing to shortage of preachers nothing other than "a day of humiliation" could be provided for some time. In February 1741 three elders and forty members in East Lothian joined the Seceders and in December they were followed by thirty more. After many disappointments they called their first minister in September 1744.

Seceder congregations were composed of the convinced who were prepared to pay for the maintenance of their church and minister. They saw no responsibilities in the surrounding community except the opportunity to gather adherents, and they disregarded the old parish boundaries. This first congregation in Haddington therefore drew its members, not only from the town, but from almost all the county. When Praying Societies "craved Gospel ordinances" and the Seceders responded, a building would be commenced, a stipend guaranteed, commonly through the promised payment of seat rents, and the new minister would preach to a congregation composed of the evangelical and the discontented from many miles around. Not content with their progress in Scotland the Seceders took advantage of discontent among the Irish Presbyterians to send preachers to Ulster from 1742 onwards and on 8 July 1746 their first Irish minister was ordained. Between 1737 and 1740 the Seceding congregations in Scotland grew from fifteen to thirty-six; by 1746 they numbered forty-five; and by 1760 they had ninety-nine, besides others in Ireland and England.[1] These congregations were controlled by their strong-willed laity. Traditional acceptance of the Westminster Confession concealed the differences among them. They had little thought of the unity of the Church and their main bonds were hostility to the National Church and a determination to have their own way.

Provincial as they were, the Seceders could scarcely be unaware that in Germany, England, Ireland, and America the decade had seen evangelical movements similar to that in Scotland. John Wesley had not commended himself to them, but George Whitefield's success as an evangelical preacher was crowned, in their eyes, by his Calvinistic orthodoxy. When Whitefield returned from his first American tour in 1741 the Seceders got in touch with him. Ralph Erskine wrote from Dunfermline to tell Whitefield about the Scottish Covenanters, the principles of the Seceders,

[1] D. Stewart, op. cit. p. 61.

and the treatment — as he saw it — which the Assembly had meted out to them. If Whitefield came to evangelize in Scotland, Erskine[1] wrote, it was to be hoped that he would confine his activity to the Seceders, not because they wished to draw profits from his services but because, if he gave any countenance to the National Church it might be supposed by some that he regarded the opponents of the Seceders as also doing the Lord's work. "Unless you came with a design to meet and abide with us . . . I would dread the consequences of your coming, lest it should seem, equally to countenance our persecutors." But Whitefield replied that he meant to come to Scotland "only as an occasional preacher, to preach the simple Gospel to all who were willing to hear him, of whatever denomination". This answer gave no satisfaction, so Ebenezer Erskine joined in the correspondence. He explained that they did not expect Whitefield to join their Associate Presbytery "unless the Father of Lights were clearing your way thereunto; which we pray He may enlighten in His time, so as you and we may see eye to eye. All intended by us is, that, when you come to Scotland, your way may be such as not to strengthen the hands of our corrupt clergy and judicatories, who are carrying on a course of defection, worming out a faithful ministry from the land, and the power of religion with it. . . . If you could find freedom to company with us, to preach with us and for us, and to accept of our advices in your work, while in this country, it might contribute much to weaken the enemy's hand, and to strengthen ours in the work of the Lord, when the strength of the battle is against us."

Whitefield evaded commitment and arrived at Leith on 30 July 1741. Though invited to preach in Edinburgh he declined to do so on the grounds that those who had first invited him should have first call upon him, so it was in Ralph Erskine's congregation at Dunfermline that he preached the following Sunday. On 5 August he met the Associate Presbytery. Ebenezer Erskine opened the meeting with prayer, and immediately the brethren came to the point by asking Whitefield for his views on Church government. Diplomatically he expressed a wish for mutual tolerance, but the Seceders pressed him for an acknowledgment of Presbyterianism as the revealed pattern of the Church. "Sir," said Ebenezer Erskine, "God has made you an instrument of

[1] J. McKerrow, op. cit. p. 154.

gathering a great multitude of souls to the faith and profession of the Gospel of Christ throughout England, and also in foreign parts. . . . Would he not therefore sustain his converts by ordaining elders as Paul and Barnabas had done?" When Whitefield replied that, being a Church of England clergyman, he could not do so, "the articles of the Presbyterian form of Church government were then read to him along with passages of Scripture in support of them; and one of the brethren addressed him at considerable length, for the purpose of showing him that neither Episcopacy nor Independency were agreeable to the Word of God".[1]

Though the Seceders denied his account, Whitefield wrote in his journal that when he asked why they wished him to preach for them alone, Ralph Erskine replied that "They were the Lord's people". "Were there no others the Lord's people but themselves?" asked Whitefield. "If not, and if others were the devil's people, they had more need to be preached to; that for his part, all places were alike to him, and that if the pope himself would lend him his pulpit, he would gladly proclaim in it the righteousness of the Lord Jesus Christ." There could be no agreement between two such divergent parties. The Seceders denounced their guest as "a wild enthusiast, who was engaged in doing the work of Satan", and they charged him with saying that they were building "a Babel which would soon fall down about their ears". Whitefield's patience may have worn thin for the moment, but soon after he went into the tent at Stirling where Erskine was preaching and sat to hear him; at the close Whitefield went into the pulpit to preach, but Erskine would not stay to hear him.

Rejected by those who had invited him, Whitefield preached in the open with his usual success and, wherever they were open to him, in the parish churches. If his visit was a warning to the Seceders that they had no monopoly of evangelical zeal, the revival at Cambuslang[2] in the spring of 1742 was even more direct.

Despite changing patterns, in some respects this is an instance of continuity in popular religious movements. Cambuslang was a Clydeside parish with Covenanting traditions and the mind of its people was at odds with that of the patron, the Duke of Hamilton.

[1] Ibid. p. 157.
[2] Arthur Fawcett, *The Cambuslang Revival*.

When the charge fell vacant by the death of its old minister[1] on 3 January 1723, the Duke, after a long interval which suggests unsuccessful negotiations, nominated Thomas Findlater, a son of the minister of Hamilton. But the Praying Societies had been active in the parish and there was prolonged opposition to Findlater. Soldiers had to be called in to keep the peace, and ultimately he withdrew and instead was inducted to West Linton in 1731.[2] A charge of misconduct against him remained unsubstantiated and it is evident that the real trouble was a difference of temperament and theological outlook; Findlater was something of a Moderate. William McCulloch was then presented, and probably he was the man the congregation had wanted for some time. He had a Galloway and Covenanting background and was of the same mind as the Praying Societies. McCulloch's heart warmed at the news of the revival in New England, accounts of the events there were read to his congregation, tracts were delivered, and McCulloch preached on conversion and the experience of being born again. At the opening of 1742 ninety heads of families in Cambuslang requested him to hold a weekly lecture on a week-night evening. The first two passed without any unfamiliar outcome, but at the third there were strange signs among the people and about fifty came to receive spiritual counsel. From this time onwards McCulloch preached daily to the crowds who flocked in. Emotional scenes took place, many conversions were made, and a record of all such cases was kept.

Summoned by the news, Whitefield arrived in June and was cordially welcomed. On the day of his arrival he preached at Glasgow in the forenoon and it was nearly midnight when he finished the third of three more sermons preached at Cambuslang. McCulloch then took his place, and it was past one in the morning when he ceased and the people were persuaded, not without difficulty, to go home.

"Persons from all parts flocked to see," wrote Whitefield, "and many, from many parts, went home convinced and converted unto God. A brae or hill, near the manse at Cambuslang, seemed to be formed by Providence, for containing a large congregation. People sat unwearied till two in the morning, to hear sermons,

---

[1] "The Cambuslang and Kilsyth Revivals, 1742. A Bibliography", *SCHS*, I, pp. 94-6.

[2] *Fasti*, I, p. 247.

disregarding the weather. You could scarcely walk a yard, but you must tread upon some, either rejoicing in God for mercies received, or crying out for more. Thousands and thousands I have seen, before it was possible to catch it by sympathy, melted down under the Word and power of God." Though Communion had been celebrated in July and therefore, by Scottish standards, might not be expected for some time to come, the Session decided to hold another in August. Some 30,000 people gathered in the fields for the great event while Whitefield and other evangelical ministers preached by turn, and about 3,000 received Communion in the tents which had been erected.[1] Once the Communion was over the excitement settled down almost as quickly as it had begun. Only the weekly lecture still continued; the crowds disappeared; and by November the parish church could again contain the Sunday congregations. There were those who, once the temporary excitement had passed, reverted to what they had been before, but long afterwards it was acknowledged that the majority of those who had been converted remained constant and were full of religious influence in their local communities.

This did not pass without adverse criticism. Sir John Clerk of Penicuik spoke for many when he complained that men neglected their work to "goe a gading after conventicles as they doe at present". He paid indirect testimony to the large numbers involved when he calculated the national loss in daily wages.[2] It is worth noting that McCulloch's elders, traditionally a highly conservative group of men, supported him up to the hilt and welcomed the revival. Among his fellow ministers in the Church of Scotland there were those who had their reservations, but none showed the bitter hostility of the Secession. Whitefield was hotly attacked. In July the Associate Presbytery, meeting at Dunfermline, appointed 4 August to be observed by all their congregations as a day of fasting and humiliation on account of "the work of delusion", as they termed the revival. "It is no wonder," the Presbytery wrote, "that the Lord hath, in His righteous displeasure, left this church and land to give such an open discovery of their apostacy from Him, in the fond reception that Mr George Whitefield has met with, notwithstanding it is notourly known that he is a priest of the Church of England, who hath sworn the

[1] J. McKerrow, op. cit. p. 164.
[2] John Clerk, *Memorials*, SHS, p. 248.

oath of supremacy, and abjured the Solemn League and Covenant, endeavours, by his lax toleration principles, to pull down the hedges of government and discipline which the Lord has planted about His vineyard in this land." From now on other revivals appeared from time to time, if on a lesser scale, at Kilsyth and elsewhere, but nothing of the sort happened again at Cambuslang during McCulloch's lengthy ministry. More than prejudice lay behind the hostility of the Seceders; they had become aware that this was a pattern of Christian life and thought widely different in some ways from that Calvinism to which they still strictly adhered. But evangelical revivalism, if it was a phenomenon which could not be fitted into the traditional pattern of Scottish Calvinism, was soon to spread across sectarian boundaries.

Though McCulloch and his colleagues had been ministers of the National Church, they were not representative of her ruling party. When Alexander Carlyle went up to Glasgow University in 1743 Hutcheson[1] was at the height of his fame as a philosopher. "He was a good looking man, of an engaging countenance. He delivered his lectures without notes, walking backwards and forwards in the area of his room. As his elocution was good, and his voice and manner pleasing, he raised the attention of his hearers at all times; and when the subject led him to explain and enforce the moral virtues and duties, he displayed a fervent and persuasive eloquence which was irresistible. Besides the lecture he gave through the week he, every Sunday at six o'clock, opened his class room to whoever chose to attend, when he delivered a set of lectures on *Grotius De Veritate Religionis Christianae* . . . on that evening he expected to be attended not only by students, but by many of the people of the city . . . and he was not disappointed." It was due to Hutcheson and his colleague Leechman of the chair of Theology, said Carlyle, that "a better taste and greater liberality of sentiment were introduced among the clergy in the western provinces of Scotland".

Not everyone shared Carlyle's estimate of the two professors. The Moderates, said one of their critics,[2] "did not refuse to sign the Confession of Faith, but they were very shy as to preaching its truths, spoke of it as containing antiquated notions, hinted in quarters where they thought themselves safe that they did not

[1] A. Carlyle, *Autobiography*, p. 78.
[2] Andrew Thomson, *The Origin of the Secession Church*, p. 188.

believe some of its doctrines, and constructed their discourses so
as to indicate an Arian or Arminian cast of sentiment which could
not be misunderstood. They flattered human nature as to its
ability to obey the moral law. What the apostles would have called
sinful pleasures they called human weaknesses." Suspicion fell
upon Leechman, not so much because of what he said, as because
of what he left unsaid. But Leechman was more than able for his
critics and had behind him a body of support infinitely stronger
than any they could muster. Even in his days as a probationer for
the ministry his sermons had been regarded as over philosophic
and far from evangelical. An elder of Glasgow Presbytery raised
before the Presbytery a complaint that a published sermon on
prayer by Leechman contained no reference to prayer being made
in the name of Christ and in 1743 William Robe of Kilsyth, who
had been McCulloch's closest partner in the Cambuslang revival,
challenged the professor's orthodoxy at the Assembly.[1] Leechman replied in detail and was vindicated, but a gulf lay between
him and his critics. The language of the Confession of Faith was
used when it suited his purpose, but his mind did not work
within its limits.

Meantime a steady stream of disputed presentations in vacancies
brought before the Assembly each year evidence not merely of a
divided Church, but of a new class whose native intelligence had
been sharpened by some country school but whose social circumstances had given no outlet for their ability, and whose
aspirations were expressed in the Church rather than the State.
In 1739 Robert Halley, a weaver, and John Gray, a mason,
appeared before the Assembly to state the case of the parishioners
of Madderty against the patron's nominee. "The two commissioners, though but poor labouring men, acquitted themselves to
the admiration of all present by their eloquence, connection, good
sense, knowledge of the constitution, forms and discipline of the
Church, advancing nothing without proper quotations. One of
them being called upon by the counsel to vouch authority for a
certain assertion, his back got up with so holy an indignation at
being interrupted, that he gave such a repartee as must have
ruffled the patience of any other than the learned gentleman."
Next year, in the case of the border parish of Bowden, "there

[1] N. Morren, *Annals of the General Assembly of the Church of Scotland*, i, pp.
46–61.

appeared Walter Heatley, the miller of Bowden's man, commissioner for the Christian people, who appealed to the 'Book of Discipline', which he held in his hand, and insisted that nothing should be determined contrary thereto or to the Scriptures of truth.''[1]

Before 1730 patrons had often failed to exercise their rights but after that date they steadily claimed them, and where presbyteries sympathized with popular objections the Assembly increasingly, under Moderate guidance, turned to supporting the rights of patrons. For a score of years the "riding committees" appointed by the Assembly or its Commission had intervened to induct nominees in disputed vacancies and thus relieve presbyteries of an unwelcome task, but in 1750 the Assembly discussed the possible ending of this policy and the need to compel inferior courts of the Church to carry out the instructions of the highest court without evasion. Every year half a dozen disputes of this kind lay before the Assembly, some returning year after year, and among these was one from the West Lothian parish of Torphichen,[2] where the Presbytery had twice failed to obey the Assembly's instructions. A long debate took place, ending in the passing of censure on the Presbytery and an instruction to its members to induct the nominee. A proposal to suspend the recalcitrant members of Presbytery had been lost and a riding committee was appointed to act. Among fourteen ministers named were William Robertson, John Home, and Hugh Blair. It was unusual at the time for younger men to address the house unless called on by the Moderator but John Home of Athelstaneford had risen to move the suspension and had immediately impressed the Assembly by his eloquence. William Robertson of Gladsmuir, who seconded him, made an even greater impression. Despite this, they got few votes at the time.

At the close there was handed in a letter of dissent[3] from the Assembly's decision; it stated that the distinguishing marks of Presbyterian Church government were the parity of ministers and the subordination of Church courts, but that obedience to the courts was qualified by the words "in the Lord", implying an appeal to conscience even against a decision of the Assembly. There had always been a strong body of opinion that Presby-

[1] N. Morren, op. cit. i, p. 354.
[2] Ibid. i, pp. 198-212, 367.   [3] Ibid. i, pp. 209-11.

terianism expressed the voice of the people through its courts, but the men into whose hands the control of the Assembly was now coming preferred to emphasize the obligation of all to accept the decision of the superior courts.

In 1749 the Rev. Andrew Richardson of Broughton[1] was presented to the vacant parish of Inverkeithing. There were strong objections and the Presbytery hesitated to act, and finally refused. In March 1752 the case came before the Commission of Assembly for[2] the third time, but by now the new leaders of the Moderates had decided that the time had come to make an example which would secure obedience among the lower courts. A motion to censure the Presbytery was defeated at the Commission but when the Assembly met in May the Lord High Commissioner actively intervened to carry the day for the Moderates and disciplinary action. It was moved and carried that the Presbytery should meet to induct the nominee on the next Thursday, that all members should be ordered to attend, and as it was known that three members were prepared to obey, the usual number of three to form a quorum was raised to five. On the appointed day the three willing members appeared, but lacking the five for a quorum they could not act. Next day the Presbytery appeared at the bar of the Assembly, were rebuked, and heard it agreed that one of their number should be deposed from the ministry. Six of their number, particularly involved, were brought before the Assembly individually. Thomas Gillespie[3] of Garnock, the last to appear, read a document defending his position. When the Assembly voted, only a single vote was cast against each of the other defendants, but 52 voted against Gillespie, while 102 abstained. Three of the others were deprived of their seats in the courts of the Church but continued in their parishes.

Gillespie received his sentence with dignity and replied briefly. "Moderator," he said, "I desire to receive this sentence of the General Assembly of the Church of Scotland pronounced against me with real concern, and awful impressions of the divine conduct in it; but I rejoice, that to me it is given on behalf of Christ, not only to believe on Him, but also to suffer for His sake." There was no obvious reason why Gillespie should have been

[1] Gavin Struthers, *The History of the Rise, Progress and Principles of the Relief Church*, p. 201. *AGA*, 1752, iv.
[2] N. Morren, op. cit. i, pp. 229ff.   [3] G. Struthers, op. cit. p. 221.

singled out. He was, in the words of Sir Henry Moncrieff,[1] "one of the most inoffensive and upright men of this time. He was equally zealous and faithful in his pastoral duties; and in his private life was irreproachable. . . . He had never entered deeply into ecclesiastical business, and was at no time a political intriguer." Probably the reason for his victimization lies in his earlier record. When he was a divinity student at Edinburgh his widowed mother joined the Seceders and persuaded her son to do so also, but the short stay of ten days in their classes convinced him that he had made a mistake, so he left them and went south to Dr Doddridge's academy at Northampton. In England he was ordained by the Independents, but in 1741 he returned to Scotland, was accepted back into the Church of Scotland without comment, and was called to Carnock. Gillespie was an evangelical. "He spoke like one who had it in his charge to convert men by every sermon."[2] And he was an opponent of patronage and of interference by the civil authorities in church matters.

It is difficult to read the accounts of Gillespie without respecting him. Unlike the Seceders, he made no verbose protests and spoke no ill of his enemies. Unlike them, he made no struggle to retain his manse or stipend. From the day he was deposed he made no attempt to re-enter his church but conducted worship, at first in the churchyard, and later on a patch of waste ground. The weather favoured him throughout the summer but as winter drew on an old barn in Dunfermline was fitted up as a church for him. Ralph Erskine died two months later, a troubled vacancy followed in his congregation for six years, and Gillespie's flock was correspondingly augmented. Strong efforts by his evangelical friends in the west to have the sentence reversed were narrowly defeated in the next Assembly. Gillespie was left to apply for re-admission, but did not do so.

To join the Seceders would now have seemed his most obvious course, but Gillespie, though not always consistent, did not share their spirit; he could not accept their insistence on scholastic Calvinism or their intolerance, was alienated by their language against their opponents, their habit of issuing "testimonies" against the National Church, and their sectarian limits on Communion. The courts of the Church, he held, should be for friendly discussion and common action rather than for compulsion of

---

[1] N. Morren, op. cit. i, p. 274.   [2] G. Struthers, op. cit. p. 200.

minorities.[1] It is to him that the Church in modern Scotland owes
the willingness of most congregations to admit all Christians to
share in the Communion. "I hold communion," he said, "with
all that visibly hold the Head, and with such only." To his great
disappointment, his old friends in the Church feared the new-
found power of the Moderates too much to assist him at Communion seasons. For six years he conducted the lengthy series of
services alone, preaching every time no less than nine sermons,
all carefully prepared in writing, and exhorting seven or eight
"tables". The Seceders formed a party and had wide support, but
Gillespie was alone. "He had scarcely the ordinary measure of
this world's policy. He was guileless as a child. His talents and
acquirements . . . were not of the very highest order. . . . He was
neither wealthy nor connected with the great. His meeting house
was mean; his congregation a few farmers, cottagers, and servants
from the country, with a sprinkling of pious and respectable
families from Dunfermline. . . . He wrestled for the liberty and
purity of Zion; the Lord gathered friends around him and he
lacked nothing. When deposed, he had even refused to take the
current half-year's stipend, because he had not fully laboured for
it, but the people did not permit him to suffer loss, because of his
scrupulous honesty. His lack was amply supplied. His congregation voluntarily fixed his stipend at £600 Scots; allowing him also
£60 Scots for a house, and otherwise consulting his comfort,
and carrying on religious ordinances. At his summer sacraments
the people would collect from £110 to £120 Scots. At that era
these were large sums. The fountain of Christian benevolence
required only to be struck, to flow copiously for his support." In
other words, he received about £65 sterling each year from a
comparatively poor congregation.[2]

In 1757 Thomas Boston,[3] minister of Oxnam and a son of
Boston of Ettrick, resigned from the National Church to become
minister of an unattached congregation at Jedburgh. The magistrates and council, all members of his new charge, walked in
procession to the new meeting-house in their insignia of office.
Boston and his congregation attached themselves to Gillespie. In
1761 a third congregation was formed at Colinsburgh, and on

[1] H. R. Sefton, "Robert Wallace: An Early Moderate", *SCHS*, xvi, p. 15.
[2] G. Struthers, op. cit. p. 254.
[3] Ibid. p. 294. *AGA*, 1756, unprinted, 1758, iv.

22 October at Colinsburgh there was formed what was called the Relief Presbytery. Scotland thus had a third dissenting Presbyterian Church. Though small in numbers it was to grow, marked always by its evangelical character and its stand for liberty. The Westminster Confession and its associated documents were retained, but were used with restraint. "The Confession of Faith and Catechisms . . . contain a collection of divine truths . . . scarcely to be equalled in any human performance. But, after all, that venerable assembly was not without their weaknesses and mistakes; and indeed they would have been more than men if they had been free from them." The Moderates were strongly of the same opinion but said less about it. In April 1754 the Seceders produced a document on the doctrine of the atonement. "Our Lord Jesus Christ," it said, "hath redeemed none others, by His death, but the elect only." Thomas Mair[1] of Orwell, who had joined them in 1737, maintained "that Christ died for all and every one of mankind sinners". For this, they put him out of their ministry.

Gillespie had taken part in forming the Relief Presbytery reluctantly. To the end of his days he retained an affection for the National Church and before his death he recommended his congregation to return to it. They did so in 1779 but the Relief Church continued, evangelical in doctrine, critical of the association between Church and State, liberal in terms of membership, and with goodwill to other Christian communities.

The older Moderates had operated the law of patronage without being reconciled to it, but they had differed from the popular party in accepting the adequacy of a call from the heritors and elders, in the terms of the Act of 1732, while the Popular Party contended for the rights of the parishioners at large, or at least of heads of families. From 1736 Argyll and his brother, Lord Islay, who controlled the administration of Scotland, entrusted the management of church business to Dr Patrick Cumming, but when Walpole fell from power Lord Tweeddale placed it in the hands of Dr Robert Wallace. Wallace was instructed that presentations were to be in favour of clerics who would be agreeable to the landlords, but that "the heritors were to be given to understand, that they must not treat the elders or other parishioners in a haughty manner, but use every honourable and conciliatory

[1] J. McKerrow, op. cit. pp. 260–6.

means to render the settlements easy".[1] When Lord Tweeddale
resigned in 1746 Cumming was reinstated. He had comparatively
little say in crown appointments, but continued Wallace's
policy of considering public opinion, for the older generation
of Moderates, while prepared to work the system of patronage
since it was the law of the land, were far from being committed
to it. This changed from the time of the Assembly decision in
the Inverkeithing case. Wallace was opposed to the treatment
given to Gillespie, and Cumming — who was in the chair — had
his reservations. The decision, he said in his closing address,[2]
had been made because of the arguments of "several young
members". The leadership of the Church was now passing to
one of these young men, William Robertson of Gladsmuir, and
under him the call was to be regarded as no more than a formality.

In Robertson the Assembly was to have as its leader a man of
European standing. The practice of choosing university principals
from the ranks of the clergy was now only a survival from the
time when the universities existed mainly for the needs of the
Church, but the appointment of Robertson as Principal of Edinburgh University was that of a scholar of the first rank. It is
doubtful whether, since the range of appointments passed beyond
the narrow circle of ministers, there has been any Principal of
a Scottish University with the international reputation which
Robertson enjoyed in his day. His work, like that of Hume and
Gibbon, has been left behind by the progress of historical research
but its literary merits equal, at least, those of Hume's history,
and in some technical respects Robertson was the superior of
both of his great contemporaries. His appointment vindicated
the intellectual claims of the Moderates and, despite the ill name
which his policy later received in Scotland, it is surprising to
find how faithful he was as a parish minister and how much, as
a man, he was well beloved.

---

[1] N. Morren, op. cit. i, p. 303.   [2] Ibid. i, p. 290.

CHAPTER FOUR

The Reign of the Moderates

The Popular Party, in eighteenth-century Church disputes, bore this name because they claimed to express popular rights and not because they spoke for the majority of the population. Every time a minister was called to a parish an opportunity was offered them to create a disturbance which would bring them publicity and adherents, but it did not follow that the majority of worshippers — and still less the majority of parishioners — would support the party of dissent. John Galt's novel, *Annals of the Parish*, puts the matter in better perspective than the accounts of contemporary historians. "The placing", said the Reverend Mr Balwhidder, of his induction in 1760, "was a great affair; for I was put in by the patron, and the people knew nothing whatsoever of me, and their hearts were stirred into strife. . . . There was obliged to be a guard of soldiers to protect the presbytery; and it was a thing that made my heart grieve when I heard the drum beating and the fife playing as we were going to the kirk. The people were really mad and vicious, and flung dirt upon us as we passed, and reviled us all, and held out the finger of scorn at me. . . . When we got to the kirk door it was found to be nailed up, so as by no possibility to be opened. The sergeant of the soldiers wanted to break it; but I was afraid that the heritors would grudge and complain of the expense of the new door, and I supplicated him to let it be as it was. We were, therefore, obligated to go in by a window. . . . Thomas Thorl, the weaver, a pious zealot in that time, got up and protested, and said, 'Verily, verily, I say unto you, he that entereth not by the door into the sheepfold, but climbeth up some other way, the same is a thief and a robber.' " Yet the opposition died down and Balwhidder had a long and happy ministry in his Ayrshire parish.

His critics would have classed Balwhidder as a Moderate. Up

to a point this is correct, but he was no party man and few of his interests ran beyond the bounds of his own parish. Yet the name would not have been inappropriate since he represented at the parish level that placid addiction to duty and freedom from enthusiasm which was found at Assembly level in the leaders of the party. Though the Moderates' control of the Assembly was firmer than their grip on the lower courts of the Church the long period of their ascendancy is proof that, on the whole, they had the support of ordinary men in the ministry and of most of their people.

In March 1752, when the Commission failed to act drastically in the Inverkeithing dispute, Robertson and his friends produced a written statement of their case which came to be regarded as the manifesto of the Moderates. Membership of a society, the argument ran, involves the acceptance of the judgment of the majority or of those entrusted with authority. The enjoyment of privilege entails the acceptance of law and order, and this is particularly so in the Church since she is not a voluntary society, but one founded by the commands of Christ. Discipline, rightly enforced, is part of her nature. Only anarchy and confusion would ensue if conscience meant the right of every man to do what seemed good in his own eyes. Where men are not prepared to face their obligations they have no right to attempt to make the best of both worlds; if they will not conform, they should go out. In Presbyterianism the equality of ministers preserves due liberty while the subordination of Church courts — the two thoughts are always associated — maintains that order which is equally essential to a civilized society. Therefore, if decisions of the General Assembly are to be disregarded they might as well not be made. In the Inverkeithing dispute the Commission of Assembly had exceeded its powers by failing to implement the instructions it had received.[1]

Logic, order, and assurance are found in every sentence of this document; it reveals, at one point, an unexpected knowledge of an obscure but telling legal precedent; it shows an ability to turn an opponent's argument against himself, an absence of un-certainty or hesitation, and a magisterial, not to say, pontifical air more calculated to command than to conciliate. Robertson's

[1] N. Morren, *Annals of the General Assembly of the Church of Scotland*, i, pp. 231–42. *AGA*, 1752, iv.

self-confidence was not based on arrogance but on ability. His prose style, clear and direct, comes like a breath of fresh air among the musty records of the time. No trace remains of the turgid rhetoric and endless Old Testament allusions of the Secession fathers. The reply[1] of his opponents is twice as long. True or not, it lacks his mastery, and had Robertson been a judge summing up after the long hearing of an intricate case no juryman would have dared to reject his guidance. Robertson lost at the Commission but won, where it mattered, at the Assembly. This decision ushered in a new era for the Scottish Church. Order was now to be enforced, and Robertson was installed as leader of the Assembly from 1762 until his resignation in 1780.[2] He maintained a personal ascendancy over the highest court of the Church such as had fallen to no other man since Carstares, "an ascendancy so stable and undisputed that, unlike his predecessors, he acknowledged no patron, and every successive government was constrained to employ, or rather to support, him on his own terms".

Robertson's strength lay not only in his great abilities but in a readiness to listen to others, to weigh the evidence and judge, not by the clamour of protest, but by the degree and quality of support. Inertia in the pew could outweigh any amount of sermons in the pulpit. As the great body of lay support had drifted away from the Covenanters in the seventeenth century and then from the Jacobite Episcopalians, so a minority body of lay opinion had launched the Secession Church, and a far larger and more influential body was now to carry the Moderates to power. For such a determined man Robertson was oddly aware of the limitations within which he had to work and had no intention of quarrelling with them. He listened to public opinion, assessed the noisy partisans by standards very different from their own and closer to those which Hutcheson had taught in Glasgow, and placed a higher valuation on that great body of the silent majority which looked for law and order and was ready to let the troublemakers go where they wished. "The natural understanding is the most whorish thing in the world," wrote Samuel Rutherford. "The understanding, even in the search of truth amongst the creatures, is a rash, precipitate, and unquiet thing." While the Seceders followed Rutherford, Robertson fully shared Hutche-

[1] N. Morren, op. cit. i, pp. 243-60.
[2] W. L. Mathieson, *The Awakening of Scotland*, p. 170.

son's confidence in the power of the human intellect,[1] and was convinced that any other way of thought would alienate the educated classes in a transformed Scotland. But his strength was also his weakness. He was a citizen of the world of his time and adapted the Church to it.

When George III came to the throne Edinburgh could be described as "a picturesque, odorous, inconvenient, old-fashioned town, of about seventy thousand inhabitants".[2] Despite the increase in population, neither its street plan nor its sewage system had changed greatly since the Middle Ages. The city still consisted of little more than one long street — stretching from the Castle to Holyroodhouse — and its associated wynds and alleys. Change was marked by the ever-increasing height of the tall lands and tenements providing cramped and insanitary accommodation for beggar, tradesman, and noble alike. But in 1767 the building of the first house in George Street marked the commencement of the New Town, separated from the Old Town by the waters of the Nor' Loch and by a whole world of thought. The nobility and wealthy rapidly forsook the evil-smelling High Street and lawnmarket for the Georgian terraces of the New Town. A house in Princes Street was advertised as having a dining-room, drawing-room, seven bedrooms, kitchen, scullery, servants' apartments, cellars, laundry, stable, coach-house and pigeon-house, and that great new amenity, "a lead cistern with a pipe within the house".[3] Whereas in the Old Town all classes had lived in proximity, if on different levels, in the same close, in the New Town no accommodation, or at least no visible accommodation, was provided for the lower classes. The Old Town was abandoned to the middle class and the working class, until even the middle class began to move out of it. By 1790 Lord President Craigie's house was possessed by "a rouping-wife, or saleswoman of old furniture . . . the house of the Duke of Douglas at the Union is now possessed by a wheelwright . . . the great Marquis of Argyle's house in the Castlehill is possessed by a hosier at £12 per annum . . . the house of the late President Dundas, who died in December 1787, is now possessed by an ironmonger as his

---

[1] H. T. Buckle, *History of Civilization in England*, iii, p. 293.
[2] Royal Commission on Ancient Monuments, *Report on the City of Edinburgh*, liii. An estimate of a population of 50,000 would be nearer the truth.
[3] Ibid. lxx.

dwelling house and ware room".[1] "Saint Cecilia's Hall," wrote Lord Cockburn[2] of his student days, "was . . . the best and most beautiful concert room I have ever seen. . . . All this was in the Cowgate! the last retreat nowadays of destitution and disease." Social distinctions had always existed in Scotland, but there had been a certain intimacy between rich and poor which was now to be lost.

Like Carstares before him, Robertson had strong Christian convictions, but saw that the world had changed. The social and intellectual revolution[3] which was reflected in the New Town of Edinburgh told that the day of the Covenant had long gone by and that the Century of the Enlightenment was in full flourish. But whereas Carstares had found it necessary to accommodate himself to the enthusiasts, Robertson knew that the time had come when he could let them go. In this he represented not only the Moderate leadership but a great body of lay opinion, and one that was overwhelmingly strong among the educated, the landed, and the moneyed classes. But Robertson realized no more than Gibbon that the whole social order of the century of the Enlightenment was on the verge of disintegration, not because of political radicalism but because of economic and industrial change. The founding of the Carron Iron Works[4] in 1759 may not have been, as has so often been said, the start of the Industrial Revolution in Scotland; but it was a portent. The Moderates were based upon the social structure of a stable agricultural community, and the transfer of trade and industry from the east coast to the west which had been in progress since the Union of 1707 was seen in the growth of the tobacco trade of Glasgow, the shipping, and the spinning and weaving of the Clyde valley. These things were to bring to an end the world which Robertson knew. Meanwhile, sedate and bewigged, as in Raeburn's portrait, he led the Church, rational, tolerant of all except the intolerant, and blind to the strength of emotion in human life.

When Robertson surveyed the Inverkeithing case he first stated the law, which was all on the side of the patron's nominee. He

---

[1] Royal Commission on Ancient Monuments, *Report on the City of Edinburgh*, lii.

[2] Lord Cockburn, *Memorials of His Time*, p. 24.

[3] Daiches, *The Paradox of Scottish Culture*, pp. 68–73.

[4] R. H. Campbell, *Carron Company*, p. 27.

then analysed the mind of the parishioners. Quite a number had accepted the nominee; others had opposed him, but without stating any clear reason, or at least any that Robertson could think so; but the majority had taken no active part in the matter. "From their neutrality, we may well conclude, both in reason and from the experience of the Church in like cases, that they are willing to acquiesce in the decisions of their superiors, and to join with Mr Richardson as their minister, as soon as he shall be settled amongst them." This common-sense viewpoint proved correct. The majority of the congregation accepted him. "Notwithstanding all the opposition and obloquy which he encountered, he was a respectable preacher, an estimable character, and an accomplished divine, whose only fault lay in accepting the presentation."[1] On the other hand, his neighbour whom the dissenting portion of the congregation called when they joined the Seceders proved to be a quarrelsome man who was never out of trouble,[2] as the historian of his own party tells. This dispute has a significance greater than that of a small-town rumpus; it marks the determination of the Moderate leadership to put an end to a troublesome party within the Church and let them go. With their success came certain gains, and some unforeseen losses.

Taken on the whole, Scottish historians have not been kind to the men who now controlled the government of the Scottish Church. Hume Brown, who had been a teacher in the Free Church School at Prestonpans where Carlyle's father had been parish minister, and who had family reasons for disliking the Moderates, compared them with the Latitudinarians in eighteenth-century England. He did not mean this as a compliment.[3] They had entered the Church, he considered, only to obtain a leisured life to cultivate literature and at Assembly time had revealed their character by meeting in a tavern. It casts a curious sidelight on Scottish historians that Hume Brown forgot for the moment that everyone else at the time, including the Seceders, had done the same.[4] Unfriendly estimates which Carlyle, the arch-Moderate, had quoted against himself with his tongue in his cheek were cited against him as objective evidence and his *Autobiography*,

---

[1] *Fasti*, II, p. 593.

[2] R. Small, *Congregations of the United Presbyterian Church from 1753 to 1900*, i, pp. 363–4. J. McKerrow, *History of the Secession Church*, pp. 515–19.

[3] P. Hume Brown, *History of Scotland*, iii, pp. 362–7.   [4] cf. supra p. 34

written largely to entertain, was accepted at face value as a complete portrait of the man and his interests. A later minister of Inveresk wrote, "From a perusal of the Kirk Session and Parochial Board Minutes, I find that Carlyle was faithful to his pastoral charge as his epitaph declares. He was much more amongst his people than his *Autobiography* leads one to imagine; and his interest in the poorest of his flock is noteworthy."[1] In 1790, when Sunday Schools were few and under suspicion, the aging Carlyle had one instituted in his parish. His church, a small medieval building, was overcrowded and towards the end of his life he fought a running fight with the heritors to have it replaced by a much larger building. Though he did not live to see it erected, it is typical of the man that he swept away a church of considerable architectural interest to make way for one which would give accommodation for his large parish. But Carlyle's *Autobiography* said nothing of his parish duties, so it was presumed that he did none.

Whatever his critics cared to think, Carlyle of Inveresk represented a tradition which had never been absent from the Scottish ministry. He combined a robust faith with tolerance and an undisguised liking for the pleasures of life as his father and his grandfather, Alexander Robeson, minister of Tinwald since 1697, had done before him. While noisy elements in the Scottish Church — too often regarded as its only authentic voice — were denouncing "promiscuous dancing" and the stage, Carlyle's parents sent him as a boy to a dancing class and took it for granted that he should take part as a student in amateur theatricals.[2] A stricter age exaggerated his failings. An Edinburgh minister told how as a child he had heard an admiring servant observe as Carlyle left the dinner table, "There he gaes, dacent man, as steady as a wall, after his ain share o' five bottles o' port", but this story is probably no more than a garbled recollection of Carlyle's own story of how Webster of the Tolbooth Kirk, a strict Evangelical, "being a five-bottle man, could lay them all under the table". It was the way of the time; a lady of Carlyle's family drew his boyhood attention because she could empty a bottle of brandy at a sitting,[3] and the favourite Biblical commentator of the age found

[1] W. L. Mathieson, op. cit. p. 210.
[2] A. Carlyle, *Autobiography*, pp. 53–4, 109.
[3] Ibid. pp. 250, 28.

nothing irreverent in observing that the wine ran short at Cana of Galilee because the twelve apostles had drunk the house dry.[1]

Carlyle is remembered as a Moderate, not because of any importance which he had in the leadership of the party, but because of the vivid record which he left of his life and times. By a curious coincidence we have two other accounts, though not of the same wide interest, from two other neighbouring ministers. Each in its own way helps to complete a portrait of the Church of the time by filling in those spaces which Carlyle left blank. Robert Sheriff, minister of the Secession congregation in Tranent, also kept a journal which was published after his death. Apart from references to his first wife whenever the anniversary of her death recurred, the journal is completely lacking in those personal reminiscences which fill Carlyle's pages, for it consists of religious meditations and of these alone. Their character echoes that of an earlier day and no one has been inclined to reprint them. It is understandable that a man like Sheriff must have taken a very dim view of Carlyle and that he must have found very little in common with his neighbour.

The third journal, that of Hugh Cunningham of Tranent, next to Carlyle's birthplace and to his parish, has not been printed but, like those of Somerville of Jedburgh and Ridpath of Stichel, holds much more of interest for the average reader. Cunningham did his best to make friends with Sheriff, but met with little response. "Drank tea with the Revd. Robert Sheriff, minister of the Associate Congregation," he noted in his diary. "Religious sentiments ought never to contract the community of love — I have often visited this gentleman — but seldom he returns my visits." Again, "the Revd. Robert Sheriff and sister Mrs. Mason drinking tea with us. Would wish to be much more intimate with Mr. Sheriff, if his views and mine more exactly corresponded — He rather stiff and not of that liberal turn I could wish in every minr. of Christ." Similarly Cunningham was prepared to co-operate with his Episcopalian neighbour in Musselburgh.[2]

Cunningham's uncle had received a very stormy welcome when inducted to Tranent in September 1740 but, like others, he lived it down, and it was the example of his faithfulness which brought

[1] J. A. Bengel, *Gnomon Novi Testamenti*, John 2:2.
[2] T. Angus Kerr, "Life and Ministry of the Rev. Hugh Cunningham of Tranent", *SCHS*, xv, pp. 54-5.

the young man to enter the ministry. After acting as assistant to his uncle, he was presented to the parish by George III in 1783. It had, in 1792, a population of 2,732 who earned a livelihood in farming, coalmining, fishing, potteries, and saltworks, and later reports on the coal miners were to show that the conditions of housing and living were grim for many. Apart from Sunday duties Cunningham's main occupation was the pastoral care of his people. He visited his parish assiduously and the many references in his diary cast a new light upon the much maligned Moderates. "Examining the inhabitants of the N. side of Elphinstone," he wrote, "highly satisfied with the attendance of the people. . . . Went round by St Clements Wells this forenoon, visited the different families . . . held a diet of examination, where I examined about a dozen . . . was informed by our maid's mother who had come from Tranent that 2 men, Geo. Hinlay and Robt. Steel were killed last night in the S. coal pit. Such an effect had this information over my spirits that I could not be happy till I . . . took a share in the troubles of the distressed friends. Accordingly set off and sympathised by prayer with both of them." He does not mention that this required a walk of many miles.

Cunningham's church, a small medieval building with two side aisles, could scarcely have contained more than a couple of hundred of his 2,732 parishioners, had they all attended; but it was only at the Communion seasons that it was unable to seat the congregation. In 1794 the Kirk Session records tell that there were about 450 communicants at seven tables. He describes a better attended but typical communion on 7 August 1786. "This being our solemn service day our church met precisely half an hour after 10 o'clock. I preached from Matt. I, v 21, And she shall bring forth a son and thou shalt call his name Jesus, for he shall save his people from their sins. Then after the necessary forms proceeded to the service of the tables — had 11 altogether and about 640 communicants. . . . Half after 4 afternoon before we could get out . . . a comfortable day. O that the fruits of holiness may appear."[1]

When Cunningham's church was rebuilt by the heritors in 1799, despite the protest of one of their number who desired a larger and better building, it was seated to accommodate 440;

---

[1] T. Angus Kerr, "Life and Ministry of the Rev. Hugh Cunningham of Tranent", *SCHS*, xv, pp. 46–7.

and the disparity between the size of the parish and the accommodation of the church disposes of the legend that all were
regularly at worship on Sundays. Until late Georgian times the
size of Scottish churches was not related to the numbers of the
population but to what came down from the Middle Ages. With
a few notable exceptions such as Burntisland or the Tron Kirk
of Edinburgh, churches which required rebuilding were recon-
structed out of the remains of the medieval churches. Midway
through the eighteenth century, however, the magistrates of
growing burghs set out to build new churches which might retain
some traditional elements in their planning but were designed
from English models. In James Gibbs' monumental church of
West St Nicholas, built in Aberdeen in 1755, the traditional
planning was retained, with a great canopied pulpit half-way
down the church looking out over a long communion table to
the fine chairs and canopied loft of the provost and magistrates.
Traditional planning apart, it was really "a mediaeval aisled nave
in classical costume".[1] The splendid church of St Andrew in
Glasgow is of much the same date but departs completely from
traditional planning. Designed by Allan Dreghorn, it is almost
entirely a copy of Gibbs' St Martin-in-the-Fields, with steeple
and pedimented portico. Its impressive interior "with tall Corin-
thian columns, rich Spanish mahogany gallery fronts and pulpit,
and the rococo enrichments of the ceiling and clock surround"[2]
tell of the new society of the tobacco lords of Glasgow. A shallow
chancel completed the building but the dominating pulpit was
set, irrelevantly but logically, on the middle of the chancel steps.
Samuel Bell's church of St Andrew, Dundee, built in 1774, retained the traditional plan of an oblong church with a tower and
spire at the west end, a pulpit in the middle of the south wall, and
an octagonal gallery opposite, but a new influence runs through
the building from its Palladian details to the gilded dragon on
top of the spire.[3]

All these show a changed outlook in ministers and congregations, but closer examination shows that they were not a sign of
universal church attendance. The average country church was
about 20 to 24 feet wide, because it was impossible to get native
timber sufficient to cover a wider stretch, and from 40 to 90 feet

[1] George Hay, *The Architecture of Scottish Post-Reformation Churches, 1560–
1843*, p. 100.   [2] Ibid. p. 102.   [3] Ibid. p. 82.

long according to the size of the parish. A clumsy arrangement of pews and lofts wasted a great deal of space, as did the stairs, long communion table, and its seats and passages. At a generous estimate Smailholm, serving a population of 551 at the time of Webster's census in 1755, could scarcely seat 200; Dalmeny with 1,103 people could seat about 200 as it then was, Gillespie's little church at Carnock had space for 140 of its 583 parishioners and Robertson's Gladsmuir could take perhaps 340 of its 1,415 parishioners. Even in a town the size of Jedburgh a thatched aisle of the Abbey, as may be seen from Adam de Cardonnel's woodcut of the building, could deal with the congregation gathered from a population of 5,816. Edinburgh, with a population of just under 50,000, was provided with eleven parish churches, three within the walls of St Giles, and two Secession churches. Glasgow had seven parish churches, three within the Cathedral, for a population of over 27,000. Yet, except on Communion Sundays, there were no complaints about overcrowding and the conclusion is obvious.

Henry Grey Graham,[1] whose scholarship was vitiated by intense prejudices, described the typical country manse at the beginning of the eighteenth century as "small, low-roofed or heather thatched . . . with brew-house on one side and stable and byre at the other, facing a dunghill which stood amongst rubbish and nettles. The windows, about two or three feet high and eighteen inches broad, were usually only half glazed — the lower part made of wooden panels, for glass then was precious — and there peered in a meagre light through walls four to five feet thick. Inside the front door, which a tall man must stoop to enter, led to a dark passage or lobby with earthen or wooden floor, a 'laigh chamber or hall' on one side, a dark earth-floored kitchen at the other, and one small bedroom. Up the creaky, narrow staircase were two bedrooms (called 'firerooms' from possessing the luxury of a hearth) and a closet or study — the doors opening into each other, as there was no space for a passage." This quite misleading account can be corrected by a glance at one of the surviving older manses such as Anstruther Easter, built in 1590, or the main part of Ormiston. Cunningham's manse at Tranent consisted of two parts, a south block of medieval

<hr />

[1] H. G. Graham, *The Social Life of Scotland in the Eighteenth Century*, pp. 280-281.

date, with barrel vaulted rooms on the ground floor and a north wing of two stories of more recent date. In 1781 his heritors demolished the medieval block and in its place erected a three-story building containing, on each of the two lower floors, two main rooms with three small apartments, and five rooms on the top floor, in addition to those already existing in the north wing. They considered various estimates and, to ensure that the work was well done, accepted the highest, which was just under £300. It had a garden of close on an acre. His Secession neighbour, Robert Sheriff, had a house of five rooms looking south across the grass between his church and the street.

Like all his neighbouring parish ministers Cunningham was receiving from the heritors a teind stipend, fluctuating with the price of grain, which made his standard of living equal to that of an East Lothian farmer and superior to that of many small lairds in the north. This set a wide financial gulf between him and the poor, but with the kirk session and the heritors he was continually making provision, even if tiny, for them. In keeping with the general Scottish custom the Tranent session limited its charity to its own people. The heritors resolved "that vagrant poor of every Denomination have no claim upon the Funds of the Parish, and discharge the application of any of the Poor's Fund for that purpose in future". Payments ran from 6d to 1s weekly. The heritors stated that they "are of the opinion that Alex. Waddel's Pension, 2s per week, is too much, recommend to Session to reduce his allowance and to find him Employment as soon as possible". Accordingly the Session instructed one of its members, "John Hedglie, to take the boy to the pottery and see and get him taken into employment, certifying that if after being so entailed, and running away, the session shall consider themselves as entirely freed from the burden of his support".[1]

Cunningham's session exercised that parochial discipline so characteristic of all churches where the Calvinist tradition had ruled, and so deeply resented in many quarters. Profanation of the Sabbath day occasionally appears as an offence in his kirk session records but, as elsewhere, discipline had now come to be concerned with hardly anything other than sexual offences. Tradition obliged sessions to exercise discipline but while there were those, especially in the west country, who were strict in the

[1] T. A. Kerr, op. cit. xv, p. 47.

matter, the Seceders were perfectly correct in holding that the Moderates took a mild view of the sins of the flesh. Discipline, in any case, fell mostly upon those likely to require kirk session assistance at some stage in their lives. Carlyle observes that Lord Grange, one of his father's elders, had various ladies at home and maintained a mistress in London. Of Lord Drummore, also an elder, and one of his father's best friends, he wrote, "After he became a widower, he attached to himself a mistress, which, to do openly as he did, was at that time reckoned a great indecorum, at least in one of his age and reverent office."[1]

While staying with his uncle as a boy Cunningham had himself attended the parish school, just round the corner, where about 60 to 80 children were taught. Other children attended schools elsewhere in the parish, making a total of about 220, and in addition there were those who attended two schools run on Sunday evenings. Along with the heritors and kirk session the minister had a responsibility for the school, frequently visited it, working on good terms with the headmaster. The headmaster augmented his small salary by acting as clerk to the heritors and session, collector of poor rates and road-money to bring in an income of about £70, about half that of the minister. Beside the school was the schoolhouse, a two-story building of five main rooms, roofed with the curved red tiles so familiar on Lothian roofs. In a community of this kind the State scarcely made itself felt, at least by government action, but the sub-systems of society operated powerfully, and in each of them the Church had integrated itself with local life and could make its weight felt, even in quarters indifferent to its faith and worship. The Seceders had standards of their own but, taken on the whole the mind of the local community and the parish church reflected each other.

As the Moderates came to power a group of ministers decided to challenge the censoriousness which claimed to speak for the whole Church but was, they held, no more than the voice of an obstreperous minority. John Home, the minister of Athelstaneford, had written a pseudo-Shakespearean tragedy entitled *The Douglas*, which he carried south in February 1755, the manuscript in one pocket of his greatcoat and a clean shirt and nightcap in the other, in the hope that Garrick might be persuaded to put it on the boards of his London theatre. No more than the title is

[1] A. Carlyle, op. cit. pp. 11, 321.

Scottish, for the culture of the Moderates had cut loose in some ways from its native roots and looked to England. In everything other than the name it bore, Home's play is no more than an aping of the second-rate efforts of eighteenth-century English dramatists. Its author was no more than a dilettante, but his country, or a part of it, was flattered at last to have produced a dramatist. "As we sat over our tea," wrote Boswell[1] at Inveraray, "Mr Home's tragedy of Douglas was mentioned. I put Dr Johnson in mind that once, in a coffee-house at Oxford, he called to old Mr Sheridan, 'How came you, sir, to give Home a gold medal for writing that foolish play?' and defied Mr Sheridan to show ten good lines in it. He did not insist that they should be together, but that there were not ten good lines in the whole play." Boswell quoted some lines from Douglas, but Johnson dismissed them with a snort as bogus rhetoric. Garrick, when he read the play, shared Johnson's opinion, so the manuscript was brought back to Edinburgh where The Douglas was performed on 14 December 1756 to rapturous applause.

Controversy at once broke out over a play written by a minister. "On the third night," says Carlyle, "I had attended the playhouse . . . being well aware that all the fanatics and some other enemies would be on the watch, and make all the advantage they possibly could against me. . . . I drew on myself all the clamours of tongues and violence of persecution which I afterwards underwent."[2] Edinburgh Presbytery at once took action. The minister of Liberton abjectly apologized for his attendance at the play, pleading "that he had gone to the playhouse only once, and endeavoured to conceal himself in a corner, to avoid giving offence . . . expressing his deep sorrow for what he had done, and firm resolution to be more circumspect for the future". He was suspended for some weeks, and the Presbytery wrote to six other presbyteries calling on them to take similar disciplinary action. From the Presbytery of Duns, where the Moderates were in control, they received a reply which is one of the unremembered curiosities of insolent literature.[3] When Carlyle returned from Dumfries in February he learned that his own Presbytery had decided to prosecute him. Knowing that their case had a legal

---

[1] James Boswell, A Tour to the Hebrides, p. 358.
[2] A. Carlyle, op. cit. pp. 329–30.
[3] N. Morren, op. cit. ii, pp. 112–32.

weakness in that the Church had never foreseen the possibility of a minister attending a theatre, he asked for a stated case, defended his action in the Presbytery, which was against him, in the Synod, where he had more success, and finally in the Assembly, where he won by 117 votes to 39.[1] Next day an Act was passed forbidding the clergy to attend the theatre but, as Carlyle commented, although Edinburgh ministers, being known, kept away from the city theatre, "yet the more remote clergymen, when occasionally in town, had almost universally attended the play-house; and now . . . when all men were convinced that the violent proceedings they had witnessed were the effects of bigotry or jealousy . . . the more distant clergy returned to their usual amusement in the theatre when occasionally in town".

This was more than an incident. Carlyle and his friends had concluded that the Puritans were only a minority, that they alienated educated opinion, and that it was hypocritical to countenance their prejudices. He was convinced that he had broken their power. "In 1784, when the great actress Mrs Siddons first appeared in Edinburgh, during the sitting of the General Assembly, that court was obliged to fix all its important business for the alternate days when she did not act, as all the younger members, clergy as well as laity, took their stations in the theatre on those days by three in the afternoon. . . . It was of great importance to discriminate the artificial virtues and vices, formed by ignorance and superstition, from those that are real, lest the continuance of such a bar should have given check to the rising liberality of the young scholars, and preventing those of better birth or more ingenious minds from entering into the profession."[2]

Robertson and his colleagues in the leadership of the Moderates had to face continual opposition in the Assembly from men who shared much of their outlook but had keen anxiety about their policy and its results. In the Assembly of 1765 it was stated that there were now 120 dissenting congregations with a total of 100,000 communicants, and that the numbers were steadily growing. Adam Gib, a Secession leader whom even his own people regarded as too much given to "asperity of language",[3] questioned these suspiciously round figures,[4] and so far as may be seen,

[1] A. Carlyle, op. cit. p. 338. *AGA*, 1757, v; cf. Unprinted Acts.
[2] A. Carlyle, op. cit. p. 339.   [3] J. McKerrow, op. cit. p. 355.
[4] N. Morren, op. cit. ii, p. 305*n*.

there were actually 87 Secession and Relief congregations at the time,[1] most of them small, so that the membership can have been no more than a fraction of the number stated; but this was bad enough. Presbyteries were therefore called on to report on the number of dissenting meeting-houses within their bounds, the strength of their membership, and the reasons for the growth of dissent, particularly in the abuse of patronage.[2] As a consequence it was reported to the Assembly of 1766 that the abuse of patronage had been a great cause of schism in the Church, that action should be taken to end it, and that there should be a conference between presbyteries and the landed gentry on the best means to do so. There was in the Church a strong party anxious to prevent the rise of sectarianism and to meet the valid objections of the Seceders, and no less a man than the Moderator for that year defended the proposals, but Robertson vigorously defended the existing practice. Patronage, he argued, had given the Church educated ministers, it was the law of the land, and the Church had her own means of controlling any abuse of it. In the end, he secured the rejection of the proposals by 99 votes to 85.[3]

Confidence among the Moderates had passed into arrogance, and a readiness to give heed to the passive majority had degenerated into an indifference to opponents. Robertson's speech is remarkable more for its defence of patronage than for any attempt to meet its critics. He had lost all interest in conciliation of those whom he could not persuade, but a deep sense of anxiety existed among his colleagues, not only at the growth of dissent and the steady destruction of the parochial system, but at the reasons behind it. The rising tide of feeling may be seen in the instance of a new minister presented to the parish of St Ninian's. For seven years the congregation, with the support of the Presbytery, opposed him. At last, in 1773, under compulsion from the Assembly[4] the reluctant Presbytery met to induct him. Many members were absent. The minister of Dollar, as Moderator, in his opening prayer did not ask for any blessing on the purpose for which they had met, and when it fell to him to give the charges — to address

[1] W. McKelvie, *Annals and Statistics of the United Presbyterian Church*, p. 32.

[2] N. Morren, op. cit. ii, p. 311.

[3] Ibid. p. 334.

[4] *AGA*, 1773, unprinted, 25 May, Sess. 5; 1774, unprinted, 26 May, Sess. 7; 27 May, Sess. 8; 1775, 30 May, Sess. 5.

the new minister — he said, "We are met here this day in obedience to the sentence of the General Assembly to admit you minister of St Ninian's. There has been a formidable opposition made against you by six hundred heads of families, sixty heritors, and all the elders except one. This opposition has continued for seven years; and if you shall this day be admitted, you can have no pastoral relation to the souls of this parish; you will never be regarded as the shepherd to go before the sheep; they know you not, and will not follow you. Your admission can only be regarded as a sinecure, and yourself as a stipend lifter. . . . Now, sir, I conjure you, by the mercy of God, give up this presentation. . . . I conjure you, by that peace which you would wish to have in your dying hour, and that awful and impartial account which in a little time you must give to God of your own soul, and of the souls of this parish, before the tribunal of our Lord Jesus Christ, give it up." But the new minister stood up in the largely empty church and replied, "I forgive you for what you have now said. May God forgive you. Proceed to execute the orders of your superiors."[1]

Though he was not yet sixty years old and had still thirteen years of life before him, Robertson followed the example of Charles V and withdrew from the Assembly and its leadership in 1780, ostensibly to devote his time to historical studies. He had accomplished what he set out to do and his decisions governed the policy of the Church until 1834. His opponents seized on his departure to reopen the question of patronage, but without success. Throughout his long reign the Assembly, as a mere formality, had annually renewed its protest against patronage, but in 1784 it dropped even this. Patronage was no longer to be regarded as a grievance. The Seceders were indifferent; they had no wish to be reconciled with a Church which they had rejected and at whose expense they were steadily growing, but the Relief Church would have been glad to be accepted as an ally of the National Church much as the Methodists might have been attached to the Church of England. The Relief Church, said the Rev. James Baine[2] of Paisley, who joined it in 1766, "does not poison our people with principles of bigotry and separation, but rather keeps them from that snare, and preserves them in as full communion with the

[1] J. Cunningham, *The Church History of Scotland*, ii, pp. 378-9.
[2] N. Morren, op. cit. ii, p. 318. *AGA*, 1766, vi.

worthy ministers of the Church of Scotland as ever. Is it candid then, or political, first to cast such men out of her communion . . . and yet to cast on them the most injurious calumny of sectaries and schismatics? The Presbytery of Relief . . . dare not decline communion with any who have the knowledge . . . of real Christianity." This was not accepted. The imposition of discipline fastened on the Church an inability to adapt itself to a changing situation, and created a running sore.

CHAPTER FIVE

The New World of Thought

Scotland had long been an unruly country. If she had kings, she had little government as it is now known. Spasmodic efforts at national defence had to be organized by the feudal landlords and the control of crime and disorder was left to the barons' courts in the countryside and to the burgh magistrates in the towns. Those elements of local government which touched the mind and the pocket of the ordinary man most closely, education and poor relief, fell to the Church, a fact which goes part of the way towards explaining the force of demands for a popular voice in the selection of ministers. Apart from occasional incidents like the Glasgow Malt Tax riots of 1725 or the astonishing Porteous riot of 1736 when the mob, led by prominent citizens in disguise, lynched the captain of the town guard for supervising an execution, the Lowlands had been reduced to order of a sort. South of the Highland line there had been no large-scale defiance of authority since the battle of Bothwell Bridge in 1679. North of the Highland Line the suppression of the Rising of 1745, the stern measures taken against the clans, the confiscation of estates and suppression of hereditary jurisdictions, the banning of the tartan and the carrying of arms, the extension of the road system and the settlement of garrisons brought order to a quarter of Scotland where it had never been known before. No one but the unfortunate objects of this treatment regarded it as other than a blessing.

"The stealing of cows," wrote an English officer[1] stationed in the north as the Highlands began to be pacified, "they call 'lifting', a softening word for theft. . . . When a design is formed for this purpose, they go out in parties from ten to thirty men, and traverse large tracts of mountains, till they arrive at the place where they intend to commit their depredations; and that they

[1] Edward Burt, *Letters from the North of Scotland*, ii, pp. 229–31.

choose to do as distant as they can from their own dwellings. The principal time for this wicked practice is the Michaelmas moon, when the cattle are in condition fit for markets held on the borders of the Lowlands. They drive the stolen cattle in the night time and by day they lie concealed with them in by-places among the mountains where hardly any others come; or in woods, if any such are to be found on their way. . . . The Highland lairds tell out their daughters' tochers[1] by the light of the Michaelmas moon.''

But when Dr Johnson visited the Highlands in 1773, less than a score of years later, he wrote, "There was perhaps never any change of national manners so quick, so great, and so general, as that which operated in the Highlands, by the last conquest and the subsequent laws. We came thither too late to see what we expected, a people of peculiar appearance, and a system of antiquated life. The clans retain little now of their original character; their ferocity of temper is softened, their military ardour is extinguished, their dignity of independence is depressed, their contempt of government subdued. . . . They are now acquainted with money, and the possibility of gain will by degrees make them industrious.'' Mistaken in this last judgment on the Highlander, Johnson was correct in observing the coming of law and order in the hitherto untamed north.

The homes of the landed gentry of Scotland had always been fortified; against invaders, against their king, and — with good reason — against their neighbours. Great houses built by the king, as at Linlithgow, or by some powerful noble, as at Crichton, took the form of a square, outwardly grim and defensive, but looking to a more pleasing courtyard within, while the poorer lairds lived in the bleak and comfortless square towers of which an example may be found in almost every Lowland parish. As the seventeenth century brought more settled times and greater prosperity, most buildings of this kind lost their strictly defensive character but still kept the age-old Scottish planning. George Heriot's Hospital, built between 1628 and 1695, has virtually the same plan as Linlithgow, however different in other ways, while Prestonfield, a laird's house of about the same period and a mile or two away, perpetuated the tower plan after the need for defence had gone.

But towards the close of the century there appeared architects

[1] i.e. They count out their dowries.

who completely abandoned Scottish tradition, taking their models from England and France, and clients prepared to pay for their work. Sir William Bruce's great house at Kinross belongs to a different world, both in planning and in detail, from earlier Scottish domestic architecture, while Hopetoun, which Bruce began in 1696 and William Adam, an able architect overshadowed by a greater son, completed, might have been the home of a French noble of the eighteenth century. The work of these men and successors such as Colin Campbell, James Gibbs, Sir William Chambers, and Robert Adam tell at a glance how great was the breach between the Scotland of the eighteenth century and the years that went before. A new pattern of society had come into being though only, as yet, in a small but powerful section of the nation. Only great wealth could pay for such houses. The beginnings of improvements in Scottish agriculture have been associated with the years following the Union[1] of 1707, but the building of these great mansions tells of a new and unwonted prosperity among landlords even before the Union. Of all the arts, architecture was the first in Scotland to display the coming of the Age of the Enlightenment, and the society which commissioned and appreciated it must have lost all sympathy with the theologizings of the seventeenth century. It was a cosmopolitan society. Scotland had long been a small and isolated country on the perimeter of Europe. During the Middle Ages she had many contacts with France, but after 1560 continental contacts were fewer, and rare indeed if Scottish mercenary soldiers and students in Protestant Holland are discounted. But now, as the effects of the Union began to be felt, the Scottish aristocracy were increasingly drawn into the circle of English life, manners, and thought, and some knowledge of the continent became the mark of every cultured gentleman so that even the half-wit Marquis of Annandale was sent to tour Europe under the oversight of no less a tutor than David Hume.

The Moderates had set out to extend this new order and discipline into the life of the Church where, rather than in the field of national politics, popular dissension found expression. The average Scotsman did not care whether Walpole or Stanhope, Newcastle or Pitt, held office in London but he had more reason to care about the kind of man who presided over his local kirk

[1] P. Hume Brown, *History of Scotland*, iii, p. 257.

commonplace. In 1731 Robert Wallace,[1] one of their early leaders,
wrote, "The debates of our time are about the foundations of
Christianity, and a question is made whether the Christian Church
is to have a being." Thirty years later he wrote, "Scepticism is in
a very flourishing footing; perhaps it has not abounded so much
in any age since the commencement of Christianity, nor has it
prevailed more in any country than Britain." Though they were,
on the whole, pragmatic rather than intellectual apologists, the
Moderates were convinced that it was necessary that the Christian
faith should be presented in such terms that it would hold the
loyalty of men in the changed world of their time. It was an effort
that had to be made if the country was not to be divided between
the upper classes and the intelligentsia, sceptical and hostile to
the faith, and the lower classes, superstitious and bigoted, but
devout in the fashion of an older day; or, at least, that is how they
saw it.[2] They came to be associated with a frame of mind, a
theological outlook which was observed rather than stated, one
which created a link between them and the men who now ruled
Scottish life, but which was almost unaware of some essential
elements in the Christian faith.

In the literature of the day Allan Ramsay and William Hamilton
of Bangour were writing more or less in the way of the older
Scotland, but it was Francis Hutcheson who spoke for the new
order in society. Calvinism was in eclipse. For long Scotland had
only heard it in second- or third-rate statements. Men had forgotten its concentration on the majesty and wonder of God, and
did not remember that what were reckoned its distinctive notes
had been sounded by St Augustine and — in some instances —
by St Thomas Aquinas. They saw only its intolerance and the
interminable trivialities of some of its scholastic exponents in the
seventeenth century. Discipline, one of its distinguishing features,
was intended to produce Christian living as the fruit of Christian

[1] H. R. Sefton, *The Early Moderates*, p. 21.
[2] Jeremy J. Cater, "The Making of Principal Robertson", *SHR*, xlix,
p. 79.

faith, but instead it had become a matter of the public punishment of offenders for sexual misconduct, leaving among the class which produced its victims the conviction that it was no more than a narrow-minded tyranny. This allied itself with the growing individualism of Christian thought and the loss of the awareness of the communal nature and unity of the Church.[1] While Hutcheson's thought moved within a Christian framework he was always the philosopher and never primarily the theologian. Rational and undogmatic, he was a humanist whose understanding of man's nature was dominated by the idea of benevolence rather than that of the fall. He was an optimist and a utilitarian, one of whose best known sayings anticipated Jeremy Bentham, fundamentally a second-rate thinker despite his attractiveness, whose limitations are exhibited by his unawareness of the place of tragedy in life. The Cambridge Platonists might have appealed to the men who heard Hutcheson lecture, but they were little known in Scotland. Instead the destructive radicalism of the Deists was making inroads among the educated laity and even, although it was not acknowledged, among the clergy. Comparatively few went to the fountain-head to read the original writers, but the outlook spread rapidly as the products of the London bookshops for the first time sold well in Scotland. Here and there, in the *Spectator* or the *Tatler*, Scottish readers might find orthodox contemporary Anglicanism, but when they came to Alexander Pope they found Deism, politely and wittily stated. Pope was a Roman Catholic, but the spirit of the age was unrestrained by ancient divisions and made progress in all denominations. There was a family of the name of Pope or — to give it the Scottish spelling — Pape or Paip, long established in Ross and Sutherland, which supplied quite a number of ministers to the Church. One of them, Hector Paip of Loth, wore his Episcopalian surplice when he preached. He continued to do this until his death in 1717, and was the last to wear this vestment within the Presbyterian Church. His son, Alexander Pope of Reay,[2] rode his pony from Caithness to Twickenham to visit his great namesake, the poet, with whom he claimed kinship. There is no hint of any difference in outlook between the two, one a nominal Roman Catholic and the other a Presbyterian minister, for each had absorbed Deism.

[1] John Kennedy, *Presbyterian Authority and Discipline*, p. 67.
[2] *Fasti*, III, p. 367.

For Pope, as for all the Deists, the fall of man was an irrelevance and the state of life of primitive man was seen as one of innocence and benevolence. This opinion, it is to be feared, was not regarded as a hypothesis but was uncritically accepted as historical.

> Nor think, in nature's state they blindly trod;
> The state of nature was the reign of God:
>
> .   .   .
>
> Pride then was not; nor arts, that pride to aid:
> Man walked with beast, joint tenant of the shade;
> The same his table, and the same his bed;
> No murder clothed him, and no murder fed.
> In the same temple, the resounding wood,
> All vocal beings hymned their equal God.[1]

The knowledge of God was held to be natural to man, and implanted in him from the beginning.

> Lo, the poor Indian! whose untutored mind
> Sees God in clouds, or hears him in the wind;
> His soul, proud science never taught to stray
> Far as the solar walk, or milky way;
> Yet simple nature to his hope has given,
> Beyond the cloud-topt hill, an humbler heaven,
> Some safer world in depths of woods embraced,
> Some happier island in the watery waste,
> Where slaves once more their native land behold,
> No fiends torment, no Christians thirst for gold.[2]

Reason and nature would therefore lead the mind to God, and no other guide was needed.

> Say first, of God above or Man below,
> What can we reason but from what we know?
> Of Man, what see we but his station here,
> From which to reason, or to which refer?
> Through worlds unnumbered though the God be known,
> 'Tis our's to trace Him only in our own.[3]

[1] Alexander Pope, *Essay on Man*, III, ll. 147–56.
[2] Ibid. I, ll. 99–108.   [3] Ibid. I, ll. 17–22.

Consequently revelation, in the Biblical sense, was superfluous and religion consisted in morality without much reference to doctrine. All forms of worship were seen as directed to the one divine Being, the First Cause of all, so that every form of intolerance and exclusiveness must be abandoned by the informed mind.

> For forms of government let fools contest:
> Whate'er is best administered is best;
> For modes of faith let graceless zealots fight;
> His can't be wrong whose life is in the right:
> In Faith and Hope the world will disagree,
> For all mankind's concern is Charity:
> All must be false that thwart this one great end;
> And all of God, that bless mankind or mend.[1]

Pope's elegant verse was widely read and admired, not only in eighteenth-century Scotland, but well into Victorian times. The Deism which he popularized was remote, not merely from the dry language of the Westminster Confession, but also, despite some superficial conformity, from the essentials of the Christian faith. The liberal distribution on his pages of those capital letters with which abstract conceptions are dignified and almost personified, tells that Deism had set out on its quest for an understanding of life from abstract concepts. It was indifferent to, and often scarcely aware of, the historical facts from which the Christian faith came. Its god was "a hypothetical abstraction, a *deus ex machina*, invoked to make the system work, but not one who was encountered personally in history and present experience".[2] Lacking a Christian basis, it achieved intellectual respectability by appealing to the authority of Sir Isaac Newton whose scientific writings portrayed an ordered universe ruled by inscrutable law, the best of all possible worlds. But if the prestige of Newton was invoked the thought was that of Leibniz. "Whatever is," wrote Pope,[3] failing to foresee Voltaire's caricature of Leibniz as Doctor Pangloss, "is right."

Despite her contacts with France before the Reformation and with the Protestant countries of Europe afterwards, Scottish thought had ventured little beyond the horizons of her national

---

[1] Alexander Pope, *Essay on Man*, iii, ll. 303–10.
[2] Colin Brown, *Philosophy and the Christian Faith*, p. 57.
[3] Alexander Pope, op. cit. i, l. 294.

tradition, but with the coming of Deism her intellectuals had moved into a climate of opinion which was truly international, even though France was its homeland and Paris its capital.[1] James Thomson, the nearest Scottish equivalent of Pope, had shed all living contact with Scottish tradition save a few picturesque memories of use in similes. His father, Thomas Thomson, minister of Ednam from 1692 until 1700 and of Southdean from 1700 until 1716, had been a man of the old school who met his death when an evil spirit or poltergeist, which he had been exorcizing from a house in his parish, retaliated with unexpected effectiveness.[2] His son has about a dozen wonderful lines of verse hidden among his writings but, on the whole, he had what might be called an anti-Midas touch, for all the gold he touched turned to commonplace. The great popularity of his blank verse amongst the landed classes of his time, and the middle and upper working classes for long after as deistic thought filtered down through society, came from the fact that it faithfully stated the platitudes of the day in simple terms.

Thomson was educated for the Scottish ministry and long hankered after a benefice in the English Church, but the most significant feature in his writings is the absence of any distinctively Christian content. In his first successful poem, written in 1725, he tells of his reading in the classics, but there is no mention of the Bible,[3] and his one attempt at Christian verse is so bad that it reveals his indifference.

> Observe the rising lily's snowy grace,
> Observe the various vegetable race:
> They neither toil nor spin, but careless grow;
> Yet see how warm they blush! How bright they glow!
> What regal vestments can with them compare?
> What king so shining? Or what queen so fair?[4]

His woolly mind had uncritically absorbed a sentimental Deism scarcely distinguishable from Pantheism.

---

[1] C. L. Becker, *The Heavenly City of the Eighteenth Century Philosophers*, pp. 33–34.

[2] James Thomson, *Poetical Works*, vii.

[3] James Thomson, "Winter", ll. 400ff.

[4] James Thomson, "Paraphrase of Matthew 6:25–34".

> These, as they change, Almighty Father, these
> Are but the varied God! The rolling year
> Is full of Thee. Forth in the pleasing Spring
> Thy beauty walks. . . .
> Then comes Thy glory in the Summer months
> With light and heat refulgent. . . .
> Thy bounty shines in Autumn unconfined,
> And spreads a common feast for all that lives.
> In Winter awful Thou![1]

Whatever theology Thomson had was drawn, not from the Bible, but, as in the case of Pope, from a popularized impression of the scientific writings of Newton, for whom he wrote a grotesque obituary.[2] A passage from the preface to the second edition of Newton's *Principia*, "we may now more clearly behold the beauties of Nature . . . and be thence incited the more profoundly to reverence and adore the great Maker and Lord of all",[3] might well have served as text for "The Seasons". If Thomson was at all representative of the divinity students of his time it is easy to see why the Seceders did not want them as ministers.

Thus Scots were painlessly introduced to a religion of nature, a version of the Christian faith, as it were, but deprived of everything specifically Christian, and armed instead with a supreme confidence in man and the power of reason. If they read Fielding's *Tom Jones*, they found it there also. It supplied much of the idealism for the Freemasonry then being founded, and it is worth noting that Alexander Ferguson,[4] whose theology scandalized the evangelically minded in 1767, was the minister in whose parish the mother lodge of Scottish Freemasonry was founded. In the public mind it came to be so intimately associated with the Christian faith in God and so long lived, that the street corner atheists of the early twentieth century still directed their arguments against it. However, at its first coming it was a congenial outlook for men whose culture was expressed by the new architecture of the Scottish upper classes, and beside it Calvinism seemed an outdated creed fit only for those classes from which

---

[1] James Thomson, "A Hymn; The Seasons".
[2] James Thomson, "Sacred to the Memory of Sir Isaac Newton", ll. 5-8.
[3] Quoted in Basil Willey, *The Eighteenth Century Background*, p. 139.
[4] *Scots Magazine*, xxix, p. 175.

the Seceders were recruited. So far as they were concerned, the age of reason had dawned, and it did not occur to them that it might have a sunset.

This optimism, which went with Deism, sprang from the fact that in eighteenth-century Scotland, as in most of Europe, the wealthy and educated enjoyed a security and felicity unknown in earlier times. Those who had never lived before 1789, said Talleyrand, looking back sadly on the age of reason, had never known how pleasant life could be. The upper classes enjoyed new pleasures and as yet retained their ancient privileges. Superstition, bigotry, intolerance, and strife belonged to the past, or so it seemed, in the enlightened century which had arrived. Thus the prevailing mood of facile assurance and complacency ran counter to that sombre awareness of the mystery and tragedy of life and death so deeply rooted in Scottish tradition and expressed in poets such as Dunbar and the writers of the ballads, but which, for the time being, found little expression.

In 1743 Robert Blair, Home's predecessor as minister of Athelstaneford, published a poem in blank verse entitled, "The Grave". Despite its incongruous eighteenth-century trappings, its "skulls and coffins, epitaphs and worms" and a superficial resemblance to moralistic writings like Edward Young's "Night Thoughts" or Hervey's "Meditations Among the Tombs", Blair's poem in places harks back to the old Scottish awareness of the tragic and mysterious. Its antecedents were not so much literary, whatever its form, as popular and traditional. Any literary merits it had were scanty, but if it counted for nothing among the educated it had a very wide circle of readers among the middle and lower classes who, like Dr Johnson, "had learned by hard experience that human life is a state in which there is little to be enjoyed and much to be endured".[1] These classes were to rise in the world, and among them what Adam Smith called "the old fanatical spirit", far from declining, was growing in self-confidence. At the close of the century Coleridge made unacknowledged borrowings from Blair, and William Blake provided magnificent illustrations for his third-rate poem, each aware that in a small way its consciousness of God, not as deified Reason, but as *Mysterium Tremendum*, had foreshadowed that spirit which was to displace the confident rationalism of the Augustan age.

[1] B. Willey, op. cit. p. 49.

Scotland received Deism, but made no material contribution to its literature, for she was to provide a sterner brand of scepticism in the writings of David Hume. Born in Edinburgh in 1711 and brought up on his father's estate in Chirnside, where Ebenezer and Ralph Erskine, the founders of the Secession, also spent their boyhood, Hume owed nothing to his background. A precocious child, he went to study Greek and philosophy at Edinburgh University when eleven years old. He seems — to put the matter kindly — to have been aware of his intellectual superiority to his tutors, and certainly was not greatly indebted to them. No shadow of Scottish tradition remained in him. Long before he ever saw France he was a man of the Enlightenment. It would seem that he had never known the Christian faith from within, but only as a spectator. After some unsettled years a legacy of £50 per annum from his father[1] enabled him to live in France, first at Rheims, and then at La Flèche in Anjou, where the traveller, in whom an intense prejudice against the Roman Church[2] was one of the few signs of a Scottish upbringing, learned of the supposed miracles of the Abbé Paris.[3] Like Berkeley, Hume produced his best work at an astonishingly early age and in 1738 he published at London his *Treatise on Human Nature*. Fully conscious of his own gifts, he was astounded at the public indifference. A warmer welcome greeted the first part of his much more commonplace *Essays* when published at Edinburgh in 1742. Convinced that this cold response arose "more from the manner than from the matter" and that he had been too hasty in publishing, he recast the first part as an *Inquiry Concerning Human Understanding*, only to be disappointed again. Despite a rising tide of criticism his *Inquiry Concerning the Principles of Morals*, as he says, came "unnoticed and unobserved into the world" in 1752.

This determined him to seek other fields. "No English author in that age was more celebrated both abroad and at home, than Hobbes," he observed.[4] In our time he is much neglected; a lively instance, how precarious all reputations founded on reasoning and philosophy. So, anxious both for public applause and for an assured income, Hume obtained the post of Librarian to the

---

[1] David Hume, *Works*, I, iv.

[2] David Hume, *National History of Religion*, VII, x, xi. *History of England*, VI, pp. 287, 323.   [3] Hume, "Of Miracles", *Works*, IV, p. 145.

[4] Hume, *History of England*, VII, p. 346.

Advocates' Library and turned to the writing of history. This might seem an odd choice for a man who had expressed such a view of the nature of causation, but Hume was not troubled about the need for consistency. Aware that Descartes and Leibniz had cast doubt on the validity of historical knowledge, Hume had shown signs of interest in the subject since he started to write.[1] This, he was convinced, was a subject to command a wide circle of readers,[2] and the event proved him correct. His *History of England*, now somewhat unjustly neglected since it is most readable, brought speedy rewards of fame and fortune. But where Gibbon was to be aided by a lively understanding of those on whom his work centred, Hume — like Voltaire — was hindered by a lack of sympathy. Words like medieval, priestly, religious, and barbaric had an emotional rather than a conceptual significance for him and he was not concerned to enquire further into them, despite an evident determination to be fair even to those, like the Covenanters, whom he disliked.

Hume's most important contributions to philosophy are to be found in the first book of the *Treatise on Human Nature*. Whereas the Deists had been filled with confidence in the power of reason Hume employed reason to demonstrate its own ineffectiveness. His was a total scepticism, or would have been had he been consistent. It was impossible to prove the existence of things outside oneself. "The idea of a substance as well as of a mode, is nothing but a collection of simple ideas, that are united by the imagination, and have particular names assigned them."[3] As he questioned the data of the senses, so he questioned that of the self. "If any impression gives rise to the idea of self, that impression must continue invariably the same, through the whole course of our lives; since self is supposed to exist after that manner. But there is no impression constant and invariable . . . and consequently there is no such idea. . . . For my part, when I enter most intimately into what I call *myself*, I always stumble on some particular perception or other, of heat or cold, light or shade, love or hatred, pain or pleasure. I never can catch myself at any time without a perception and never can observe anything but the perception. . . . Were

[1] Hume, *Treatise on Human Nature*, I, iii, p. 4; I, iii, p. 13. *Works*, I, pp. 115, 193–6.

[2] Hume, "On the Study of History", *Works*, IV, pp. 528–33.

[3] Hume, *Treatise on Human Nature*, I, i, p. 6. *Works*, I, p. 33.

all my perceptions removed by death, I should be entirely an-
nihilated. . . . I may venture to affirm of the rest of mankind, that
they are nothing but a bundle or collection of various perceptions."[1] But Hume's most famous paradox was his denial of
causation. "There is no object," he says, "which implies the existence of any other if we consider these objects in themselves, and
never look beyond the ideas which we form of them. . . . The
necessity, which makes two times two equal to four, or three
angles of a triangle equal to two right ones, lies only in the act
of the understanding, by which we consider and compare these
ideas; in like manner, the necessity of power, which unites causes
and effects, lies in the determination of the mind to pass from
the one to the other."[2]

"Hume's philosophy, whether true or false," says Bertrand
Russell,[3] "represents the bankruptcy of eighteenth century reasonableness. He starts out, like Locke, with the intention of being
sensible and empirical . . . but arrives at the disastrous conclusion
that from experience and observation nothing is to be learned.
There is no such thing as a rational belief." Hume, he says elsewhere, "represents, in a certain sense, a dead end. In his direction
it has been impossible to go further. To refute him has been, ever
since he wrote, a favourite pastime among metaphysicians. For
my part I find none of their refutations convincing; nevertheless
I cannot but hope that something less sceptical than Hume's
system may be discoverable."[4] In other words, as Hume himself
said of Berkeley, his arguments "admit of no answer, and produce
no conviction".[5] And of this, no one was better aware than Hume
himself.[6] "Whether your scepticism be as absolute and sincere as
you pretend," says a character in one of his dialogues, "we shall
learn by and by, when the company breaks up. We shall then see,
whether you go out at the door or by the window; and whether
you really doubt if your body has gravity, or can be injured by its
fall; according to popular opinion, derived from our fallacious
senses, and more fallacious experience."

---

[1] Hume, *Treatise on Human Nature*, I, iv, p. 6. *Works*, I, pp. 320–1.
[2] Hume, *Treatise on Human Nature*, I, p. 14. *Works*, I, p. 200.
[3] Bertrand Russell, *History of Western Philosophy*, p. 645.
[4] Ibid. p. 634.
[5] Hume, *Inquiry Concerning Human Understanding*, p. 12. *Works*, IV, p. 181.
[6] Hume, *Dialogues Concerning Natural Religion*, p. 1. *Works*, II, p. 426.

Hume's comprehensive scepticism extends to all the major points of religious belief, despite the elaborate irony with which from time to time he pays tribute to convention. It is hard to see why he restricted his open attacks to the Roman Church and avoided explicit repudiation of the New Testament, for the days of intolerance had passed and the implications of his writings were evident to everyone likely to read them. In the *Natural History of Religion* he set out to attack the Deist teaching that the noble savage, as yet uncorrupted, had worshipped one God, the Creator. Since he was no more of an anthropologist than his opponents and had no intention of investigating the mind of contemporary primitives he drew on classical literature. "It is a matter of fact incontestable," he wrote,[1] "that about 1,700 years ago all mankind were polytheists." Religion had arisen from the anxious fears of primitive man alone in an unfriendly universe, the changing and inconsistent phenomena of which he ascribed, not to natural causes, but to a number of unseen and superhuman beings.[2] Monotheism arose when men began to think of one divine being as their particular patron, to be cajoled or lauded; but it was seldom found in a pure state. Many evils had arisen from religion. "The greatest crimes have been found . . . compatible with a superstitious piety and devotion." In particular, as monotheism increased, so did intolerance.[3]

When he rewrote the *Treatise of Human Nature* as the *Inquiry Concerning Human Understanding* Hume inserted his famous chapter on miracles. A wise man, he says, proportions his belief to the evidence. Where our experience is not uniform, evidence can only point to probability, but "a miracle is a violation of the laws of nature; and as a firm and unalterable experience has established these laws, the proof against a miracle, from the very nature of the fact, is as entire as any argument from experience can possibly be imagined".[4] He urges that there is not, in all history, a miracle sufficiently attested, that humanity is credulous, that miracles are related "among ignorant and barbarous nations", that many bogus miracles are known, and that falsehoods are only too hard to disprove with the passage of time. "Upon the whole, then, it appears,

[1] Hume, *Natural History of Religion*, p. 1. *Works*, IV, p. 437.
[2] *Nat. Hist. of Religion*, xiii, ii. *Works*, IV, pp. 498, 442.
[3] *Nat. Hist. of Religion*, v, viii, xiv, ix. *Works*, IV, pp. 465, 471, 508, 474.
[4] Hume, *Inquiry Concerning Human Understanding*, x. *Works*, IV, p. 133.

that no testimony for any kind of miracle has ever amounted to a probability, much less to a proof."[1]

In his will Hume bequeathed his manuscripts to Adam Smith[2] with instructions that he should publish the *Dialogues Concerning Natural Religion*, till then unprinted. The setting is the library of Cleanthes, a philosopher. Demea, a spokesman for "rigid inflexible orthodoxy" — possibly modelled on that George Home of Chirnside who had tutored Hume in his boyhood — explains that he first teaches a child implicit devotion. A child should be introduced to natural theology only when he has learned to discount philosophy because of — and here one may presume that Hume ironically refers to himself — "the strange, ridiculous conclusions which some of the greatest geniuses have derived from the principles of mere human reason".[3] Philo, the representative of "careless scepticism", mockingly commends the wisdom of the simple Demea, since life is indeed an inscrutable mystery. Thereafter Cleanthes and he, with occasional protests and interjections from Demea, debate the force of scepticism, the being and attributes of God, and the value of the arguments involved. Cleanthes offers some succour to Demea by arguing from design in the universe, but when he affirms that this in itself is a sufficient foundation for religion, Demea replies indignantly that it must be a slight fabric which can be erected on so tottering a foundation.[4] But against the argument that the universe has a transcendent Creator Philo offers the thesis that it is an organism of which the Deity is the soul, and then, as an alternative, the atomic theory of Epicurus.[5] Turning to the mystery of evil, both natural and moral, in the universe, he tentatively concludes that nature provides evidence to attribute neither goodness nor malice to its Creator.[6] At this Demea reacts violently. "Are you secretly, then, a more dangerous enemy than Cleanthes himself?" "And are you so late in perceiving it?" replied Cleanthes.[7] "Believe me, Demea, your friend Philo, from the beginning, has been amusing himself at both our expense; and it must be confessed that injudicious reasoning of our vulgar theology has given him but too just a

---

[1] David Hume, *Inquiry Concerning Human Understanding*, x. *Works*, IV, p. 150.   [2] Hume, *Works*, I, xxviii.
[3] Hume, *Dialogues Concerning Natural Religion*. *Works*, II, pp. 423–4.
[4] Ibid. II, pp. 473–4.   [5] Ibid. II, p. 489.
[6] Ibid. II, p. 527.   [7] Ibid. II, p. 528.

handle of ridicule. . . ." "Blame not so much," interposed Philo, "the ignorance of these reverend gentlemen. They know how to change their style with the times. . . . As men have now learned to form principles and to draw consequences, it is necessary to change the batteries, and to make use of such arguments as will endure at least some scrutiny and examination." "I could observe," says the narrator, "that Demea did not at all relish the latter part of the discourse; and he took occasion soon after, on some pretence or other, to leave the company."

Hume was a kindly man, and well liked. When he set up house in the New Town of Edinburgh in 1770 at the corner of David Street, as it was intended to name it, and St Andrew Square, the housemaid told him one morning that some one had chalked "St David Street" on the wall. "Never mind, lassie," he said. "Many a better man has been made a saint o' before." Many anecdotes circulated relating to his supposed atheism or supposed belief.[1] At the close of the *Natural History of Religion*[2] he had written, "The whole is a riddle, an enigma, an inexplicable mystery. Doubt, uncertainty, suspense of judgement, appear the only result of our most accurate scrutiny concerning this subject." But it may be that his final words were those of Philo,[3] when he resumed the discussion with Cleanthes after Demea had gone out in dudgeon. "If we are not contented with calling the first and supreme cause a God or Deity, but desire to vary the expression; what can we call him but Mind or Thought, to which he is justly supposed to bear a considerable resemblance? . . . And here I must also acknowledge, Cleanthes, that as the works of Nature have a much greater analogy to the effects of *our* art and contrivance, than to those of *our* benevolence and justice, we have reason to infer, that the natural attributes of the Deity have a greater resemblance to those of men, than his moral have to human virtues. But what is the consequence? Nothing but this, that the moral qualities of man are more defective in their kind than his natural abilities. For, as the Supreme Being is allowed to be absolutely and entirely perfect, whatever differs most from him, departs the farthest from the supreme standard of rectitude and perfection. These, Cleanthes, are my unfeigned sentiments on this

---

[1] H. G. Graham, *Scottish Men of Letters in the Eighteenth Century*, pp. 35–59.

[2] Hume, *Natural History of Religion. Works*, IV, p. 513.

[3] Ibid. IV, pp. 536–7.

subject . . . but, in proportion to my veneration for true religion, is my abhorrence of vulgar superstitions; and I indulge a peculiar pleasure, I confess, in pushing such principles, sometimes into absurdity, and sometimes into impiety." Despite the last paragraph of the Dialogues, which commends Cleanthes, this may be Hume's own last word, but his continual use of irony leaves it, as no doubt he would have wished it to remain, an open question.

As for the reaction of the Church to Hume, when the Assembly of 1755 met, there was published a pamphlet[1] attacking him and Lord Kames, an elder who had made some unguarded excursions into theology. "You deposed a minister who disowned your authority, but enrol as a member of your courts an elder who has disowned the authority of Almighty God; and that some of you at least live in the greatest intimacy with one who represents the blessed Saviour as an impostor, and His religion as a cunningly devised fable. May your conduct be such as fully to wipe off all these reproaches." But the Assembly disappointed the writer by doing no more than recommending ministers to be vigilant against infidelity.[2] Next year there was a full debate, not on the floor of the house, but in a committee. No question of censorship was involved, but that of personal discipline. Hume, it was argued, was no Christian and therefore the Church had no authority over him. To this it was replied, quite accurately, that he had never repudiated his baptism, but after two days of heated debate no action was taken.[3] From the Reformation until the close of the Second Episcopate the Church had seen herself as empowered to act against any citizen, but this decision was clear evidence that she now saw herself as a voluntary society. No minister of standing had raised the case against Hume. It was the work of George Anderson, an obscure man without a parish. Now almost eighty years old, the contemporary of the unhappy boy who was hanged for atheism in 1696, he had lived to protest that ministers were openly friendly with David Hume.[4]

The Moderates were of opinion that a reply was made not only to Hume but to infidels in general by their success in establishing the intellectual status of the clergy as that of men who must be

---

[1] N. Morren, *Annals of the General Assembly of the Church of Scotland*, ii, pp. 54–61.   [2] *AGA*, 1755, iv.

[3] N. Morren, op. cit. ii, pp. 86–98. R. M. Schmitz, *Hugh Blair*, pp. 29–35.
[4] cf. supra p. 14; cf. *Fasti*, iii, p. 114.

respected. "Soon after the Rebellion of 1745," Carlyle wrote,[1] "Lord Elibank took up his residence in Scotland, and his seat being between Dr Robertson's church and John Home's, he became intimately acquainted with them, who cured him of his contempt for the Presbyterian clergy, made him change or soften down many of his original opinions, and prepared him for becoming a most agreeable member of the literary society of Edinburgh."

But, apart from making it plain that a man did not need to be ignorant or superstitious to be a Christian, the Church produced replies to the challenge. Hume, wrote Dr George Campbell of Marischal College, Aberdeen, had argued that miracles were contrary to the uniform experience of humanity. "It is strange," Campbell said, "that the author has not favoured us with the definition of a term of so much moment to his argument. This defect I shall endeavour to supply. . . ."[2] Campbell distinguished two kinds of experience: firstly, our own personal experience, which the faculty of memory recorded for us; and secondly, what he called *derived experience*, namely, that which lay outside our own limited scope but which we accepted on the testimony of others. Hume's argument had depended on the first alone. In his essay the words "contrary to experience" had meant only something which we had not yet personally experienced,[3] and he was thus enabled to beg the question by arguing as to what could not be without determining whether it actually had been.[4] The evidence for the Gospel miracles, said Campbell, was not restricted to the writers of the Four Gospels, but was demonstrated by the very existence of the Church, "of the numberless proselytes that were daily made to a religion, opposing all the religious professions then in the world".[5] Whether he knew it or not he was, in fact, repeating an argument of St Thomas Aquinas, but without advancing to his conclusion that the continued existence of a believing Church in the world was the one standing miracle.[6] There was no reason to associate either fraud or credulity with the first converts,[7] and yet there existed no evidence, from friend

[1] A. Carlyle, *Autobiography*, pp. 279–80.
[2] G. Campbell, *A Dissertation on Miracles*, p. 29.
[3] Ibid. p. 33.   [4] Ibid. p. 45.   [5] Ibid. p. 57.
[6] Thomas Aquinas, *Summa Contra Gentiles*, I, vi, i.
[7] G. Campbell, op. cit. p. 63.

or foe, which did not associate Jesus with miracles. Any man who argued that miracles were essentially impossible ought therefore to have dealt frankly and unevasively with evidence which plainly stated that they had been witnessed. Campbell ended by quoting the famous passage in which Hume observed that the Christian faith had been founded on miracles and could not be believed today without one. "Whoever is moved by faith to assent to it is conscious of a continued miracle in his own person, which subverts all the Principles of his understanding, and gives him a determination to believe what is most contrary to custom and experience." Campbell observed a trifle tartly that it is difficult to reply adequately to a proposition that is not squarely stated but ironically implied. Were Hume's words true in their literal sense, there would be either an abundance of miracles, or else no believers; if the first were true, then experience could hardly be argued as grounds for disbelief in past miracles, and if the second be true, "if there be not in the world any who believe the Gospel because, as Mr Hume supposes, a miracle cannot be believed without a new miracle, why all this ado to refute opinions which nobody entertains?"[1]

There was a friendly exchange of comment between Campbell and Hume who, as a matter of principle, left his writings to speak for themselves and refused to enter into controversy. Similarly there was a friendly exchange between Hume and Thomas Reid, first minister of New Machar and afterwards professor of Philosophy at Aberdeen and Glasgow. Once a follower of Berkeley, Reid abandoned his idealism in reaction to Hume's scepticism, and his *Inquiry into the Human Mind on Principles of Common Sense* is an attempt to reaffirm our convictions on the existence of an external world. He insists that the mind has an immediate perception that the sensations of external objects are real. Though he counts today "as a non-starter as compared with Hume",[2] Reid was a man of great influence in his day and for long after, virtually the founder of a Scottish school of philosophy. The *Essay on the Nature and Immutability of Truth* by another Aberdonian, James Beattie, wakened more public response by its virulent polemical tone, and stirred the normally placid victim to irritation. But it has been written that "Beattie's poetry is better

[1] G. Campbell, op. cit. pp. 133–4.
[2] G. E. Davie, *The Democratic Intellect*, p. 299.

THE NEW WORLD OF THOUGHT 101

than his divinity"[1] and only those who have read his now neglected poem, "The Ministrel", will take the measure of what this
implies. However, he received many honours and tributes.
Oxford University bestowed upon him the degree of D.C.L. and
what is probably Sir Joshua Reynolds' worst painting shows
Beattie attired in his academic robes and holding his famous book,
while a rather pretty angel of truth and justice thrusts the evil
figures of infidelity into the Stygian gloom beneath.

The numbers affected by philosophical controversy were small;
but the pulpit reached more. Hugh Blair of the High Kirk of
Edinburgh was the outstanding preacher of his time, largely
because he had taken great care to adapt himself to it. A century
afterwards his reputation had sunk. "His sermons were exceedingly popular," wrote John Mackintosh,[2] "though it is difficult
to discover the reason why they were so." So high was his
standing that the Magistrates created a Chair of Rhetoric for him
in the University, and so complete his decline that the copy of his
lectures which the writer borrowed had lain in the University
Library for 120 years with the pages uncut. He was a man of wide
reading and of equally wide sympathies who could commend a
Roman Catholic[3] to his Presbyterian students as the best model
for a preacher. He spoke with pontifical assurance, not hesitating
to patronize Voltaire as he commended him[4] even if, lacking in-
fallibility, he compared MacPherson's "Ossian" to the "Iliad".[5]
The first requirement in preaching, he wrote, is that the preacher
should himself be a good man who believes what he preaches. He
should have a clear view of what he intends, and should set out
to be popular, not in the bad sense of the word, but in the sense
that he makes an impression on the mind of the ordinary man.
Every sermon should be confined to a single subject. No sermon
should ever be read. Generalities and long words should be
avoided. The preacher must have sufficient imagination to put
himself in the place of his listeners; and he should know when to
stop. A dry sermon can never be a good one. The purpose of
preaching, he said, is "to infuse good dispositions into the
hearers, to persuade them to serve God, and to become better

[1] J. Cunningham, *The Church History of Scotland*, ii, p. 366.
[2] J. Mackintosh, *The History of Civilization in Scotland*, iv, p. 215.
[3] Hugh Blair, *Lectures*, p. 390.   [4] Ibid. pp. 496, 610, 644.
[5] Ibid. pp. 41–2. R. M. Schmitz, op. cit. pp. 42–60.

men", and the best applause it can have is the impression made. After hearing Massillon preach, Louis XIV said to him, "Father, I have heard many great orators in this chapel; I have been highly pleased with them; but for you, whenever I hear you, I go away displeased with myself; for I see more of my own character."[1]

It is a mistake to accept at face value the adverse judgments[2] often made on Blair's sermons. Once allowance has been made for the language and mannerisms of a bygone day, it will be found that they are direct and forceful, designed to commend the Christian faith to the man of his time. Deeper notes may be found in his Communion sermons, but on the whole Blair spoke to the man of the world in his own language. In a sermon on the Middle-aged Man he[3] said, "One of the first questions, therefore, which every man who is in the vigour of his age should put to himself is 'What am I doing in this world? What have I yet done, whereby I may glorify God, and be useful to my fellows? Do I properly fill up the place which belongs to my rank and station? Will any memorial remain of my having existed on the earth; or are my days passing fruitless away, now when I might be of some importance in the system of human affairs?' Let not any man imagine that he is of no importance, and has, upon that account, a privilege to trifle with his days at pleasure. Talents have been given to all; to some, ten, to others, five; to others, two. *Occupy with these till I come*, is the command of the great Master of all."

For many years Hugh Blair had as his colleague in St Giles Robert Walker, a preacher of a different stamp. "Walker," says an unjust and most uncharacteristic comment from the usually generous Carlyle,[4] "was a rank enthusiast, with nothing but heat without light." So far as style and vocabulary go, there is little or no difference between the two. Both copy the standards of Augustan prose. Some early editions of Hume's works are prefaced by a list of so-called Scotticisms for the benefit of readers on the wrong side of Tweed, but the sermons of Blair and Walker would seldom have needed such aid. In a day when the judgments of the bench were still being delivered in broad Scots this steady use of standard English in the pulpit must have done much to

[1] Hugh Blair, *Lectures*, pp. 377–93.
[2] W. G. Blaikie, *The Preachers of Scotland from the sixth to the nineteenth century*, pp. 231–5.
[3] H. Blair, *Sermons*, III, p. 66.   [4] A. Carlyle, op. cit. p. 247.

destroy the use of Scotland's native speech in educated circles. Walker's sermons[1] were different, not in style, but in content; they were Biblical and expository where Blair's were not, and a more evangelical outlook runs through them, though it is worth noting that Walker was no more a strict Calvinist than was his colleague. For the most part Walker did not draw the fashionable worshippers who listened to Blair, but on Sunday evenings he held prayer meetings in his manse to which the pious Lady Glenorchy used to take her convivial husband. Lord Glenorchy had given standing orders to his servant that "if he was to dine in company beforehand, his servant, when he came to attend him to his carriage, should offer him the wrong side of the surtout and, if he objected, carry him to the meeting but, if he tried to put it on as it was, to carry him home".[2]

Each in his own way commended the faith. The poorer classes came to hear Walker and an elder of St Giles commented that "it took twenty-four of Mr Walker's hearers to equal in contribution one of Mr Blair's".[3] But despite this, and despite Carlyle's comment, it was with men of Walker's outlook rather than his more famous colleague, that the future of the Church lay for, whatever their other achievements, the Moderates' statement of the Christian faith was in some respects an inadequate one.

The eighteenth century had been an age of achievement in Scotland in every field from architecture to philosophy, but it is a striking fact that in the long and varied list of distinguished names there is not one theologian of international reputation. "The clergy of England," said Dr Johnson[4] at Talisker, "have produced the most valuable books in support of religion, both in theory and practice. What have your clergy done since you sunk into Presbyterianism? Can you name one book of any value in religion written by them?" We could not. Said he, "I'll help you. Forbes wrote very well, but I believe he wrote before Episcopacy was quite extinguished," and then pausing a little, he said, "Yes, you have Wishart *Against* Repentance." At Auchinleck[5] Johnson returned to the same subject, and challenged Lord Auchinleck

[1] Hugh Watt, "Robert Walker of the High Church", *SCHS*, xii, pp. 82–96.

[2] Henry MacKenzie, *Anecdotes and Egotisms*, i.

[3] H. G. Graham, op. cit. p. 123.

[4] James Boswell, *A Tour to the Hebrides*, p. 215.   [5] Ibid. p. 376.

"to point out any theological works of merit written by Presbyterian ministers in Scotland. My father, whose studies did not lie much in that way, owned to me afterwards that he was somewhat at a loss how to answer, but that luckily he recollected having read in catalogues the title of *Durham on the Galatians*; upon which he boldly said, 'Pray, sir, have you read Mr Durham's excellent commentary on the Galatians?' 'No, sir,' said Dr Johnson. By this lucky thought my father kept him at bay, and for some time enjoyed his triumph; but his antagonist soon made a retort, which I forbear to mention." But Lord Auchinleck's patriotism had been better than his memory, for the work he had seen listed in the catalogue — though Johnson did not detect this — was *Durham on Revelation*.

The reason for the failure of the Moderates to write any theology of distinction is tolerably plain. They were restricted by the Westminster Confession. They did not hold its doctrines, but could not say so in public. In Ireland the Non-Subscribing Presbyterians protested that their only objection was to confessional statements as such and not to Christian doctrine, but they were under suspicion of moving away from orthodoxy, especially as regards the doctrine of the person of Christ.[1] Similarly the Moderates were suspected of unacknowledged deviations. It was their silence on certain topics, rather than anything they said, which gave grounds for this. In particular, they were under suspicion on the subject of the doctrines of the fall and of original sin, of grace, salvation, and the atonement.[2] In 1753, the year after Robertson's victory at the Assembly, there was published an anonymous satire entitled "Ecclesiastical Characteristics". It was, in fact, the work of John Witherspoon, then minister of Beith, but later to be President of Princeton, a member of the first Congress, one of the founding fathers of the Republic, and the only clergyman among the signatories to the Declaration of Independence. Witherspoon[3] assailed the manners of the Moderates, the company they kept, their easy-going ways, and their secular outlook. He offered them "The Athenian Creed".

"I believe in the beauty and comely proportions of Dame Nature, and in Almighty Fate, her only parent and guardian; for

[1] W. T. Latimer, *History of the Irish Presbyterians*, pp. 146–56, 171–2.
[2] Andrew Thomson, *The Origin of the Secession Church*, p. 188.
[3] A. L. Drummond, "Witherspoon of Gifford", *SCHS*, XII, p. 190.

it hath been most graciously obliged (blessed be its name) to make us all very good.

"I believe that the Universe is a huge machine, wound up from everlasting, and consisting of an infinite number of links and chains, each in a progressive motion towards the zenith of perfection . . . and that I myself am a little glorious piece of clockwork, a wheel within a wheel, or rather a pendulum within this grand machine, swinging hither and hither by the different impulses of fate and destiny; that my soul (if I have a soul) is an imperceptible bundle of exceedingly minute corpuscles much smaller than the finest Holland sand. . . .

"I believe that there is no ill in the Universe . . . that those things vulgarly called *sins* are only *errors* in judgement, and foils to set off the beauty of Nature, or patches to adorn her face; that the whole race of intelligent beings, even the devils themselves (if there be any) shall finally be happy, so that Judas Iscariot is by this time a glorified saint. . . .

"In fine, I believe in the divinity of Lord Shaftesbury, the saintship of Marcus Antoninus, the perspicuity of Aristotle, and the perpetual duration of Mr Hutcheson's works, notwithstanding their present tendency to oblivion. Amen."

In other words, Witherspoon taunted the Moderates with holding a creed akin to Deism, with believing in God and morality, but with an indifference to Christ other than as an example, and to the doctrines of the atonement, forgiveness and redemption. In 1767 an aged minister Alexander Ferguson of Kilwinning, a former student of Simson in Glasgow, published an article in the *Scots Magazine*[1] which showed that the suspicions were fully justified. Ferguson had no use for the doctrines of the fall, of human depravity, and the vicarious sacrifice of Christ. He distinguished sharply between the Bible and theology. No Church, he held, had the right to impose a detailed Confession except in so far as it could be justified from Scripture, and subscription to the Confession must therefore be made, not in the sense that it is absolutely true, but only in so far as it is Scriptural.[2] Parliament had enacted the Confession only that it might be a test of conformity to the Presbyterian establishment. This, as all his readers should have known, was perfectly true. But Ferguson combined

[1] *Scots Magazine*, xxix, p. 175.
[2] W. L. Mathieson, *The Awakening of Scotland, 1747–1797*, pp. 217–18.

a plea for theological liberty with the repudiation of important Christian doctrines. Yet no one of standing paid any heed to his challenge to orthodoxy. Instead one of Witherspoon's former parishioners, James MacConnell,[1] the town drummer of Beith, brought a complaint before the Presbytery. The Presbytery retorted that MacConnell was illiterate and that it was none of his business. Ferguson was then interviewed and the case dismissed. Ferguson's congregation had been listening without complaint to his sermons for close on half a century and evidently shared his outlook; so, it seems, did the Presbytery. It was left to one of the socially underprivileged to complain, and one of them had the courage and initiative to do so.

Less than a score of years later Dr William McGill, minister of the second charge of Ayr, published in 1786 *A Practical Essay on the Death of Christ*. Whereas Ferguson had something like a Unitarian outlook McGill[2] had the merit of having attempted to state in fresh language the doctrine of the purpose of God, and the person and work of Christ. His work had its defects, but it was not these so much as his obvious divergence from the Westminster Confession which brought down on him the wrath of the Seceders. Writing under the pseudonym of "A Friend to Truth", Dr John Jamieson, best known because of his dictionary of the older Scottish tongue, bitterly assailed McGill in a pamphlet entitled *Socinianism Unmasked*, and a second attack was made by James Moir, the Seceder minister of Tarbolton.[3] McGill's prosecution in the church courts wakened great public interest in Ayrshire and far beyond, but ended in a compromise and the acceptance of his explanations and apologies, to the undisguised disappointment and wrath of the Seceders.[4]

Between these two cases there had been a change in public opinion. The Moderates had taught Scotland to be tolerant; they had taught that Christian conduct was more needful than theological exactitude; and by personal influence they had commended the faith in the century of the Enlightenment. Very largely, they had accepted the rationalistic theology current in England. But Scotland had produced, in David Hume, the most merciless critic

---

[1] *Fasti*, II, p. 182. *New Statistical Account of Scotland*, v, p. 587.
[2] Alexander McNair, *Scots Theology in the Eighteenth Century*, pp. 21–74.
[3] Ibid. pp. 75–95.
[4] *Fasti*, II pp. 93–4. J. McKerrow, *History of the Secession Church*, pp. 359–69.

of this rationalistic theology with its dependence on miracles and the argument from design. Hume may have had little effect in creating active disbelief in Scotland, for Christians had not reached their faith as the last step in a chain of argument, but he had discredited Deism and a theology which had more in common with Deism than it cared to admit. After him Scottish disbelief was to be, not deistic, but atheistic. In the same way he, or rather the whole eighteenth-century assault on the Christian faith, of which he was a part, caused Christians to reconsider the ground on which they stood or, to use his own phrase, "to change the batteries".[1] In one respect, Hume's scepticism had been consistent with the Scottish outlook. An element of natural theology had been retained by John Calvin,[2] but it is, in the sense in which geologists use the word, an erratic in his system of thought, unrelated to the terrain on which it rests. The same is true of the Westminster Confession. The revelation of God in His Word was central for each. This could not be said for the theological outlook of the Moderates, and Hume's scepticism produced within the Church a questioning of their position, a return to more Scriptural thought, and a more Christocentric way of Christian faith. It is a strange fact that even among the Seceders[3] the life and death of Christ — as distinct from the consequences — found little place in preaching midway through the eighteenth century. Among the Moderates it was even more so. There is truth in Hume's jest after listening to Carlyle[4] preaching in Athelstaneford church, "What did you mean by treating John's congregation today with one of Cicero's academics. I did not think that such heathen morality would have passed in East Lothian." But a change had come. Between the hearing — or rather the casual dismissal — of Ferguson's case in 1770 and the stir aroused by McGill's book in 1786 the rationalistic theology of the Moderates had lost its hold upon the Church. Consequently theology of the type produced by Paley never had much appeal in Scotland.

Along with this change in the outlook of the Church which may, not unfairly, be described as the growth of an evangelical outlook, came a change in the influence of the different social

[1] Hume, *Works*, II, p. 528.
[2] John Calvin, *Institutes of the Christian Religion*, I, v, pp. 1–3.
[3] W. G. Blaikie, op. cit. p. 209.
[4] A. Carlyle, op. cit. p. 290.

classes within the Church which the formerly dominant classes saw with distaste. "The General Assembly was deserted by the most respectable part of the landlords, in whose place men of an inferior station and narrow and bigoted principles have been allowed to fill that court. . . . Through the indifference of the laity and the inattention of Government, the wild party have been gaining ground, while many of the wisest and most experienced of the moderate party have been disgusted with neglect, and have discontinued their attendance at the Supreme Court. Young men of low birth and mean education have discovered that livings may infallibly be obtained by a connection with the most insignificant voter for a member of parliament, and superior spirits perceiving that the most distinguished among the moderate clergy had not for many years power of recommendation to benefices, have generally betaken themselves to other professions."[1] This comment from a disgruntled spectator in 1780 tells that the reign of the Moderates was ending.

Lord Cockburn, whose heart lay with the Moderates, was of the same opinion when he looked back in old age. "Principal Robertson's ecclesiastical policy tended to divide our ministers into two classes; one, and that by far the largest, had no principle superior to that of obsequious allegiance to patrons; the other, devoting itself entirely to the religion of the lower orders, had no taste or ambition for anything higher. . . . The old historical glory had faded. . . . It was chiefly a lower description of men who were tempted to enlist in the ecclesiastical service."[2] It did not occur to Cockburn to relate what he here described to the fact that, as he noted elsewhere, the Church had simultaneously been gaining in Scotland.[3] It would be naïve to accept the judgment of either commentator at face value or to accept the conclusion that "patronage contributed rather to the declension of the clergy than to their rise".[4] What is seen here reflected complex changes in both the outlook and the social structure of the community. The eighteenth century had begun to die before its span of years was ended.

Many comments have been made upon the influence of Calvinism on the Scotland of the time, without first considering the

[1] H. G. Graham, op. cit. p. 99n.
[2] Lord Cockburn, *Memorials of His Time*, pp. 139-40.
[3] Ibid. pp. 35-7.   [4] W. L. Mathieson, op. cit. p. 228.

preliminary question of how Calvinist eighteenth-century Scotland was. The element of Calvinism most consistently accepted
was its indifference to the concept of the State as known in the
modern world, that of an omnicompetent authority. All Scotland
still regarded education and social welfare as the responsibility
of the Church. In the words of R. H. Tawney,[1] "the real State in
Scotland had been represented, not by Parliament or Council, but
by the Church of Knox". Otherwise Calvinism had traditionally
expressed itself in three fields of church life — discipline, order,
and doctrine. As regards the first of these, kirk session discipline
was enforced in every parish of Scotland,[2] but it was restricted in
two respects. In the first instance, its scope, once very broad, had
virtually been reduced to sexual offences. A famous entry[3] in the
kirk session records of Mauchline exhibits its character in the late
eighteenth century.

"1788, July 30, Jean Armour, Robert Burns their recent affair not
settled. August 5, compeared Robert Burns with Jean Armour his
alleged spouse. They both acknowledged their irregular marriage,
and their sorrow for that irregularity, desiring that the Session
will take such steps as may seem proper to them in order to the
solemn confirmation of said marriage. The Session taking this
affair under their consideration agree that they both be rebuked
for their acknowledged immorality, and that they be taken
solemnly engaged to adhere faithfully to one another as husband
and wife, all the days of their life. In regard the Session have a
title in law to some fine for behoof of the poor, they agree to refer
to Mr Burns his own generosity. The above sentence was accordingly executed, and the Session absolved the said parties from any
scandal on this account.

Robt. Burns
Jean Armour
William Auld, Modr.

Mr Burns gave a guinea-note for behoof of the poor."

The other respect was less obvious. The application of

---

[1] R. H. Tawney, *Religion and the Rise of Capitalism*, p. 124.
[2] Andrew Edgar, "The Discipline of the Church of Scotland", in R. H.
Story, *The Church of Scotland*, v, pp. 466–556. *AGA*, 1707, xi, Form of Process.
[3] *Fasti*, ii, pp. 123–4.

discipline had social limits, since it was easier to deal with Robert
Burns than with Gavin Hamilton.

Secondly, while Presbyterian church government was established by the law of the land and Episcopalianism had shrivelled
to a tiny group, Scottish Presbyterianism, like its counterparts
on the continent, had changed its character. It was no longer a
revolutionary movement. Originally it had been a vehicle for the
expression of the will of local congregations, whereas under
Robertson's régime it became an instrument for controlling them.
Thirdly, so far as doctrine and theology went, there were powerful
elements in the national life which were either outside the
National Church or retained only a nominal connection with her.
The parishioners of that Alexander Pope who went south to visit
his great namesake, we are told, were "Episcopalians in name but
heathens in reality".[1] Even within the ministry and membership
of the Church, doctrinal Calvinism was the outlook of no more
than a minority. When Alexander Gillies[2] was licensed by the
Presbytery of Stranraer on 1 January 1766 he signed the Confession of Faith, "erroribus exceptis", and the Presbytery accepted
him on this basis. Few were so open about the matter, yet this
represented the outlook of many. The Shorter Catechism might
be taught in all schools and the Institutes of Calvin might dominate the theological classrooms, but Calvinism held no place in the
minds of the moderates, and its doctrines of election and predestination were scarcely consistent with the preaching of the
Evangelicals.

Probably only among the Seceders was Calvinism a dominant
influence. Even among them the leaven of new thought was
working. In 1745 they began to debate whether the burgess oath
which required an acknowledgment of "the true religion professed within this realm" might legitimately be taken by their
people, and in 1747 they split over this into Burghers and Antiburghers.[3] Party feelings ran so high that the Antiburghers
brought the Burgher leaders to the bar of their Synod and, when
they failed to appear, deposed and excommunicated them, including those fathers of the Secession, Ebenezer and Ralph Erskine.
In 1795 a greater issue arose[4] over subscription to the West-

[1] Donald Sage, *Memorabilia Domestica*, p. 43, cf. supra p. 86.
[2] *Fasti*, II, p. 180.
[3] J. McKerrow, op. cit. pp. 208–38.   [4] Ibid. pp. 578ff.

minster Confession and became known as "The Old Light and New Light Controversy", or — to give it the Scottish form — "Auld Licht and New Licht". This phrase goes back to the Pilgrim Fathers, but the Seceders drew it from Ireland where it had first been used by the Rev. John Malcolm[1] of Dunmurry in a sermon, printed in 1720, *Personal Persuasion No Foundation for Religious Obedience*. As in Ireland, so in Scotland, the phrase referred to the inability of eighteenth-century Presbyterians to accept every word of the Westminster Confession. It was a sign that even in one of its strongholds Calvinism was on the defensive. In 1768 John Brown of Haddington became Professor of Divinity for the Associate Synod — the Burghers. Brown had been brought up, not on the *Institutes* of Calvin, but on the standard textbook of seventeenth- and early eighteenth-century Calvinism, the *Institutio Theologiae Elencticae* of François Turretin,[2] but he ceased to use Turretin and produced a series of lectures of his own based on an incessant searching of the text of Scripture. What he gave to his students in these lectures was passed on to a much wider audience in his *Dictionary of the Bible* and, above all, in *The Self-Interpreting Bible* — "Brown's Bible" — which passed through twenty-six editions and became the mainstay of devotion in countless homes. While it was consistent with Turretin's theology instead of emphasis being placed, as in Calvin, on the eternal decrees of God, it was laid upon the historical activity of God, first in the Old Testament covenant — the covenant of works — and then, in that of the New Testament — the covenant of grace, Brown turned the mind of his students and readers directly to the Bible.[3] As for the West Highlands, later the home of scholastic Calvinism and the literal acceptance of the Westminster Confession, throughout much of the eighteenth century, so far as they were anything other than pagan, they were the countryside first of the Episcopalians[4] and then of the Moderates. The rich farm land of Easter Ross was not characteristic of Highland society, and it is the only district beyond Moray where late seventeenth- and early eighteenth-century

[1] T. Witherow, *Historical and Literary Memorials of Presbyterianism in Ireland*, pp. 217–25. W. T. Latimer, op. cit. p. 147.
[2] A. L. Drummond, *The Kirk and the Continent*, p. 144.
[3] R. MacKenzie, *John Brown of Haddington*, pp. 133, 203–22.
[4] J. B. Craven, *Journals of Bishop Forbes*, pp. 65–120.

houses of the type so common in Fife and the Lothians may be found. Here Calvinism struck its first roots in the north[1] through such men as Thomas Hog of Kiltearn.

There is a strange contrast between the backwardness of Scotland at the opening of the century and its cultural achievements half a century later. It must be asked whether there is any relationship between this and the teaching of the Scottish Church. Men like David Hume and Adam Smith owed nothing to Calvinism. Even a lesser but possibly more representative man like Adam Ferguson, who has been regarded as the founder of modern sociology,[2] shows a religious outlook totally divorced from Scotland's supposedly Calvinist tradition, though a minister of the Church even if unplaced in a charge. The religion of nature filled his mind. "The will of God is, no doubt, of supreme authority; and where it is known, we need not recur to any other. But, if it has pleased Him that His will, at least in the first intimation of it, should be declared by means of the order established in His works. And in our conduct of life the opposite natures of right and wrong are our safest guides, in every particular instance, to the performance of what the will of God has required. It is in search of a model, and of a patron of what is *previously* known to be right, that we arrive at our best and our highest conceptions of the Supreme Being."[3] He was concerned with the argument from design, the immutability of God, the order of the universe, and the reasonableness of belief in the immortality of the soul,[4] and it was this very attenuated version of the Christian faith, little removed from Deism, which shaped the thought of the men who made the Scottish contributions to literature, history, and philosophy. If any credit for the cultural achievements of eighteenth-century Scotland can be assigned to religious elements it must be to this rationalistic and untheological faith. Any contribution of Calvinism can have been no more than its indirect influence as a mould of character through education and habits of discipline. Much the same would seem to be true of the men who made the first Scottish contributions to advances in mathematics,

[1] John McInnes, *The Evangelical Movement in the Highlands of Scotland, 1688–1800.* Hugh Miller, *My Schools and Schoolmasters,* xiv.

[2] Paul Hazard, *European Thought in the Eighteenth Century,* p. 232.

[3] Adam Ferguson, *Principles of Moral and Political Science,* i, p. 167.

[4] W. C. Lehmann, *Adam Ferguson and the Beginnings of Modern Sociology,* p. 136.

medicine, and chemistry in the same period.[1] The Scotland of these achievements, the Scotland which produced the *Encyclopaedia Britannica* at Edinburgh between 1768 and 1781, moved in a different world of thought from traditional Calvinism and those classes in which it still was active.

[1] A. G. Clement and R. H. S. Robertson, *Scotland's Scientific Heritage*, pp. 22–50.

CHAPTER SIX

The Changing Face of Society

When Dr Webster of the Tolbooth Kirk made his pioneer census in 1755, almost but not quite the first in Europe since Roman times, he estimated the population of Scotland at 1,265,380. Scotland had about one-fifth the population of England and half that of Ireland. By 1801, when the first government census was taken, Scotland had 1,608,420 inhabitants,[1] and there is reason to hold that in the first half of the century there had been an increase comparable with that of the second. Though small compared with what was to follow, this is a sign of growing prosperity, since the population was limited by the stern necessity of earning a living in a poor country. Many a Scottish minister, writing in the First Statistical Account, made simple observations akin to those later more systematically expressed by Malthus. As in Ireland, where the increase was even more rapid until the disastrous years of the potato famine after 1840, this increase had depended, in the first instance, on improvements in agriculture.

The ancient nobility of Scotland had been men of war. When Aeneas Sage was a divinity student his curiosity led him to go to Fetteresso in 1715 to see the Old Pretender, Scotland's rightful king. "His countenance," Sage[2] told, "was considerably above the common cast of faces, and was even royal, but it had a pale, sickly hue, expressive of weakness. His fierce and mailed followers, the Earls of Mar and Marischal, Cameron of Locheil, General Hamilton, and others, stood around him, with heads uncovered, and to these men of bold and vigorous spirit he yielded himself much as would a child to its nurse." But Sage had seen the last of the feudal barons, and their descendants of the next generation were to be, not warriors, but improving landlords.

[1] *Scottish Population Statistics*, SHS, p. 82.
[2] D. Sage, *Memorabilia Domestica*, p. 4.

Sir John Clerk of Penicuik was not of ancient lineage but, like many other Lothian landlords, was the grandson of a man who had made money in the previous century, bought an estate, and settled down to the life of a country gentleman. "By my improvements," he wrote in his memoirs,[1] "I have made the estate my father left me of much greater value and extent; and amongst other things I am persuaded I have, within these thirty years, planted more than 30,000 trees, which in time may be of considerable value. About this time [the year was 1730] I got my tenants at Penicuik to divide their lands, for till now all of them were in run-rig. This I found a very difficult matter, for that few tenants could be induced to alter their bad methods of agriculture. . . . I altered the face of the Moor of Loanhead by inclosures with hedges and ditches, whereas before nothing grew here but whins and heather, nor did I pay any rent at all." Similarly Cockburn of Ormiston was intensely critical of the bad farming of old-fashioned tenants. "His husbandry," he wrote of one,[2] "goes no further than to get bad grain one year and worse the next." He granted long leases to his tenants and set an example by rebuilding steadings, planting turnips, and introducing new seeds. Further north, in Aberdeenshire, Grant of Monymusk[3] introduced the rotation of crops, and the planting of turnips, clover, and rye grass. His farming was better than his prose. "There is," he wrote, "as certain and large estates to be got in husbandry as in any employment; and where more probably than in this country where it is little understood and ready sale and good prices for everything, and no business of life is more rational, more quiet and agreeable, afford profit with greater certainty and less risk, if but tolerably attended to without fatigue and things put into method."

This brought wealth, and with wealth social changes. Whereas under the last of the Stewart kings Scotland had been a nation of peasants, by the close of the eighteenth century she was mainly an agrarian society divided into a comparatively small group of large landowners, a much larger number of capitalist farmers, and a still larger number of landless labourers. Rural society became stratified, and it became increasingly harder for a man

[1] John Clerk, *Memorials*, SHS, pp. 136–7.
[2] Cockburn, *Letters to His Gardener*, SHS, p. 17.
[3] *Monymusk Papers*, SHS, lvii.

to make his way by industry — or by marriage — from one group
to a higher one. Scottish farming,[1] which had been primitive at the
start of the century, by the close was the envy of Europe. Everywhere the prosperity of this new and independent class of farmers
was to be seen. "Their dwellings," said the Rev. John Mitchell,
looking back on Ayrshire life towards the end of the century,
"assumed an improved and more comfortable aspect; those reared
about this time were constructed on a better plan, warmer and
more convenient, more roomy and more tidy in appearance.
Formerly they were put down anywhere, apparently at random;
now the site was chosen with a view in part to its dryness, the
prospect which it commanded, and the facilities it afforded."
Those, like the family of Robert Burns, who could not succeed
in making farms pay well, were few indeed. At the close of the
century what had once been reckoned good houses were in turn
being replaced by still bigger ones, and in the Lothians a prosperous farmer would have scorned not merely Woodhead, the early
home of the Bairds of Gartsherrie, later to be great coal and iron
masters, but the High Cross[2] farm to which they moved in
1808.

But if some peasants were enriched, others were impoverished,
if not absolutely, yet comparatively. "In the district of Galloway,
where the basis of the population is Celtic, the idleness and consequent poverty of the people was peculiarly great. There was a
prodigious number of small tenantry, of very indolent character,
and who were accustomed to 'run out' or exhaust their land to
the last extremity, cropping it two years for one of lea, of course
without manure, and being at the same time generally several
years behind in their rents. . . . The landlords, anxious to introduce
a better system, began to subdivide and enclose their lands, in
order to stock them with black cattle, and to eject tenants hope-
lessly sunk in idleness and poverty."[3] This "Levellers' Revolt",
as it was called, had religious leadership. As among the Protesters of the previous century, there were signs of class warfare,
for the underprivileged and dispossessed were identical with a
religious group alienated from the leadership of the Church. They
were led by "a certain mountain preacher" who denounced the

---

[1] T. C. Smout, *A History of the Scottish People, 1560–1830*, p. 291.
[2] Ibid. facing p. 223.
[3] R. Chambers, *Domestic Annals of Scotland*, iii, pp. 492–3.

gentry "for, as he termed it, making common property".[1] When the magistrates of Kirkcudbright attempted to disperse the Levellers by reading the Riot Act, they retaliated by reading the Solemn League and Covenant with its implication that uncovenanted magistrates and clergy had forfeited all authority. Their unnamed leader was a follower of John Hepburn,[2] minister of Urr from 1689 till 1723, a consistent opponent of all legislation after 1690 and a violent man often under discipline from Assembly and Privy Council alike. At the time of the Rising of 1715 he raised a volunteer corps and marched at their head under a banner inscribed "For the Lord of Hosts". "What families," he preached, "are more corrupt and ungodly than those of many noblemen and gentlemen?" There was breaking of dykes and killing of cattle on summer nights. Dragoons were sent in and there was a skirmish, but provocation was avoided, and the attacks died out. This was the only major protest of the century against rural change. It is worth noting that the local Presbytery showed no sympathy and that the leadership came from "the hill men or society people", for the national Church was not to lose the support or good will of the labourers.

Compared with the farmhouse, the labourer's cottage was a miserable place. Alexander Somerville[3] described the Berwickshire home where his parents brought up eight children at the close of the century. "It was about twelve feet by fourteen, and not so high in the walls as will allow a man to get in without stooping. That place without ceiling or anything beneath the bare tiles of roof; with no floor save the common clay; without a cupboard or recess of any kind; with no grate but the iron bars which the tenants carried to it, built up, and took away when they left it; with no partition of any kind save what the beds made; with no window save four small panes at one side — it was this house, still a hind's house at Springfield for which, to obtain leave to live in, my mother sheared the harvest and carried the stacks." These conditions outlasted the century, and the oldest and poorest of farm cottages still surviving in the Lothians, though now

[1] T. C. Smout, op. cit. p. 362.
[2] *Fasti*, I, pp. 607–8. "Remarkable effects sometimes attended his ministry, especially in prayer, which sometimes continued for hours together, while he was equally fervent in preaching."
[3] Alexander Somerville, *Autobiography of a Working Man*, p. 10.

disused, resemble those designed by Hamilton[1] on improved lines in 1822.

There had been a time on the land when few lived in anything better, but this contrast between farmhouse and farm cottage was now a sign of a deep social cleavage. In addition, the old fixity of the population had begun to be lost; a time had been when men died in the parish in which their forefathers had been born; but the landless labourer, and especially the poorest, was now beginning to shift from farm to farm at any term day. It became increasingly difficult for a minister or elder to have fellowship, as distinct from formal contact, with shifting labourers. Dr Robertson of Whittinghame, it is said, when visiting his parish in Victorian times, used to get out of the carriage to go into the farmhouse, but he sent his driver to the cottage door to summon the labourer and his wife to come out to speak to the minister. As Cunninghame's diary shows, it would be a libel to suggest that this was general in the century of either man, but it cannot be denied that a kind of social gulf had begun to open. The Seceders, especially in the west, might draw occasional recruits from the farmers, who could travel across country by pony and trap, and were both able and willing to pay for their church; but the farm labourer went to the church that was within walking distance and to the one where he would not have to pay; he still felt that the parish kirk was his kirk and its minister his minister. More and more, with some exceptions, the Secession churches drew the responsible and the convinced while the parish churches drew the poor and dependent.

In the towns the increasing prosperity of the surrounding countryside supported a growing middle class of craftsmen, merchants, and professional men from tailors and grocers to men like Duncan Forbes[2] who were at home in the company of the highest in the land. Until now Edinburgh and the Lothians had led Scotland, but at this point there began a shift of enterprise and leadership to Glasgow and the west. Glasgow produced a new class of wealthy merchants, independent of the native Scots economy, in the tobacco lords. In 1724 4,192,576 lb. of tobacco were brought to the Clyde and of this 3,053,570 lb. were re-exported, mostly to France. This encouraged the growth of the

---

[1] Thomas Ferguson, *The Dawn of Scottish Social Welfare*, pp. 2–3, 45–6.
[2] T. C. Smout, op. cit. p. 362.

Clyde as a shipping centre. In 1692 Glasgow had fifteen ships of 1,182 tons. In 1718 the first Glasgow ship crossed the Atlantic. By 1735 there were 67 ships of 5,600 tons trading from the Clyde and by the time of the American War of Independence 386 ships of 22,892 tons.[1] The names of the new streets built to the west of the old medieval city tell by their names the political outlook of the citizens and the source of their wealth. Brunswick Street, Hanover Street, and Frederick Street tell of Whig politics, and Virginia Street, Jamaica Street, and Plantation of American trade. A new moneyed class had come into existence, one which might acquire land for reasons of prestige, but which did not depend upon it as did the older nobility. Many of its members were committed to the Church by strong conviction, but they had little place in the conduct of its affairs. Unless they bought land, they had no place among the heritors, who controlled so much of country church life. In the burghs the Town Councils, who had power in the town churches akin to that of the heritors in the country, like the kirk sessions of the National Church, were self perpetuating, nominated their own successors, and did not always open the door to new-comers. Only in the Secession, where elders were elected, was the road to lay office open. On the other hand, the heritors, who were financially responsible for the Church, had once reflected the wealth of the nation, but now they were only a section of it; yet they paid for the Church while the new rich were more or less free of the burden. The landed interest no longer spoke for the nation as a whole, but its power in the Church remained much the same.

The Scottish Church of Covenanting times had held the traditional ecclesiastical view of usury, but this was forgotten by the end of the century when a Scot, William Paterson, was mainly responsible for the founding of the Bank of England in 1694. In 1695 the Bank of Scotland was founded, followed by the British Linen Bank, the Royal Bank, and others, like the Ship Bank of Glasgow which has now vanished. All these issued their own notes. With the notable exception of Douglas, Heron, and Company, whose bankruptcy brought many Ayrshire families to disaster, all flourished. Nothing tells better the new-found prosperity of Scotland than the splendid Georgian bankhouses built around the end of the eighteenth century in country towns.

[1] Henry Hamilton, *The Economic Evolution of Scotland*, p. 4.

Already Scotland, once the home of idleness and poverty, was becoming dedicated to money-making. She was displaying the outlook later proclaimed by Samuel Smiles in *Self Help*. There had been a silent revolution in ethics. "If a man desires to be religious," wrote Ralph Erskine,[1] "God must have his whole heart; and he through grace must give it, and make a continual trade of religion; if a man desire to be rich, the world will oblige him to rise early and sit up late and eat the bread of carefulness; yea and employ his head and his heart, and all about the world. And therefore God and the world cannot be served by one and the same man." But while the most active classes in eighteenth-century Scotland had heard about the difficulty of serving both God and mammon, they were convinced that no good thing could be done without trying. "You've forgotten the grandest moral attribute of a Scotsman, Maggie," says one of Sir James Barrie's[2] characters, "that he'll do nothing which might damage his career." Acquisitiveness, which had been regarded as a temptation or a sin, was now on the highway to being regarded as a virtue, and its success as a mark of divine favour. In Glasgow and the Clyde valley, now becoming the heart of Scotland's commercialism, the leaders of industrial growth were to be self-made men, risen, like their counterparts in Manchester and Westphalia, from very modest circumstances.[3] Benjamin Franklin, America's exponent of this new ethic of hard work and money-making, though himself, in Weber's words, "a colourless deist", tells in his *Autobiography* how in his boyhood his Quaker father[4] drummed into him the words, "Seest thou a man diligent in his business? He shall stand before kings." Many of those who created the industrial revolution in the west of Scotland were men who shared both Franklin's Christian upbringing and his deistic outlook, but the numbers of convinced Christians among them were markedly higher than among the intellectual circles where David Hume and Adam Smith moved. If they had deviated from the ways of their fathers, it was in ethics rather than in theology.

Economic and political factors combined to introduce the industrial revolution in the west of Scotland before it made much

[1] Ralph Erskine, *Works*, ii, pp. 541–2.
[2] James Barrie, *What Every Woman Knows*, Act 2.
[3] Max Weber, *The Protestant Ethic and the Spirit of Capitalism*, p. 65.
[4] Ibid. p. 53. Proverbs 22:29.

impact on the continent[1] and appropriately, therefore, Scotland also made great contributions to the early scientific study of Political Economy. In his "Discourses" and "Essays" David Hume turned his mind to the subject and he would be better remembered as an economist today, as would be Sir James Steuart of Coltness and Lord Lauderdale, had they not been overshadowed by the great name of Adam Smith. Born at Kirkcaldy in 1723 Smith was one of many students drawn to Glasgow by Hutcheson's reputation, and all his life he remained indebted to his teacher. From Glasgow he went to Balliol as a Snell Exhibitioner but, though he used his time well, he formed a poor impression of the staff and their scholarship. "In the university of Oxford," he later wrote,[2] "the greater part of the public professors have, for these many years, given up altogether the pretence of teaching." In 1751 he returned to Glasgow, first as professor of Logic and then of Moral Philosophy, but he interpreted the field of his work so widely that in his closing lectures he "examined those political regulations which are founded, not upon the principle of *justice*, but that of *expediency*".[3] He was a popular lecturer and the number of his students increased every year.[4] "No discipline," he wrote[5] with pardonable complacency, "is ever requisite to force attendance upon lectures which are really worth the attending, as is well known wherever any such lectures are given." In particular, since the close association between the university and the commercial life of the city is one of the factors in the industrial growth of Glasgow, it is worth noting that considerable numbers of merchants were known to attend his lectures.[6] Out of these Glasgow lectures there came in time his epoch-making *Inquiry into the Nature and Causes of the Wealth of Nations*.

If Fife, his native county, had once been Covenanting country Adam Smith had moved far from its tradition. It is said that in his Oxford days he considered taking orders in the Church of England,[7] but if there is any truth in the story he must have seen

[1] Arthur Birnie, *An Economic History of Europe 1760–1930*, pp. 1–13.
[2] Adam Smith, *The Wealth of Nations*, p. 342; cf. Gibbon's similar estimate, *Autobiography*, pp. 40, 42.
[3] John Rae, *Life of Adam Smith*, p. 55.
[4] Adam Smith, *Theory of Moral Sentiments*, viii.
[5] Adam Smith, *The Wealth of Nations*, p. 343.
[6] Adam Smith, *Theory of Moral Sentiments*, viii.   [7] Ibid. iv.

it, like the youthful Charles Darwin, as no more than a leisured life suitable for a gentleman of education. Under suspicion as a close friend of David Hume, he was something of a Deist, believing in God as "the great Director of Nature",[1] in the moral law, and in an immortality in which virtue would be rewarded,[2] but without any interest in the distinctively Christian doctrines of the Trinity, the Incarnation, the Atonement, and the Holy Spirit.[3] One passage in his writing casually reveals that he had no clue as to what is involved in worship,[4] and so far as his lectures on ethics show, he might never have read the New Testament.

The catalogue[5] of his library, a Scottish parallel to that of Gibbon, still survives. Not everything in a library reflects its owner's mind but Adam Smith's library was one of his especial pleasures and was chosen with care. As one might expect, it was strong on the classics, on economics, history and geography and, surprisingly, on poetry. In philosophy ancients such as Plato and Aristotle were on his shelves, and moderns such as Berkeley, Locke, Hutcheson, Hume, and Reid, but it is the great names of the Enlightenment — D'Alembert, Bayle, Buffon, Condillac, Diderot, Helvetius, Montesquieu, Newton, Rousseau, and Voltaire — which mark the collection. Only Leibniz, Maupertuis, and D'Holbach are missing. In contrast to this is the virtual absence of all the great names in Christian writing. A Bible was on the shelves, but so was a Koran. Origen and Pascal no doubt were represented as philosophers and Massillon as a master of rhetoric. St Francis of Assisi in an odd volume and another odd volume of Van Maestricht's *Theologia* are doubtless the accidents to be found in any library. When set beside such other elements as the great edition of Voltaire in sixty-nine volumes, this omission is significant. Its owner was uninterested in the Christian faith.

One qualification must be made. Adam Smith credits the Neoplatonists with teaching that the supreme attribute of God is love. Many ancient fathers of the Church, he says, though without offering names or references, thought so also, as did the Cambridge Platonists. "But of all the patrons of this system, ancient or modern, the late Dr Hutcheson was undoubtedly, beyond all

[1] Adam Smith, *Theory of Moral Sentiments*, pp. 119, 321.   [2] Ibid. p. 226.
[3] John Rae, op. cit. pp. 129, 310-14.
[4] Adam Smith, *Theory of Moral Sentiments*, p. 184.
[5] James Bonar, *A Catalogue of the Library of Adam Smith*.

comparison, the most acute, the most distinct, the most philosophical, and, what is of the greatest consequence of all, the
soberest and most judicious."[1] It is a strange comment on the
doctrine of the Scottish Church in the eighteenth century that
one of the two greatest Scotsmen of the age should know no
other source for the teaching that God is love.

Though guardedly expressed, some of his opinions on the
Church in Scotland can be detected. The Christian faith, he held,
was intended "not so much to render the people good citizens in
this world, as to prepare them for another and a better world in
a life to come",[2] so it is a paradox that his own interest in the
Church was largely concerned with its financial structure and its
place in society. On the whole, he had respect for the ministers
of the National Church and considered that this was general, and
that the cause could be traced to their very limited incomes. "This
mediocrity of benefice has, however, some very agreeable effects.
Nothing but exemplary morals can give dignity to a man of small
fortune. . . . He is obliged to follow that system of morals which
the common people respect the most. Their kindness naturally
provokes his kindness. . . . The Presbyterian clergy, accordingly,
have more influence over the minds of the common people, than
perhaps the clergy of any other established church."[3] Yet they
had their opponents, for in Scotland, he wrote, as "in every
civilized society . . . there have been always two different schemes
or systems of morality current at the same time, of which the one
may be called the strict or austere, the other the liberal or, if you
will, the loose".[4] The former flourished among the working people
where small sects encouraged strict morals; and against these
sectarians the clergy of the larger church "when attacked by a set
of popular and bold, though perhaps stupid and ignorant enthusiasts, feel themselves perfectly defenceless".

But while there is no doubting his preference for the Moderates
as against the Seceders, as an observer of the religious life of
Scotland Adam Smith saw, or thought he saw, advantages in
sectarianism. It "might, in time, probably reduce the greater part
of them to that pure and rational religion, free from every mixture
of absurdity, imposture, or fanaticism, such as wise men have, in
all ages of the world, wished to see established". He credited

[1] Adam Smith, *Theory of Moral Sentiments*, p. 406.
[2] Adam Smith, *The Wealth of Nations*, p. 353.   [3] Ibid. p. 364.   [4] Ibid. p. 356.

Quaker Pennsylvania, as no one would ever have credited George Fox, with having produced "philosophical good temper and moderation". Meantime, the clergy needed to be restrained, and patronage provided the instrument for this. Placing the right to elect their pastors in the hands of the people led to the election of fanatical men, and the Act of 1712 had restored patronage "on account of the confusions and disorders which this more popular mode of election had almost everywhere occasioned. . . . Yet the Church requires sometimes (for she has not in this respect been very uniform in her decisions) a certain concurrence of the people. . . . She sometimes, at least, from an affected concern for the peace of the parish, delays the settlement till this concurrence can be procured. The private tampering of some of the neighbouring clergy . . . and the popular arts which they cultivate . . . are perhaps the causes which principally keep up whatever remains of the old fanatical spirit, either in the clergy or in the people of Scotland." This is an indirect admission that in a divided community the nomination of the clergy was in the hands of the adherents of the élite culture while Christian conviction was strongest among the adherents of the mass culture.

Buckle shared the contempt of David Hume and Adam Smith for the Presbyterian tradition in Scotland. "The peculiarity of Scotland," he wrote,[1] "is that . . . the industrial and intellectual progress has continued without materially shaking the authority of the priesthood. . . . The country of such fearless thinkers as George Buchanan, David Hume, and Adam Smith, is awed by a few noisy and ignorant preachers." But in some measure he was aware of the unconscious limitations of the great minds of the Enlightenment. He wrote of Hume[2] that "one of the capital defects of his mind was a disregard of facts. This did not proceed . . . from an indifference to truth. . . . In him, a contempt for facts was merely the exaggerated result of a devotion to ideas. He not only believed, with perfect justice, that ideas are more important than facts, but he supposed that they should hold the first place in the order of study, and that they should be developed before the facts are investigated." Similarly he observed that the apparently empirical character of *The Wealth of Nations* was de-

---

[1] H. T. Buckle, *History of Civilization in England*, iii, p. 185.

[2] Ibid. iii, p. 338. C. L. Becker, *The Heavenly City of the Eighteenth Century Philosophers*, pp. 91–5.

ceptive. Adam Smith had worked from general principles and merely used facts as they proved convenient to illustrate his theme. Though Buckle thought primarily of his economics, this holds equally true of Smith's comments on the Church, for his analysis is not as objective as it seems, but is the product of a rationalist outlook. Popular disorders in the election of ministers had not preceded and caused the Act of 1712, but had been a result of it; and his surmise that the growth of sectarianism would lead to the adoption of "the religion of nature" and the decay of fanaticism proved the reverse of the case.

But the fact that Adam Smith shared the illusions of the Enlightenment, that he failed to observe the seeds of dynamic change present in his society, underestimated the power of the masses and the strength of the irrational in human life, and supposed his writings to have a freedom from presumptions which they did not possess, cannot detract from the importance of *The Wealth of Nations*. It is one of the most significant and influential books ever produced in Scotland; significant because it tells something of the new form of society emerging, and influential because it went far to mould the shape of European society. By the time it issued from the press the confident rationalism of the first half of the century was already under challenge, and the first signs had appeared to tell that the leadership of the intellectual life was to pass from France to Germany. The risings of 1715 and 1745 have been regarded as the last flickering embers of the ancient association with France, but so far as intellectual life was concerned French influence was dominant in Scotland all through the eighteenth century. But the concern of Romanticism with the emotions and the hidden springs of action had already appeared in the writings of Rousseau, and the emergence of Goethe and Kant was soon to point to the rise of German thought. Deism continued to have an effect on the popular mind — as in the case of Robert Burns — but from 1740 onwards it ceased to count for so much among leaders of thought. Bolingbroke, who died in 1751, was the last professed Deist of any note in England. When his writings were published by his executor, David Mallet, in 1754, they had a badly dated character. "Sir," said Dr Johnson,[1] "he was a scoundrel, and a coward: a scoundrel for charging a blunderbuss against religion and morality; a coward, because

[1] James Boswell, *The Life of Samuel Johnson*, i, p. 160.

he had not the resolution to fire it off himself, but left half a crown to a beggarly Scotchman, to draw the trigger after his death!"

It was somewhat late in the day, so far as the Enlightenment was concerned, when Adam Smith's great book, one of its most characteristic products, appeared in 1776, yet its foundation was an unquestioned acceptance of the Deism which had seen its heyday when Smith was a student. Deism had moulded his mind, not so much as it had been stated by Toland or Anthony Collins, as in the popularized form given to it in the verse of Pope. Through all he wrote on economics ran "the strong faith that nature was known and tamed",[1] and it transferred and applied to economic and social life the conviction that men lived in an ordered universe, ruled by divine law for the ultimate good of all who permitted an impartial and benevolent Providence to work for the well being of all.[2] Part of the secret of Smith's immediate success was the fact that he transferred to an untilled field no novel principle but one already familiar and commonplace. What Smith had heard as a student in the salons could now be recognized at once in the street and the shop where it was to be given a practical application. The new commercial society, the beginnings of which Adam Smith observed, was to be of the utmost importance to the life of the Church in Scotland; but the interpretation which he placed upon it was to be of at least equal importance since it went far to shape the social order in which, to an ever-increasing degree, she had to live and work. "Smith's work," said Pulteney[3] in 1797, "would persuade the present generation and govern the next." This proved correct. *The Wealth of Nations* was read and acted upon both by the industrialists of Glasgow and men, like Pitt, at the head of government.

Adam Smith's insistence upon the merit of individual enterprise, the benefits of competition, and the need for complete freedom from government interference was the message which a rising industrialism had longed to hear, for those who were creating the fortunes of the new Scotland had made their way, unassisted, by their own hard work. For all Smith's writings on the power of sympathy, in practice he restricted moral considerations to private life and divorced them from business and social matters.

[1] J. Steven Watson, *The Reign of George III*, p. 329.'
[2] J. Bronowski and Bruce Mazlish, *The Western Intellectual Tradition*, p. 352.
[3] J. S. Watson, op. cit. p. 329.

Thus he helped to bring about a society prepared to function without interference either from ethical considerations of religion or social considerations of government. Religion was banished to a private sphere, where it would not have contact with business. Since the publication of the *First Book of Discipline* in 1560 there had always been strong elements of social consideration in the religious life of Scotland, but Adam Smith's teachings heralded a century in which ruthlessness in industry and commerce could be, and often were, combined with evangelical devotion and private charity on a large scale.

Self-love, the new teaching ran, would in the end be the best possible service to the community. "Every individual is continually exerting himself to find out the most advantageous employment for whatever capital he can command. It is his own advantage, indeed, and not that of the society, which he has in view. But the study of his own advantage naturally, or rather necessarily, leads him to prefer that employment which is most advantageous to the society."[1] Out of this came the new bourgeois ethic of nineteenth-century Scotland, an essentially individual ethic, since it was every man's duty to get on in the world and make a place for himself. By contrast, the working-class ethic remained a communal one, where each felt that he could only aid himself by aiding his neighbour. "Union is strength" became the motto of the Co-operative Movement which, with the Trade Unions, was a natural expression of this outlook. But Scotland's great economist had convinced the managerial class that competition was good for trade and served the general good by providing the needs of man at the cheapest price. "The price of monopoly is, upon every occasion, the highest which can be got. The natural price, or the price of free competition, on the contrary, is the lowest which can be taken, not upon every occasion, indeed, but for any considerable time together."[2] Combinations, whether of masters or men, were not in the public interest. Those of workmen were forbidden by law but masters were "always and everywhere in a sort of tacit, but constant and uniform, combination, not to raise the wages of labour above their actual rate".[3] Attempts to organize trade unions had the odds heavily against them, but the worker had at least the consolation that employers

[1] Adam Smith, *The Wealth of Nations*, p. 198.
[2] Ibid. p. 28.   [3] Ibid. p. 30.

could not force wages below the level at which it was possible to maintain life.

Convinced as he was of the power of rational argument, Adam Smith does not seem to have realized how strong were some other inducements to follow such teachings. He under-estimated the attractive force of his doctrines of competition and free trade. "To expect, indeed, that the freedom of trade should ever be entirely restored in Great Britain," he wrote, "is as absurd as to expect that any Oceana or Utopia should ever be established in it."[1] But he was mistaken; the taste of freedom con-vinced economic interests that unrestricted private enterprise was the path for society. Business must be left to take its own course, and if the weakest must go to the wall this was no more than an unavoidable incident in the general advance. Government should stand aside and let economic forces run their own course. "The recovery of a great foreign market will generally more than com-pensate the transitory inconveniency of paying dearer during a short time for some sorts of goods. To judge whether such retaliations are likely to produce such an effect, does not perhaps belong so much to the science of a legislator, whose deliberations ought to be governed by general principles which are always the same, as to the skill of that insidious and crafty animal, vulgarly called a statesman or politician, whose councils are directed by the momentary fluctuations of affairs."[2] Since the laws of Pro-vidence operated for the ultimate good of all, a free economy, unrestricted by social or ethical considerations, would promote the welfare of the whole community.

The interference of the State in industry or commerce, he summed up, "retards, instead of accelerating, the progress of the society towards real wealth and greatness. . . . All systems, either of preference or of restraint, therefore, being thus completely taken away, the obvious and simple system of natural liberty establishes itself of its own accord. Every man, as long as he does not violate the laws of justice, is left perfectly free to pursue his own interest his own way."[3] By twentieth-century standards the part played by government in the industry and commerce of the time was small indeed, but as the Scottish economy steadily expanded the principles of Adam Smith were allowed to rule it

[1] Adam Smith, *The Wealth of Nations*, p. 207.
[2] Ibid. p. 206.   [3] Ibid. p.311.

until, in the nineteenth century, they became the fiscal policy of the State. Principles apart, Scotland scarcely possessed the machinery for State participation in her economic life, for after 1746 the Lord Advocate and — until 1827 — leading politicians of the day known as "the Managers" were responsible for the day-to-day conduct of the country's affairs so that until the institution of the Scottish Office in 1885 there was little effective administration of Scotland.[1]

At the time of the Union, Glasgow had been a quiet country town, dominated by its university and comparable with St Andrews rather than with Edinburgh. In the well-known words of Daniel Defoe,[2] it was "one of the cleanliest, most beautiful, and best built cities in Great Britain", a description which the Industrial Revolution was to render ironical before the century ended. Steady growth followed the Union. New markets were opened up and small industries founded, but it was the tobacco trade with Virginia which brought wealth to the city. Its numbers increased, at first slowly, and then rapidly. In the year of the Union, Glasgow had about 13,000 people. In 1710, 129 weddings were recorded and the annual number remained under 150 until 1740, but from then on there was a rapid increase to 271 in 1750, 367 in 1780, and 480 in 1790. Simultaneously the number of baptisms rose from 470 in 1710 to 657 in 1740, 901 in 1750, and 1,449 in 1790.[3] In other words, it was a city of young people in which, as the mid-century approached, the rate of increase suddenly quickened. As yet it was more of a merchant city than an industrial one and the Clyde, which had opened the American trade to its citizens, more like a salmon river than a harbour. As a result of the colonists' reaction to the Stamp Act of 1765, Glasgow's American trade suffered, but it was the outbreak of the War of Independence in 1775 which brought ruin to the tobacco trade. In 1775 Glasgow imported nearly 46,000,000 lb. of tobacco and re-exported all but some 3,000,000 lb. to the continent, but her total imports fell to about 7,500,000 lb. in 1776, and to 295,000 lb. in 1777.[4] The trade had gone, and gone for ever. These events did not take the Glasgow merchants by

[1] R. H. Campbell, *Scotland since 1707*, p. 4.
[2] T. C. Smout, op. cit. p. 380.
[3] James Cleland, *Annals of Glasgow*, i, p. 359.
[4] H. Hamilton, *The Industrial Revolution in Scotland*, pp. 120–1.

surprise, and if they lost their income they retained their very considerable capital, which had now to be redirected. Aided by the foundation of the Glasgow Chamber of Commerce[1] in 1783, the first of its kind in Britain, they expanded the West Indian trade. Scottish banking[2] had been centred on Edinburgh and was conservative in an unwillingness to provide for industrial expansion, and it was just recovering from the crisis year of 1772, but its facilities for credit now combined with the sudden release of capital in Glasgow and found a suitable field in the rising cotton industry.

Earlier Scottish ventures in the textile trades had been in linen and woollens. In 1710 Scotland produced 1,500,000 yards of linen and in 1720 she exported to England alone some £200,000 worth of linen goods.[3] To some extent, especially where the finer cloths were concerned, these interests suffered from English competition after 1707[4] but under the encouragement of the Board of Trustees the linen trade as a whole flourished. It is a very odd fact that Christian Shaw of Bargarran, who was responsible for the prosecution of the Renfrewshire witches, made a second place for herself in Scottish history by the improvements which she introduced into the linen[5] trade. In towns such as Stirling, Kilmarnock, and Ayr the woollen trade was carried on and such goods as tartans, tweeds, hosiery, bonnets, blankets, and carpets were produced.[6] These industries were domestic, spinners and weavers worked — for the most part — at home, and the work was therefore widely distributed.

England produced the inventions which made cotton a great industry. In 1770 Hargreaves patented the spinning-jenny which multiplied the amount of yarn that could be spun. Further improvements were made by Arkwright, who applied water power to the running of his mill at Cromford in 1771. Crompton's mule, invented in 1775, produced a thread which was both fine and strong. By 1785 his machine was being used in Scotland, and what had once been an industry of the Far East was now to

[1] J. Cleland, op. cit. i, p. 36.
[2] R. H. Campbell, op. cit. pp. 68–75, 133–5.
[3] J. Mackintosh, *The History of Civilization in Scotland*, iv, p. 373.
[4] R. H. Campbell, op. cit. pp. 54–63.
[5] R. Chambers, op. cit. iii, pp. 510-11.
[6] J. Mackintosh, op. cit. iv, p. 369.

become the start of the factory system[1] in the West. Scotland, and the Clyde valley in particular, possessed the capital, the skills, and the water power for the new industry, and any shortage of manpower could be met by migration from Ireland and the impoverished Highlands. The first effective cotton mill in Scotland was built at Rothesay in 1779 and others followed in many parts, but particularly in Lanarkshire and Renfrew. Though the steam engine had been invented by James Watt in 1769 and made a commercial proposition in 1785, it was slow to displace water power in the cotton mills. It was used for the first time at Glasgow in 1792; by 1800 only 8 of the 128 cotton mills in Scotland used steam,[2] but by 1831, 107 did so in Glasgow alone.

These economic changes had far-reaching results for the social life and — in the long run — for the religious life of Scotland. With the rapid development of industry there came the rise of a new capitalist class in the west of Scotland. The social structure of Edinburgh reflected the older Scottish life with a considerable number of resident gentry and a high proportion of professional men,[3] but Glasgow was becoming the city of industry and newly-made wealth. None of the new industrial magnates were the sons of the old aristocracy and few came from the families of professional men. John Burns, the pioneer steamship owner, and Robert Carrick, who began as a clerk in the Ship Bank in the Stockwell of Glasgow and died in 1815 leaving £500,000, were both ministers's sons, but this was exceptional.[4] More typical were James and William Campbell, the mill owners, Charles Tennant of the St Rollox chemical works, and William and James Baird, the iron masters, who were the sons of small farmers, or James Watt, the son of a shipwright, J. B. Neilson, the son of a colliery engineman, or Robert Napier, the son of a smith. Some of these men made their names and their fortunes after the opening of the new century but as a class they shared much in origin, character, and achievements with one of the earliest examples of the type, David Dale.

[1] H. Hamilton, *The Industrial Revolution in Scotland*, pp. 122–3.

[2] Ibid. p. 132. Lord Cockburn commented that between 1785 and 1825 there were probably more steam engines in Glasgow alone than in the whole of Europe. *Journal*, ii, p. 5.

[3] T. C. Smout, op. cit. p. 381.

[4] Ibid. p. 388.

Dale[1] was born in 1739, the son of a village grocer in Stewarton. After starting work as a herd boy, and then as a weaver, he became clerk to a silk mercer in Glasgow. About 1763 he took a shop in the High Street for £5 annually, rented half of it to a watchmaker, obtained the support of a moneyed partner, and so set up in business as a linen and yarn merchant. He tramped the countryside buying up small quantities of thread from farmers' wives and from these small beginnings he first became an importer on a large scale and then ventured into the cotton trade.[2] In 1783 he built the first large cotton-spinning mills in Scotland at New Lanark, and later others at Stanley in Perthshire, Spinningdale near Dornoch, Blantyre in Lanarkshire, and Catrine in Ayrshire. He was now a magnate of the first rank, controlling an industrial and commercial empire from his new Georgian house beside Glasgow Green, strong willed and self-assured, if not always consistent, the pattern of the self-made man.

Dale was a man of strong Christian conviction but, in this as in everything else, very much an individualist. He had a keen eye for money and was given to speculation so that, despite his wealth, he was three times almost bankrupted, and it was suggested that he was "trading on too narrow a margin, too near the verge of bankruptcy, which, had it taken place, would have involved others in injury and suffering, and brought discredit on his Christian character".[3] In business matters, he was as hard as nails, and he was blamed for holding "his assistants and other people with whom he did business to the letter of their contracts in circumstances where one might have expected greater generosity in a man of his benevolence". On the other hand, he was lavish with his generosity, and what he made with one hand he gave away with the other. During times of distress he chartered ships to import grain which he then sold cheaply to the poor. He was credited with many secret acts of private generosity, and he gave great support to religious causes. Something of this ambiguity appears in his dealings with his work people.

His mills required a great amount of unskilled labour, and as no great strength was necessary he was therefore mainly an em-

---

[1] Stewart Mechie, *The Church and Scottish Social Development, 1780–1870*, pp. 4ff.

[2] H. Hamilton, *The Industrial Revolution in Scotland*, p. 125.

[3] S. Mechie, op. cit. p. 13.

ployer of women and children. It was said that the ideal employee would have been a widow with a large family, and New Lanark had 34 such widows in 1793, and Catrine had 44 in 1819.[1] But the most obvious source of suitable cheap labour lay in the orphan children with whom Scotland abounded. At New Lanark David Dale built a barracks in 1797 capable of holding 500 children who worked from six in the morning till seven in the evening, six days a week, with an interval of half an hour for breakfast and an hour for dinner.[2] "The directors of the public charities," wrote Robert Owen, Dale's son-in-law, "from mistaken economy would not consent to send the children under their care to cotton mills, unless the children were received by the proprietors at the ages of six, seven, and eight. And Mr Dale was under the necessity of accepting them at those ages, or of stopping the manufacture which he had commenced."[3] On the other hand, by the standards of the time Dale's care for his workers was highly enlightened, for he retained an element of the paternalism which marked the great estates. Catrine and New Lanark, if a trifle bleak, offered a good standard of housing, and the mills were well designed. His child labourers, if hard worked, were at least better housed, better dressed, and better fed than was usual in poorer working-class households. As for their education, "the children, both those fit for work and those who are too young for it, have the privilege of attending the school gratis, the former in the evenings, the latter through the day. Three professed teachers are paid by Mr Dale for this purpose, and also seven assistants who attend in the evenings, one of whom teaches writing. There is also a Sunday School at which all the masters and assistants attend." Unfortunately the schooling at the end of a long day's labour brought little reward. "This kind of instruction," Robert Owen wrote, "when the strength of the children was exhausted, only tormented them without doing any real good — for I found that none of them understood anything they attempted to read, and many of them fell asleep during the school hours."[4] This paternalistic exploitation won glowing praise from many contemporary observers but, understandably, chilly comment from later times.

[1] T. C. Smout, op. cit. p. 408.   [2] S. Mechie, op. cit. p. 7.
[3] Robert Owen, *A New View of Society*, p. 117.
[4] Robert Owen, *Life of Robert Owen*, i, p. 60.

Dale had been brought up in the National Church, but when the magistrates of Glasgow won a dispute regarding the patronage of the city churches in 1763[1] he left to join a newly-founded congregation of the Relief Church. Five years later when John Barclay of Fettercairn, a licentiate of the Church of Scotland who became the leader of a small sect known as the Bereans, visited the city, Dale accepted his congregationalist principles. Two ministers, James Smith of Newburn and Robert Ferrier of Largo, had resigned their charges on similar grounds to found a group known as the Old Scots Independents. Ferrier and Dale both became elders of their Glasgow congregation and from 1769 until his death in 1806 Dale regularly preached.[2] In other words, though sincerely Christian, he was a born dissenter, an individualist with little sense of the Church as a community, whose religious outlook "reflected the individualism and activism which rise out of the economic life".[3] Throughout the following century many other self-made men were to swell the ranks of Scottish dissent.

At the other end of the economic scale the employees of such men as Dale were also going out of the National Church, but for a different reason. The introduction of the factory system did not mean the immediate disappearance of the individual spinner and weaver, working in his own cottage, but improvements in machinery inevitably drew workers from domestic employment into the mills. Spinning passed from the fireside to the factory but the former household workers were not sufficient to meet the demands for new industrial labour and a steady movement of population commenced. The family of Peter Carmichael[4] had been small farmers at Knockando in Morayshire and Mortlach in Banffshire. "Those who have read of the condition of Strathspey in 1782 and the year following," he wrote, "will not wonder at my grandfather then leaving the district and preparing to follow his brother to America. . . . Going forth from Speyside with his wife and family my grandfather went to Greenock and took ship there for America, but a few days after sailing they were

[1] R. Small, *Congregations of the United Presbyterian Church from 1753–1900*, ii, p. 32. James Cleland, op. cit. ii, pp. 408–11.

[2] S. Mechie, op. cit. p. 11.

[3] H. Richard Niebuhr, *The Social Sources of Denominationalism*, p. 88.

[4] *Dundee Textile Industry, 1790–1885*, SHS, p. 4.

shipwrecked on the coast of Ireland, losing everything but their lives. They returned to Scotland and my grandfather began afresh and must in some measure have redeemed his fortune, for at his death he left some property in Glasgow. . . . My father, after what must have been a good schooling, was trained as a mechanic, a term then used in the strict sense to denote a man who worked in metal as distinguished from a mill-wright who worked in wood. As a young man he got ample employment at the cotton mills being erected in the neighbourhood of Glasgow. . . ."

Carmichael's family came from Speyside and prospered, but while details of the new industrial class are anything but clear, it would seem that most of them — apart from migrants from the countryside — came from the West Highlands and Ireland, and remained poor. The contrast between the figures in Dr Webster's census of 1755 and those of the Old Statistical Account almost forty years later tell of a growing population in the Gaelic counties. Out of 21 parishes on the western seaboard of Ross and the islands north and west of Skye, all but 6 doubled in population between 1755 and 1841; in 9 the increase exceeded 150 per cent; and in 5 the numbers trebled.[1] While the landlords welcomed this growth, it also brought problems for their patriarchal society. Poor standards of cultivation and shortage of good land meant poverty and a low standard of living for which emigration was the only solution. But it was not the occasional and much lamented departure of an emigrant ship for Canada[2] so much as the unnoted and unplanned but persistent drift of a hungry people to the mills of the Clyde valley which carried off most Highlanders. "The people here marry young," said one writer in the Old Statistical Account. "They have an uncommonly numerous offspring. This is the reason why the Highlands are a nursery for raising so many useful hands for the countries below them. It is almost incredible to tell what swarms leave the country every year, and go to the south for service. Almost all the boys from ten to fifteen go to tend sheep or cattle, and learn a little English. Many of them afterwards go into service or to handicraft employments, and never return. Besides these, crofters, cottagers, and day labourers, who can earn no bread at home, set

[1] Malcolm Gray, *The Highland Economy*, p. 60.
[2] J. MacInnes, *The Evangelical Movement in the Highlands of Scotland 1688–1800*, pp. 133ff.

out for the great towns to get employment."[1]

A time had been when the Highlanders stood very lightly to the Church but in the second half of the eighteenth century a succession of revivals and evangelical movements made deep impressions in the north,[2] and the records of the General Assembly tell of unceasing endeavours to provide ministers, schoolteachers, and Gaelic religious literature. Many of those who came south to work in the mills were therefore devout. Some, like the family of David Livingstone, made their homes in communities too small to support a Gaelic church, but in Glasgow a Gaelic church was founded in 1772 in Ingram Street, and a second in Duke Street in 1798, while one was founded in Greenock in 1792.[3] As for those who lacked such strong convictions, there is only too much reason to suppose that, deprived of the support of their family background and traditional culture, and taken from a pastoral and patriarchal society into the slums of industrial towns, they swelled the numbers of those who had lost all active contact with the Church.

If the Highlanders formed an alien group in Lowland Scotland this was even more true of most of the immigrants from Ireland, since they were Roman Catholics. Apart from a few titled families and their dependants who maintained a loyalty, sometimes little more than political or sentimental, to the Church of the Old Pretender, the Roman Catholics of Scotland were few and obscure in the century and a half following the Reformation. Dr Webster's census of 1755 recorded 265 in Edinburgh, a Peebleshire group of 22 dependent on the Stuarts of Traquair, and 384 in Dumfries and the Stewartry dependent on the Maxwell and Herries families. Otherwise there were none in the Lowlands save 2 in Lanarkshire and 3 in Renfrewshire. Further north occasional families were found until the north-east where, almost alone in Protestant Scotland, under the leadership of the house of Huntly nearly 10,000 had kept an unbroken loyalty to the Roman See. The population of Aberdeen, wrote the far from impartial Samuel Rutherford,[4] "consisteth either of Papists, or men of Gallio's naughty faith". In the West Highlands were another 5,400 Romanists. It is often

[1] Malcolm Gray, op. cit. p. 64.
[2] J. MacInnes, op. cit. pp. 124–63.
[3] *Fasti*, II, i, pp. 32, 34, 241.
[4] Samuel Rutherford, *Letters*, "To Lady Boyd".

thought that they, too, had never wavered in loyalty to Rome, but this is not so. For long the Reformed Church was unable to staff the wild parishes of the north-west as she might have wished. Dr Donald MacLean[1] found it impossible to reduce to order the accounts of Roman Catholic conversions in Lochaber, and failed to recognize that the population, nominally Christian, was in fact quite pagan, though ready to offer a welcome to any itinerant evangelist and to bring the unbaptized in hundreds to priest or minister alike. The fact that ultimately South Uist, Barra, and some nearby parts of the mainland became Roman Catholic was due to the effective work of the Franciscan mission from Bona-margey in County Antrim in 1624.[2]

Between 1690 and 1800 Scotland's Roman Catholics, it has been estimated, declined from 50,000 to 30,000.[3] Probably this higher number can only be reconciled with that of Webster by assuming that it included many purely nominal adherents. Until 1781 any Glasgow Romanists were served by a priest from Drummond Castle in Perthshire, a fact which tells its own story, but from then onwards Bishop Geddes regularly visited Glasgow from his Edinburgh home. In 1783 he was relieved for a time by Dr Alexander Geddes, the author of a translation of the Bible, and the first priest since the Reformation to get a doctorate from a Scottish university. "Your little flock here," he wrote, "will get into a bad habit of hearing mass every Sunday, and will take ill to their old period of six months." His congregation had grown to 15 and he expected it soon to reach 20. The Rev. Alexander MacDonell of Badenoch followed some of his flock to Glasgow and canvassed a number of Protestant millowners for support in an effort to bring others to a place where they could get enough or, at least, a little more to eat. He was successful, and on 21 October 1792 the first post-Reformation Roman Catholic church was opened in Glasgow with a congregation of more than 200. A number of manufacturers, headed by David Dale, had guaranteed the rent of temporary premises and promised £30 annually

[1] Donald MacLean, *The Counter-Reformation in Scotland, 1560–1930*. Norman MacLeod, *Reminiscences of a Highland Parish*, p. 119.
[2] J. L. Campbell, "The Irish Franciscan Mission to Scotland", *Franciscan College Annual*, 1952, pp. 7–24; *Innes Review*, iv, pp. 42–8; v, pp. 33–8.
[3] James Darragh, "The Catholic Population in Scotland", *Innes Review*, iv, pp. 49–59.

for the priest's salary. By 1797 a church and presbytery had been built and the congregation was well established.

But it was not to the native adherents that the Roman Church in Scotland owed its rebirth. Since early in the eighteenth century a few Irish had been settling in Scotland. Soon after its formation in 1727 the Board of Trustees brought James Adair from Belfast with his son and twenty weavers to introduce the linen trade into Galloway.[1] In 1777 the penal statutes against Irish Roman Catholics were repealed and in 1778 English ones obtained relief, but, despite the sympathy of Principal Robertson, the proposal to extend emancipation to Scotland roused wide opposition,[2] and strong resentment frustrated the attempt of the Moderate leadership to obtain some form of approval from the Assembly.[3] On 2 February 1779 the Edinburgh mob sacked a chapel recently erected in Leith Wynd and, on the following day, with complete immunity, the house and chapel of Bishop Hay. Similar disturbances began in Glasgow, but there the magistrates acted more speedily to prevent damage to property. But the times were changing even if prejudices died hard, and in 1793,[4] partly as a consequence of the French Revolution and partly as a result of the diplomacy of Bishop Hay, Scottish Roman Catholics received their legal rights. In the interval since the riots Irish immigrants had begun to arrive in the textile parishes of the West of Scotland and to awaken some anxiety through their religion and alien ways.[5] About 7,000 came to Scotland in 1796 from County Armagh after the massacre of the "Diamond", many of them to settle around Neilston and Barrhead.[6] 1798 saw a marked increase as a consequence of the harsh measures taken after the suppression of the rising of that year.[7] Those who came from Antrim and Down were Presbyterians[8] but many Roman Catholics from Wexford and Wicklow arrived in Ayrshire. From 20 May till the end of 1795 there were 20 baptisms at the Glasgow chapel. In 1798 there were 83 and 93 in the next year, and from then onwards

---

[1] H. Hamilton, *The Industrial Revolution in Scotland*, p. 82.

[2] John Cunningham, *Church History of Scotland*, ii, pp. 385ff.

[3] *AGA*, 1778, 28–9 May.

[4] William Ferguson, *Scotland; 1689 to the Present*, p. 232.

[5] T. C. Smout, op. cit. p. 264.

[6] James E. Handley, *The Irish in Scotland*, p. 44.

[7] R. H. Campbell, *Scotland since 1707*, p. 180.

[8] J. M. Barkley, *A Short History of the Presbyterian Church in Ireland*, p. 40.

there was a steady rise to 155 in 1805, 379 in 1810, 471 in 1815 and 583 in 1820.[1]

This was an event of primary importance in the religious and social history of Scotland. Presbyterian immigrants from Northern Ireland were of the same religious outlook and social character as those among whom they settled and soon merged in the general population. The Irish Roman Catholics remained distinct. Many may have lapsed from the faith and morals of their fathers in a strange industrial environment, but whereas the Church of Scotland and the Seceders equally began to lose their grip on the poor of the new slums the Roman Church followed its people and retained their loyalty. The unprecedented factor in Scottish life as the eighteenth century drew to a close was the explosive increase in the number of industrial jobs available and the numbers, particularly in the Highlands and Ireland, who had no alternative save to seek such employment. The industrial revolution[2] brought the workers together in adventure and misfortune in the horrid environment which it was steadily creating, destroying the ethics and order of the older trade guilds even as it violently displaced the newcomers from the paternalism, social supports, and Christian faith of the countryside. As their numbers grew and their self consciousness increased, they were to develop attitudes different from or hostile to those of the rest of society both in religion and in politics. They were to become Ishmaelites, their hand against every man and every man's hand against them. The undisturbed section of the community had little understanding of those who had been torn from their social roots and thrown into the *melee* of industry, and even less sympathy. For the Irish, ill-educated, underprivileged, and accustomed to more squalid conditions or obliged to accept them, this was doubly true. They lived in the deepest level of poverty that Scotland could offer. "To what class of society do the Irish in Glasgow and its neighbourhood belong?" Bishop Scott[3] was asked in early Victorian times. He replied, "I must answer that all those with whom I have been acquainted belong to the poorer and almost the lowest class of society." Most of them, he told, were cotton weavers or labourers.

[1] J. E. Handley, op. cit. p. 54.
[2] T. C. Smout, op. cit. p. 392.
[3] J. E. Handley, op. cit. p. 65.

There was much hostility to the newcomers. "The Irish labourers," wrote the parish minister of Lennoxtown,[1] "have imported their custom of pigging—as many persons occupying a room at night as can find space to lie in it—a practice equally inimical to health and to decency." This comment, like many others, dates from some forty years after the start of the problem, for Scotland launched itself upon the new venture of industrialism with neither planning nor foresight, but only the conviction that an economy unrestrained by ethical or social considerations would automatically bring its own rewards. The consequences were not foreseen; but the Irish got much of the blame for a situation of which they were no more than the victims. "The Irish weavers," said one observer,[2] "are a little in advance in the career down hill, for they are the main cause of pulling the Scotch down after them. Of course they are in a slightly better condition than in their own country, which is precisely the reason why they take the lead in the career downwards, having less natural repugnance to privations which they have been previously in some measure inured to; when a manufacturer desires to lower his wages, it is ten to one but the Irish are the first to accept his terms." "They have," said another,[3] "eaten up our public charities, filled our prisons, crowded the calendar of crime, and destroyed the appearance and character of many an old Scots village. Dark shadows marked the advent of the Irish among these scenes of peace and prosperity—shadows which have darkened into sullen, gloomy clouds." This criticism came from more than prejudice or national intolerance. It arose because the Irish, "possessed", in the words of the parish minister of Whithorn, "of nothing but a number of naked, starving children", were obliged in desperation to tolerate even worse conditions than the poorest Scots would endure. They were prepared to live on potatoes where Scots aspired to porridge. The degradation of the Irish immigrants produced a reaction of distaste. A social gulf, as large as that between Lazarus and Dives, separated them from the literate Scots and prevented any sympathetic understanding of their faith. Scottish concepts of Roman Catholicism were formed, not from the Roman Catholics in their midst, but from tradition and popular history.

[1] Quoted in S. Mechie, op. cit. p. 18.
[2] Quoted in R. H. Campbell, op. cit. p. 186.   [3] Ibid. p. 192.

In these grim circumstances the Roman Catholic Church performed an astonishing feat. Their priests followed their people. When numbers grew they started their own schools. In October 1817 the Catholic Schools Society was founded in Glasgow with the support of Protestant manufacturers. "The manufacturers of this country," said Kirkman Finlay,[1] "could never have gone on without the emigration from Ireland, or the assistance of Irish weavers; and, having them, would they retain them in an ignorant and debased state, or help them to attain to the character of a population who were able to read and write?" Despite resentment at Protestant support the Society weathered the storm and by 1825 had five schools with 1,400 pupils. Churches, too, were built, this time with exclusively Romanist support. The most striking was St Andrew's[2] in Glasgow, commenced in 1814 and, despite damage by hooligans, completed in 1816 at a cost of £15,000. Set in a commanding position on a splendid site overlooking the Clyde, this great church, seating 2,200 persons, was a visible tribute to the achievement of those who had begun their work among a mere handful of poverty-stricken immigrants barely a quarter of a century before. Glasgow's Episcopalians could still be accommodated in the little church of St Andrew's by the Green, built in 1751 and Presbyterian to every eye, save in its altar, orchestra, and organ gallery; but the new Roman Catholic community had built by far the largest church in the city except the cathedral which, in any case, could hardly have been claimed as Presbyterian workmanship.

[1] J. E. Handley, op. cit. p. 125.
[2] J. Cleland, *Annals of Glasgow*, i, pp. 66–7.

CHAPTER SEVEN

The New Century

On a Sunday morning in 1769 Mr James Monteith, a wealthy Glasgow manufacturer who lived in the village of Anderston, a little to the west of the city, was walking to church. He was a Seceder, and an elder of the Antiburgher congregation which had split away from the original Secession church in Glasgow in 1754. But before he could reach his own church at the old Havannah, at the corner of Duke Street and High Street, a heavy shower came on. Mr Monteith went into the open doorway of the Tron Kirk, which he happened to be passing, and then, as the rain continued, stayed there for the service. For this he was rebuked by his own uncompromising session, and in dudgeon he joined with a friend to found a new church in Anderston.[1] His conduct illustrates both the strength and weakness of the Seceders, their devotion and responsibility, their obstinacy and total lack of any sense of the communal nature of the Christian Church. Even the disputes of this cantankerous if pious people led to their growth. Led by laymen with a keen business eye, they consistently placed their churches on sites with a good prospect of capital development, and advanced from comparative poverty to prosperity. Their steady growth was a sign, not merely of opportunism and vitality, but of widespread dissatisfaction among the new classes of society with the National Church, both in her administration and in her preaching.

On the other hand, the Church of Scotland, inhibited by an establishment which had been intended to strengthen her, and saddled with the Westminster Confession as a doctrinal standard, could do little either to found new congregations or to enter new fields of thought. Based on a structure planned for a rural society, as Scotland became more industrial and urban with every passing

[1] J. B. Primrose, "The Mother Anti-Burgher Church of Glasgow". W. McKelvie, *Annals and Statistics of the United Presbyterian Church*, pp. 291–300.

year, she found herself faced with unsurmountable problems in educating the children and supporting the poor of the new slums. No longer secure in the nominal adherence of the whole population, she saw her social responsibilities gradually assumed by secular authority.[1] Collections in the plate at the kirk door ceased to provide for local poverty as once they did and local assessments were made for poor relief. Country schools, supported by heritors and sessions, and those organized by the S.P.C.K. in the Highlands since 1709, though limited by poverty, could cope in a fashion, but in the areas of rapid growth neither the Church nor private enterprise could meet the clamant need.

Those who flocked with their families into the industrial towns of Scotland from the Highlands and Ireland were not finding them to be the Eldorados of which they had dreamed. A time had been when the handloom weaver was very well off by Scottish standards. He was not overworked, he ate well and he dressed well, and since his ranks contained many men of native intelligence he often bought books, especially of poetry and religion, was independent in his churchmanship, and often was concerned with some small independent sect. Of the many minor poets who came from this background, Robert Tannahill of Paisley was longest remembered. Weavers became amateur students of botany, ornithology, and geology, and were known for enquiring minds. But all this was coming to an end, for the markets for their products were limited, too many workers were entering this field, and over all hung the shadow of the competition of the mills whose products were much cheaper and every bit as good. Twice in the first decade of the new century the weavers petitioned parliament to fix minimum wages. When rebuffed, they formed a trade union. After local negotiations they drew up a wage scale and table of prices which the Court of Session approved, but the refusal of the Glasgow manufacturers to accept it brought off the great strike of 1812. In February 1813 the Glasgow leaders of the strike were arrested, tried, and — despite the earlier support of the Court of Session — sentenced to terms of imprisonment of from four to eighteen months.[2] This broken strike was a turning-point

[1] T. Ferguson, *The Dawn of Scottish Social Welfare*, pp. 176–93. J. E. Graham, *The Poor Law of Scotland Previous to 1845*, pp. 64–5.
[2] T. C. Smout, *A History of the Scottish People, 1560–1830*, pp. 422–6. W. L. Mathieson, *Church and Reform in Scotland, 1797–1843*, pp. 136–40.

in their history. Men who had been comfortably off were steadily reduced to hopeless poverty in a declining trade. "I remember," said a witness before a Royal Commission in 1834, "in former times that the weaver could sit down to a tea-breakfast, and have his butter and ham like an ordinary furnished table; but the general breakfast now is porridge and buttermilk, and the dinner potatoes and possibly a herring, or any cheap article; as for broth or flesh meat, it is a very rare thing that is in a weaver's house." Weavers ceased to own their own houses as once they had done. In desperation many took to drink. After 1820 they ceased to take a leading part in politics or in literary activities. They ceased to attend church and became embittered.

In particular, the children of weavers suffered. "They are poor, neglected, ragged children," said a report in 1833. "They are seldom taught anything and they work as long as the weavers, that is, as long as they can see; standing on the same spot, always barefooted, on an earthen, cold, damp floor, in a close damp cellar, for thirteen or fourteen hours a day. They can earn two shillings per week, and eat porridge if their parents can afford it, if not, potatoes and salt."[1] In the factories wages were also low and hours long. Intimate family life had been traditional in Scotland, but under the factory system the father was an absentee for most of the week. His interests were restricted to his work and the public house, and he saw his family only at night and on Sundays. Family ties were loosened and morals deteriorated. Sheriff Alison held that three-quarters of factory girls lost their virginity before they were twenty.[2] Families who were being forced down the ladder by economic pressures found themselves obliged to accept the most degraded type of housing. Whatever hovels the poor of rural Scotland may have known had at least the advantage of the open countryside and clean air at the door, but the new poor were crowded into unspeakable quarters. Health deteriorated, infectious diseases spread, and the death rate was high. A Glasgow doctor told how in 1818 he visited a narrow close, from four to five feet wide, flanked by houses five stories high. The collected filth lay in a pool from which there was no drain, and animals were housed among the human beings. "I saw one closet, measuring twelve feet by less than five, on the floor of which he told me six people had lain, affected with fever, within these two

---

[1] T. C. Smout, op. cit. p. 427.   [2] Ibid. p. 415.

days, and where I saw the seventh inhabitant now confined."[1]
Such evidence could be multiplied. "The streets or rather lanes
in which the poor live," says another observer, "are filthy beyond
measure; excrementitious matter and filth of every description is
allowed to lay upon the lanes. . . . The houses are ruinous, ill-
constructed, and to an incredible degree destitute of furniture. In
many there is not an article of bedding and the body clothes of
the inmates are of the most revolting description."[2] A glance at
the back of many early nineteenth-century tenements in Glasgow
will show that they were built, even then, with no sanitary accommodation, and that this was only added in late Victorian
times.

Poverty and squalor had always been found in Scotland, but it is
not an illusion to say that they had been somewhat alleviated by
a certain neighbourly kindness. Now the classes were segregated
and the evils accumulated in certain restricted areas. Simultaneously the standards of the middle class rose so that there were
created two worlds, as it were, within the one society, one knowing nothing of the other. While the poor of Glasgow lived in the
dark wynds behind the High Street and the Saltmarket, the
splendid terraces of the New Town of Edinburgh were being
built and other Scots were being housed behind the magnificent
facade of Moray Place. The paradoxical situation arose that while
the religious life of the upper classes was improving under
evangelical influence and the reaction to the French Revolution,
there was a section of the community which was becoming pagan.

The Lothians knew nothing of the depravity of Glasgow, but
when Hugh Miller[3] came to work there as a mason he wrote, "I
must in justice add that all the religion of our party was to be
found among the Seceders. Our other workmen were really wild
fellows, most of whom never entered a church. A decided reaction had already commenced within the Establishment, on the
cold, elegant, unpopular Moderatism of the previous period —
that Moderatism which had been so adequately represented in
the Scottish capital by the theology of Blair, and the ecclesiastical
policy of Robertson; but it was chiefly among the middle and
upper classes . . . and so the working men of Edinburgh and its

[1] Ferguson, op. cit. p. 56.
[2] S. Mechie, *The Church and Scottish Social Development 1780–1870*, p. 29.
[3] H. Miller, *My Schools and Schoolmasters*, xv–xvi.

neighbourhood, at this time, were in large part either non-religious, or included within the Independent or Secession Pale." In the middle of the eighteenth century it was the Highlands that had been pagan. "Sabbath," according to a popular writer, "never got aboon the Pass of Killiecrankie." But the situation was now reversed. "It is in the great towns that paganism now chiefly prevails. . . . It is mainly during the elapsed half of the present century that this change for the worse has taken place in the large towns of Scotland. In the year 1824 it was greatly less than half accomplished; but it was fast going on. This course of degradation is going on in an ever-increasing ratio; and all that philanthropy and the Churches are doing to counteract it is but as the discharge of a few squirts on a conflagration. . . . The ever growing masses of our large towns, broken loose from the sanction of religion and morals, may yet terribly avenge on the upper classes and the Churches of the country the indifferency with which they have been suffered to sink."

In 1831 David Stow reckoned that out of Glasgow's 200,000 inhabitants 30,000 were Roman Catholics who provided as best they could for their children's education, a quarter of the rest were able to pay, a half fulfilled their responsibilities as well as they could with more or less inadequate means, but the remainder allowed their children to grow up in ignorance and anarchy. To this disinherited and rootless class belonged "the careless, half-infidel and turbulent artisans and labourers" and below them, the utterly demoralized, composed of "ballad singers, and match sellers, thieves, and pickpockets". Two-thirds of the children, he considered, might be described as educated, but only one-third could read "pretty well", and of these "very few understood the meaning of what they read". As for their knowledge of the Christian faith, one in six of those whom he questioned "had never heard the name of Jesus but from the mouth of profane swearers". The Roman Catholics had at least known of the person of Christ, but when questioned on the patriarchs, prophets, and apostles some had replied politely enough, "Sir, we don't know anything about these gentlemen."[1]

Thus there existed the paradoxical situation that while the general state of the nation was showing steady progress a substantial section was being relentlessly forced down into misery

[1] L. J. Saunders, *Scottish Democracy, 1815–1840*, pp. 278–9.

and godlessness. Private charity was scanty and ineffective, the ancient systems of welfare were incapable of carrying the burdens of a new age, and such reaction as there was lay in the twin fields of resentment and reform.

Before the nineteenth century, central government had had limited effects on Scottish life; instead the structure of local institutions had ordered society. Ever since the event which Glasgow's annalist,[1] writing in 1818, could still describe as the "detested treaty", the Scottish members at Westminster had been a negligible element in Scottish life. They were regarded as corrupt and sycophantic, and the narrow and antiquated franchise on which they were elected lay open to manipulation. As late as 1820 the voters' roll for the country constituencies numbered only 2,889 in all, and even this contained many "parchment barons", who served only to increase their superior's power. Thus in Lanarkshire the 66 authentic voters were outnumbered by 95 dependants of the Hamilton family.[2] Edinburgh's member was elected by the 33 members of its self-perpetuating Town Council. Glasgow's Town Council sent a delegate to join with others from Renfrew, Dumbarton, and Rutherglen in electing a member for the four. Occasional demands for the reform of this ridiculous situation began to be heard in the second half of the eighteenth century. Lord Buchan protested in 1768 against the manner of election of the sixteen representative peers, and the Court of Session made an assault on electoral abuses, only to be frustrated by the House of Lords in 1770.[3] Demands for burgh reform, sponsored by manufacturers and professional men excluded from urban administration but with no inclination to extend the franchise to the unpropertied classes, were more radical and tenacious. Since 1766 Henry Dundas had manipulated the Scottish electorate in the interests of the government. In the summer of 1788 he reported to Pitt that the outlook was "very favourable", and he was vindicated by the results of the election of 1790 when 34 out of the 45 Scottish members returned were under his control.[4] But at this point the coming of the French Revolution suddenly revealed that the older Scottish society, which had been

[1] J. Cleland, *Annals of Glasgow*, ii, p. 61.
[2] T. C. Smout, op. cit. p. 219.
[3] W. Ferguson, *Scotland: 1689 to the Present*, p. 242.
[4] Ibid. p. 247.

so largely indifferent to parliament, was being brought to dissolution by economic and social changes.

As various references in the poetry of Robert Burns reveal, Scotland at first welcomed the Revolution cordially and then had serious second thoughts, but there remained in Scotland a body of sympathizers with the objects, as distinct from the methods, of the Revolution. It was in the decade after the fall of the Bastille that Scottish radicalism, as it was to be known in the nineteenth century until the rise of the Labour Party, was born. Tom Paine's *Rights of Man* was widely read. Newspapers, of which there were eight in Scotland in 1782, multiplied in response to popular interest, and in 1790 there were twenty-seven. Too costly for the average working man, they were frequently bought by joint subscription and read in reading-rooms or clubs, or even at the smiddy or the cobbler's shop. While there were a few leaders with upper-class connections the initiative of protest now passed to a new revolutionary radical element drawn from urban artisans and the lower middle class. Walter Bagehot[1] was of opinion that the English lower classes "did not analyse very much; they liked to have one of their 'betters' to represent them; if he was rich, they respected him very much; and if he was a lord, they liked him the better". England, he held, did not have an unrepresented class of skilled artisans who could form superior opinions on national matters, and ought to have the means of expressing them. This was not true of Scotland.

A bad harvest and the rising price of bread increased discontent in 1792. In December the Friends of the People held a convention at Edinburgh under the leadership of a young advocate, Thomas Muir of Huntershill. On 2 January Muir was arrested, but was released on bail. He used his temporary freedom to visit France. On arriving back in Scotland in August he was arrested and, after a notorious trial, sentenced to fourteen years' transportation to Botany Bay. In September 1793 Thomas Palmer,[2] a Unitarian minister in Dundee, was sentenced to seven years, and a few months later, sentences of fourteen years on the other leaders deprived the movement of any who could act as spokesmen. A folk-memory of these events, more dependent on

[1] Walter Bagehot, *The English Constitution*, Preface to the Second Edition, xi, xiii.

[2] A. MacWhirter, "Unitarianism in Scotland", *SCHS*, XIII, pp. 102–3.

tradition than documents, persisted in Scottish radical families till late Victorian times, but for the moment, savage repression had broken the back of incipient radicalism.

Scottish working-class radicalism may not have been orthodox but on the whole it was not anti-Christian. On the other hand, horror at the excesses of the Revolution was widespread among those who, till now, had encouraged sceptical thought. The philosophers of the eighteenth century had set before men the question of whether they lived in a world ruled by a beneficent mind, or in one ruled by an indifferent force, and the second answer had become fashionable. At the same time the philosophers had been ambitious to be esteemed as "men of virtue". "It is not enough," said Diderot[1] referring to the theologians, "to know more than they do; it is necessary to show them that we are better, and that philosophy makes more good men than sufficient or efficacious grace". But now events had suddenly confirmed the Christian apologists' charge that unbelief would unsettle the foundations of morality and social order, and many who had accepted the philosophers' claim to be pillars of virtue and society quickly decided that it was calamitously bad. They saw that "the revolution" meant anarchy in government and atheism in religion;[2] they abhorred the one and took second thoughts about the other. Rationalism and heterodoxy came to be looked on with suspicion. Evangelicalism, which in any case was in the ascendant, came to be seen as a useful force in restraining the people and ordering society.

The difference between the outlook of the ruling classes in the last decade of the century and that of thirty years or so before can be seen in John Galt.[3] On the Sunday following the news that the French had executed their king, Mr Balwhidder preached "one of the greatest and soundest sermons". Next Monday, Mr Cayenne, the local mill owner and no pillar of the kirk, sat as a justice of the peace to hear "two democratic lads" on a charge of high treason. They admitted that they were reformers. "Was not," they said, "our Lord Jesus Christ a reformer?" "And what the devil did He make of it?" cried Mr Cayenne, bursting with passion. "Was He not crucified?" "I thought, when I heard these

[1] Quoted in C. L. Becker, *The Heavenly City of the Eighteenth Century Philosophers*, p. 81.
[2] Ibid, p. 165. [3] John Galt, *Annals of the Parish*, xxxiv.

words, that the pillars of the earth sank beneath me," wrote Mr Balwhidder. "Soon after there was a pleasant re-edification of a gospel-spirit among the heritors, especially when they heard how I had the comfortable satisfaction to see many a gentleman in their pews that had not been for years within a kirk door."

This reaction to the Revolution brought a halt, for the time being, to any prospect of political reform, but it was plain that European life would never be quite the same again. Changes could not be indefinitely postponed. In particular, the relations between Church and State called for reconsideration.

Scottish Calvinists had seen Church and State as little more than two aspects of the one community. Since his concept of the Church had been determined by each believer's acceptance of its teachings[1] Calvin had applied a credal test and had wished to penalize failure by loss of citizenship. The Westminster Confession inherited this. Church and State were jointly entitled to proceed against those who denied Christian principles by word or act[2], and the civil magistrate had a responsibility for maintaining unity and peace in the Church, and purity of doctrine, worship, and discipline. Some elements of this outlook survived the legislation of 1688, but the Union of 1707 in practice put an end to them. Not since the heyday of the Covenant, which Kirkton regarded as "Scotland's high noon", had the Calvinist view of Church and State been fully realized, and yet this teaching was still supposed to be the mind of the Church. With the coming of the Enlightenment and the social changes of the Industrial Revolution the discrepancy between this teaching and actual practice was obvious to all save the most doctrinaire, and signs began to appear that the nature of the Church as a spiritual community and her relationship with the secular community were being reconsidered.

The Relief Church had always been critical of the Confession at this point. "National churches," wrote its spokesman, Patrick Hutchison[3] of Canal Street Church in Paisley, "were foreign to the nature and constitution of the Christain Church." "The civil magistrate has no more right to dictate a religious creed to

---

[1] John T. McNeill, *History and Character of Calvinism*, p. 141.

[2] *The Confession of Faith*, xx, iv; xx, iii.

[3] R. Small, *Congregations of the United Presbyterian Church from 1753 to 1900*, ii, pp. 519–20.

his subjects, than they have a right to dictate a religious creed to him."[1] In 1795 the Antiburghers began a long debate[2] on this issue which ended in their modifying their adherence to the Confession and the consequent loss of Thomas McCrie and some others. Meantime the Burghers came to the same decision more promptly, but with a similar result.[3] Thus both branches were divided into what was called a "New Licht" and a much smaller "Auld Licht". It would be a mistake to dismiss this impatiently as yet another of their interminable arguments and schisms, for it meant that at long last this conservative body had begun to open its mind to new thought. This was the beginning of the end of their divisions. In 1820 the two "New Licht" bodies[4] united, and in 1847 they were joined by the Relief Church to form the United Presbyterian Church.[5] Further, as thorough-going Calvinists noted with indignation,[6] the Seceders had realized that seventeenth-century documents were of limited relevance in a changed world. They were prepared to reconsider the nature of the Christian Church and to question the tenets of scholastic Calvinism in the light of the New Testament and the world in which they lived.

A second feature of this new look at the Church was an awakening interest in Foreign Missions. After the Reformation the task of world evangelism had tacitly been resigned to the Roman Church. "Heretics are never said to have converted either pagans or Jews to the faith, but only to have perverted Christians," wrote Cardinal Bellarmine,[7] "but in this one century the Catholics have converted many thousands of heathen in the new world." In the century of the Covenant, Scots, isolated from foreign parts and absorbed in fighting each other, fully lived up to this bad beginning, but the Scottish ministers sent out to Darien were expected to extend their work to the natives, and in 1732 the directors of the S.P.C.K. (Society for Promoting Christian Knowledge), whose main work lay in the Highlands, engaged three mission-

---

[1] G. Struthers, *The History of the Rise, Progress and Principles of the Relief Church*, p. 312.

[2] J. McKerrow, *History of the Secession Church*, pp. 372–82.

[3] Ibid. pp. 578–617.

[4] Ibid. pp. 645–60.

[5] A. Thomson, *The Origin of the Secession Church*, pp. 160–1.

[6] J. MacLeod, *Scottish Theology*, pp. 235–42.

[7] Quoted in Stephen Neill, *A History of Christian Missions*, p. 221.

aries to work among the American Indians.[1] Until the last decade of the century Foreign Missions scarcely crossed the mind of Scottish churchmen, but in 1792 the Missionary Society of the English Baptists was founded, in 1795 the London Missionary Society,[2] and in 1796 missionary societies were founded in Edinburgh, Glasgow, and other Scottish towns under the leadership of Dr John Erskine and Sir Harry Moncrieff. These societies crossed denominational frontiers, for the organization of the Scottish Churches was so based on local congregational life and lacking in central bureaucracy that none of them had an executive structure capable of launching a Foreign Mission.

At the General Assembly of 1796 a proposal that the Church should "contribute to the diffusion of the Gospel over the world" met with a chilling response.[3] It was argued that the Gospel could be preached only to the civilized, that missionary societies were supported by people from different denominations, that they would export sectarianism and, that they were associated with radical political elements and agitation against the slave trade; so the Assembly dismissed the appeal.[4] In March 1797 the Glasgow Missionary Society sent its two first missionaries — Campbell, a weaver, and Henderson, a tailor — to Sierra Leone; but neither had adequate preparation of any kind and their expedition was a fiasco. Six months later the London, Glasgow, and Edinburgh societies each sent two more men to West Africa. Greig, one of the Edinburgh men, was murdered in 1800 after two years of faithful work, Brunton, his companion, was invalided home soon after, and the two Glasgow men died of fever. Neither then nor afterwards did their country give much thought to the first Scotsmen to die in Africa for the faith.

Those who sponsored Foreign Missions were under suspicion, and not without cause, of sympathy with the French revolution. They were also associated with an evangelicalism which had much in common with the tradition lingering on from the Cambuslang Revival. In 1796 Charles Simeon and Rowland Hill, Anglican Evangelicals, preached in Perthshire and met James Haldane, the younger brother of Robert Haldane of Airthrey in

---

[1] J. MacInnes, *The Evangelical Movement in the Highlands of Scotland 1688–1800*, p. 138.   [2] S. Neill, op. cit. p. 252.

[3] W. L. Mathieson, op. cit. pp. 77–82. Hugh Watt, "Rax Me That Bible", *SCHS*, x, pp. 54–5.   [4] *AGA*, 1796, 27 May, Sess. 8.

Stirlingshire. Both brothers were deeply devout and idealistic men who had, at one stage, been sympathetic to the Revolutionary cause, and then had entertained thoughts of becoming missionaries in India. Until now Scottish evangelicalism had been led by ministers, but the Haldanes broke new ground by becoming lay preachers. In 1798 they sold Airthrey for £46,000 and decided to devote their lives and all they had to the spread of the Gospel. Since they did not hesitate to criticize the defective teaching of parish ministers they provoked widespread resentment until the Assembly of 1799 passed an Act[1] restricting preaching to ministers, and warned their congregations against itinerant evangelists. By 1805 the Haldanes claimed to have trained 200 lay preachers, whom they largely supported and, between 1798 and 1810 their expenditure on these and other projects amounted to over £70,000.[2] Large tabernacles were built in Edinburgh, Glasgow, and Dundee for their followers. Wherever they could they started Sunday Schools which consequently fell under suspicion from the National Church and from the Seceders alike. "There have arisen among us," said the Assembly's pastoral letter of 1799, "a set of men whose proceedings threaten no small disorder to the country. They assume the name of missionaries, as if they had some special commission from heaven; they are going through the land as universal itinerant teachers, and as superintendents of the ministers of religion; they are introducing themselves into parishes, without any call, and erecting in places Sunday Schools without any countenance from the Presbytery of the bounds or the minister of the parish; they are committing in these schools the religious instruction of youth to ignorant persons, altogether unfit for such an important charge; and they are studying to alienate the affections of the people from their pastors, and engaging them to join their new sect, as if they alone were possessed of some secret and novel method of bringing men to heaven."[3] It is to the Haldanes that the existence of the Baptist and Congregational Churches in Scotland owes much, and the mission halls under lay leadership in such places as the fishing villages. Their work is a sign of rising dissatisfaction with a clerically organized church.

The three issues involved in these matters, the relationship of

[1] Ibid. 1799, v.   [2] W. L. Mathieson, op. cit. p. 67.
[3] A. Edgar, *Old Life in Scotland*, ii, pp. 125-6.

Church and State, Foreign Missions, and the place of the laity, were all to be of importance in the century now opening. If Scotland had surrendered her central government in 1707 — as distinct from local administrative functions — she had retained her independence in the three great national institutions of the Church, Law, and Education. But the social disorder now commencing was to bring violent tension between the Church and the Law within the lifetime of a man, and the case of Professor John Leslie highlighted the beginning of similar tension between the Church and Education. Education has always been a function of the Church in newly evangelized and primitive lands; the medieval universities of Scotland were the creation of the Church and existed for little more than the training of clergy; and the post-Reformation universities of Scotland had scarcely escaped from this position. Their bonds with the Church — or rather, with the ministry — were close. By modern standards, their students were pitifully few, and most of them aspired to be ministers. Medicine and Law might lead an independent life, but the faculty of Arts was almost as completely staffed by ministers as was that of Divinity. Even among the non-ministerial members of staff quite a number came from clerical homes; men like Colin MacLaurin, the foremost mathematician of his time, and Matthew Baillie, the first to treat pathology as a subject in itself, had been brought up in manses. Nor had the secularism of the eighteenth century ended this partnership, for the leaders of the Moderates had been fully at home in the rationalistic world of intellectual Scotland.

But with the growth of specialization and intensive scholarship the dominance of the ministry in the universities was coming to an end. In February 1805 Thomas McKnight of Trinity College Church was a candidate for the vacant chair of Mathematics in Edinburgh University; his qualifications were adequate, if not much more, and he was willing to resign his parish if the Town Council, the patrons of the chair, should elect him. But the Moderate leaders in Edinburgh Presbytery made their support for him conditional upon his retention of his parish and when this became known Dugald Stewart and John Playfair protested vigorously to the Town Council and began to canvass support for John Leslie.[1] Leslie's qualifications were higher than those

[1] Ian D. Clark, "The Leslie Controversy, 1805", *SCHS*, xiv, pp. 179–97.

of McKnight, but he was regarded as a Whig, and rumours began to be spread that a favourable comment which he had made on a passage from Hume in his "Essay on Heat" implied heterodoxy or scepticism. On 9 March the Presbytery reminded the Senate of the University that its members were obliged, if need be, to sign the Confession of Faith, but the Senate retorted effectively that in practice this had been allowed to lapse by no less a person than Principal Robertson. Two days later a minister warned the Lord Provost that the clergy would oppose Leslie's appointment, and the Provost informed him that the election would take place on 13 March, but next day when the ministers were meeting they learned that the Council was actually in session and making the appointment. They hurried to the council chamber but were informed that the Council, who had tributes to Leslie's orthodoxy before them, were about to appoint him despite their protests.

A division now appeared among the ministers. When they met on 22 March the Evangelicals were prepared to accept Leslie's election, but the Moderates were determined on a fight. When the matter was brought before Edinburgh Presbytery — for the first time — on 27 March, the Moderates carried the day by only two votes. In the third week of May the case reached the Assembly after much propaganda on both sides, and to the general astonishment the decision of the Evangelicals to accept Leslie's appointment was accepted by 96 votes to 84. Here was a landmark in the history of the Assembly, for the Moderates, who for so long had controlled it, had for the first time in living memory lost an important decision and the Evangelicals at last had hope that the Moderates would become only a minority party. Further, while the Evangelicals had been associated with the middle and lower classes of no account in the intellectual world, it was now their turn to be associated with secular thought while the Moderates appeared obscurantist. That rationalistic theology which stemmed from Hutcheson and had dominated the Scottish mind for the best part of the century was in retreat, and the evangelical outlook, which was dependent on Scripture, looked to revelation and was comparatively indifferent to a rapprochment with secular knowledge, was in the ascendant. A sidelight is cast on this by the different attitude of the two parties in the Church to pluralities, the holding of academic appointments by parish ministers. As early as 1779 the appointment of George Hill, Professor of Greek in St Andrews, to one of the town churches, had been unsuccess-fully opposed.[1] With the opening of the new century such appoint-ments were consistently opposed by Evangelicals on the grounds that no man could effectively carry out parish and university duties simultaneously.[2] Thomas Chalmers, at that time the young minister of Kilmany and still a Moderate, thought otherwise, and while the Leslie case was in progress he drafted a pamphlet defending pluralities. "The author of this pamphlet," he wrote,[3] "can assert, from what to him is the highest of all authority, the authority of experience, that after the satisfactory discharge of his parish duties, a minister may enjoy five days in the week of uninterrupted leisure, for the prosecution of any science in which his taste may dispose him to engage".

The importance of the Leslie case for the Church in nineteenth-century Scotland was not the beginning of the disappearance of ministers from non-theological chairs in the universities, but the growing conviction, not only in Scotland but in England and the Reformed Churches of Holland, France, Germany, and Switzer-land, that the old categories of "general" and "special" revelation, dependent on Nature and Scripture respectively, had been shaken by the arguments of Hume and — though his influence was still scarcely felt in Scotland —Kant, and that the Christian faith must be vindicated on other grounds. This decline of the old rational-istic theology was associated with the coming of the romantic movement. The family of Robert Burns had Episcopalian roots. He did not like Calvinists, and sympathized with clergy whom others might have called Socinians. This sympathy was not the fruit of independent thought but the acceptance — by a man otherwise not much interested — of any convenient theological criticism of those who troubled him locally. By contrast, Sir Walter Scott, who was reserved about his theological predilec-tions, in his poetry and novels created a romantic sympathy for the medieval Church and its worship so that the moneyed classes of Scotland, whose fathers would have identified medievalism with barbarism, now subscribed to the Bannatyne and Maitland clubs and were proud to have on their shelves the printed records

---

[1] J. Cunningham, *The Church History of Scotland*, ii, p. 389.

[2] Ibid. ii, pp. 438–42.

[3] H. Watt, *Thomas Chalmers and the Disruption*, p. 3. Lord Cockburn, *Memorials of His Time*, p. 125.

of the ruined abbeys even if they did not read them. This had no effect on the fortunes of the Roman Church, but it brought new interest in the worship of the Scottish Episcopal Church whose numbers, aided by old family traditions and the new custom of sending the sons of the aristocracy to England for education, began to grow. Scott himself, an elder of the kirk, was drawn to the liturgy[1] and found his way back to the Church of his fore-bears. As the poetry of Wordsworth became known it radically altered the concept of nature, or perhaps it would be truer to say that it caught the changed mood of the public mind. Nature was no longer seen as the sphere of inexorable laws so much as the supreme manifestation of the sublime and beautiful, the con-templation of which drew the soul in wonder to God. And when Scots read Coleridge, "Aids to Reflection" and the "Confessions of an Inquiring Spirit" set before them concepts of the Church as the divine community and of Scripture as evoking faith, penitence, love, and hope. Thus, as the influence of the Moder-ates, once the party of education and scholarship, declined, and the masses of the poor began to drift away from the Christian faith, these new forces began to draw the mind of the intelligent enquirer towards a more evangelical statement of the faith.

In *Peter's Letters to His Kinsfolk*, written in 1816, J. G. Lockhart[2] wrote, "As for the Church . . . in regard to its influence among the mass of the people, I am inclined to entertain a very high respect — the truth is, the clergy of Scotland are, at the present day possessed of comparatively little power over the opinions of the best educated classes of their countrymen. One very efficient cause of this want of influence is, without doubt, the insignificant part they have of late taken in general literature; their neglect, in other words, their strange and unprecedented neglect of an engine, which among a people whose habits at all resemble those of the present Scots, must ever be, of all others, the most exten-sive in its sway." But the facts were not so straightforward. The Scottish clergy had indeed lost the prestige which had been given to them by such men as Dr Robertson; their influence among the masses was confined to the traditional section of the population and was rapidly being lost in the industrial areas; but the influence of the Christian faith was steadily increasing among the new

---

[1] J. G. Lockhart, *Life of Sir Walter Scott*, pp. 758–9.
[2] J. G. Lockhart, *Peter's Letters to His Kinsfolk*, i, pp. 83–4.

middle classes and intellectual classes when compared with the century of the Enlightenment.

Lord Cockburn made a more mature assessment. "It is not unusual," he wrote[1] about 1825, "for certain persons to represent Scotland, but particularly Edinburgh, as having been about the beginning of this century very irreligious. . . . As to the comparative religiousness of the present and the preceding generation, any such comparison is very difficult to be made. Religion is certainly more the fashion than it used to be. There is more said about it; there has been a great rise, and consequently, a great competition, of sects; and the general mass of the religious public has been enlarged. On the other hand, if we are to believe one half of what some religious persons themselves assure us, religion is now almost extinct. My opinion is that the balance is in favour of the present time. And I am certain it would be much more so, if the modern dictators would only accept of that as religion, which was considered to be so by their devout fathers."

This gradual change of mind can be traced in one undistinguished but fairly representative family of ministers. Alexander Findlater[2] was minister of Strathaven from 1693 till 1695 and afterwards, at first of the second charge of Hamilton and then, until his death in 1735, of the first charge. His son, Thomas,[3] was the nominee of the Duke of Hamilton, whom the people of Cambuslang successfully rejected as their minister before McCulloch — of the Revival — was called. Rejected by Cambuslang, Thomas Findlater became minister of West Linton in Peeblesshire in 1731. His son, Charles,[4] became assistant and successor to his father in 1777, and in 1790 transferred to the nearby parish of Newlands. In 1828 his wife was accidentally burned to death and the bereaved husband occupied his loneliness in making a meticulous catalogue of his library.[5] It is plain that he was a scholarly man who cared for his books and that his father and grandfather had been the same. While there are occasional books in this list which have been inherited or acquired second hand, it is plain that the great majority had been acquired more or less

[1] Lord Cockburn, op. cit. pp. 36–7.
[2] *Fasti*, II, pp. 259, 261, 263.
[3] Ibid. I, p. 247.
[4] Ibid. I, pp. 247, 248, 253, 254.
[5] MS. Catalogue, *penes* Newlands Kirk Session.

soon after publication. There was a Greek New Testament on the shelves but, as other evidence would confirm, little sign of any other interest in Greek. By contrast, there was a wide range of Latin classics ranging from a Plautus of 1519 to a Tacitus of 1818. As was to be expected, volumes of sermons had steadily been added and there was a good array of commentaries and theology, but the wide interests of the family were revealed by the number of books on other subjects. Shakespeare, Milton, and the conventional poets of the eighteenth century, Dryden, Pope, Young, Thomson, and Falconer, were present. Charles Findlater had bought a copy of the *Poems* of Robert Burns and Scott's *Minstrelsy of the Scottish Border*. Scott's Waverley novels had not been purchased, but some standard novels, like *Don Quixote* and *Gil Blas*, were on the shelves. So, unexpectedly, were Petronius and Rabelais. There were books on the practical subjects which interested the eighteenth-century country clergy, agriculture, medicine, law, political economy, and a few on cookery.

Alexander Findlater, unless a copy of Samuel Rutherford's *Letters* be reckoned an exception, had no interest in those Covenanting writers beloved by his Lanarkshire parishioners. Instead he bought Anglican sermons such as those of Sherlock and Tillotson. The standard textbooks of theology, Calvin, Turretin, and Witsius, seem to have dated from his student days, but he had a copy of Madame Bourignon's notorious book, quite a number of Anglican theologians, and a few unexpected writers such as Pascal and Leibniz. His son's outlook, very like that of his father, explains the hostility of the congregation at Cambuslang. He had little in common with them. In his days at West Linton the son had the wide ranging interests and tastes of a typical Moderate. He read Shaftesbury, Bolingbroke, Hume, Voltaire, and Gibbon, as well as an apologist like Bishop Butler. It would appear that he was particularly interested in Hume's argument on miracles, for he owned not merely a copy, but also several replies. Charles, the grandson, was keenly interested in science and its relationship with the Christian faith, and he had an interest in political economy and radical politics which got him into trouble with the government. But the most striking feature of the library is the fact that as life went on he bought books of an increasingly evangelical tone. He had been interested enough to buy McGill's questionable essay on the death of Christ, but he also had devotional writings like Scoughal on *The Life of God in the Soul of Man*, Willison's *Balm of Gilead*, and the sermons of Sir Henry Moncrieff. He even had a volume of Thomas Chalmers. Probably he would have been called a Moderate by his critics but, if so, the word now carried a meaning far removed from the time when it could have been employed to describe his father by his Cambuslang opponents.

CHAPTER EIGHT

Chalmers in Glasgow

An awareness of most of these problems — if not all of them — and a response — if not always the right one — is found in the outstanding churchman of his generation, Thomas Chalmers. Born in 1780 at Anstruther into the large family of a small-town business man, he went to school at the age of three, to St Andrews University before he was twelve, into the Faculty of Divinity at fifteen, and at nineteen was licensed as a probationer, so young that no presbytery would have considered ordaining him. He was very precocious, but otherwise immature, and in some respects these qualities remained with him all his life. His abilities were considerable, but his gusto, enthusiasm, and will to communicate were greater still, and all his days he retained the commendable but embarrassing zeal of youth for tackling problems which others might shirk but which he was unable to solve. His short-comings are obvious and all too easily seen; he commenced many tasks but completed none of them; those who differed from him, such as W. P. Alison on Poor Relief and Matthew Leishman of Govan at the Disruption, may well have been right; but the fact remains that no Scotsman of the century made a mark on the life of the country which can compare with his.

Conscious of his own capacity, he had considerable ambitions but these, at first, were academic. Before he was inducted to the parish of Kilmany in 1803 he taught Mathematics at St Andrews for the ailing professor and hoped to retain the appointment. But the professor, whom he had publicly rebuked for giving class certificates without his approval, not unnaturally had other intentions. Chalmers then commenced a class of his own, and next turned to Chemistry. He applied for the vacant chair of Mathematics at Edinburgh in 1805, and made his first venture in Political Economy.[1] But these interests declined into second place

[1] H. Watt, *Thomas Chalmers and the Disruption*, pp. 1–26.

with a drastic change in his religious outlook which took place towards 1809 under a number of influences, the death of a sister, his own ill health, the reading of Wilberforce's *Practical View of Christianity* — at that time the best-known statement of the evangelical outlook — and another book almost unknown in Scotland but congenial to Chalmers because of the writer's part in Mathematics — the *Pensées* of Pascal.

Writing to his former parishioners[1] after he had left Kilmany, Chalmers told what it meant to him. "I cannot but record the effect of an actual though undesigned experiment, which I prosecuted for upwards of twelve years among you. For the greater part of that time, I could expatiate . . . upon all those deformities of character, which awaken the natural indignation of the human heart against the pests and the disturbers of society. Could I . . . have got the thief to give up his stealing, and the evil speaker his censoriousness, and the liar his deviations from truth, I should have felt all the repose of one who had gotten his ultimate object. It never occurred to me that all this might have been done, and yet every soul of every hearer have remained in full alienation from God. . . . During the whole of that period I made no attempt against the natural enmity of the mind to God, while I was inattentive to the way in which this enmity is dissolved, even by the free offer on the one hand, and the believing acceptance on the other, of the gospel salvation. . . . It was not till the free offer of forgiveness through the blood of Christ was urged upon their acceptance, and the Holy Spirit given through the channel of Christ's mediatorship to all who ask Him, was set before them . . . that I ever heard of any of those subordinate reformations. . . . You have at least taught me, that to preach Christ is the only effective way of preaching morality in all its branches; and out of your humble cottages have I gathered a lesson, which I pray God I may be enabled to carry with all its simplicity into a wider theatre, and to bring with all the power of its subduing efficacy upon the vices of a more crowded population." These words were written after he had been nominated by the Town Council and inducted to the swarming parish of the Tron Kirk in Glasgow on 21 July 1815.[2]

Chalmers was not a thinker of the first rank. His genius lay in

[1] Thomas Chalmers, "Address to the Inhabitants of the Parish of Kilmany", *Works*, xii, pp. 108-10.   [2] H. Watt, op. cit. p. 41.

the fact that he committed himself to the needs and tasks of his day, and a ready audience awaited a man who was able to state clearly the issues half formed already within their own minds. He was to be the prototype of the Victorian popular preacher, but with one important difference. It had been a central tenet of the Moderates that for its full development humanity required the independent cultivation of the intellectual as well as the spiritual life.[1] The Evangelicals had not been disposed to recognize holiness in this sense of *wholeness*, and had insisted that a minister should have no other interest to compete with that of the saving of souls. Chalmers carried with him into his evangelical days the old Moderate conviction of the importance of the intellectual life, even if it was now forced into second place. What differentiated his preaching, which drew rapt crowds to the Tron Kirk, from that of his Victorian successors, was that he did not confine himself to a strictly evangelical message, but that he set out to explore contemporary problems and issues in the course of his sermons. Many of them were, in effect, lectures on subjects in the setting of Christian interpretation, not delivered dispassionately, but urged upon his hearers with all the force of his personality. If he may be compared with a greater man, it may be said that the great volume of Chalmers' writings, produced in a life of ceaseless activity, was due, like those of Augustine, to the fact that he produced his weekly discourses, not to be thrown aside, but to be published. As writings, they suffer through this. What may have sounded eloquent, does not read well. Chalmers made sure that his audience would understand the trend of his thought by the old preaching device of saying the same thing several times in different words, and his interminable repetition and verbosity repel the reader and distract attention from what was all important and evident to the first listeners, the highly intelligent and relevant train of thought.

The congregations to which Chalmers preached were largely composed of the middle and upper classes of the commercial city of the west, and it was to this class that he primarily spoke.[2] These men appealed to him. He was sensitive to the virtues shown by many of them who lacked his evangelical outlook,[3]

[1] W. L. Mathieson, *Church and Reform in Scotland, 1797–1843*, p. 268.
[2] T. Chalmers, "On the Dissipation of Large Cities", *Works*, vi, pp. 157–8.
[3] T. Chalmers, "On the Mercantile Virtues", *Works*, vi, pp. 23–5.

even while he called for a prayerful devotion which should be carried from the home into daily business.[1] His personal sympathies and prejudices were the same as theirs, and he had no sympathy with the radical agitators of working-class background. "We hold nothing to be more unscriptural," he wrote,[2] "than the spirit of a factious discontent with the rulers of our land . . . we trust that the mighty interval of separation between the higher and the lower orders of our community will, at length, be broken down, not by any inroad of popular violence — not by the fierce and devouring sweep of any revolutionary tempest — not even by any new adjustment, either of the limits of power, or the limits of property . . . but as the fruit of that gradual equalisation in mind and in manners, to which even now a sensible approach is already making on the part of our artisans and our labourers." Chalmers could have no illusions as to the magnitude or intensity of the problem at the door of his own church. Bad harvests, high prices, and unemployment following the end of the Napoleonic Wars brought bitter agitation among the poor and disfranchised for political and economic reform. In Scotland a number of trials for sedition in the course of 1817 brought no great satisfaction to the government.[3] In August 1819 the massacre of Peterloo revealed the intensity of feeling and the nervousness among the ruling classes; eleven people were killed and some four hundred wounded. In panic the government passed repressive legislation, "the Six Acts", and in February 1820 the twenty-seven members of a Glasgow radical committee were arrested on suspicion of planning revolution. Pathetic attempts at a rising in April 1820 — the "Radical War" — ended in three executions.[4]

To Chalmers, it appeared at times that society lived on the edge of a precipice. "After all that police, and refinement, and the kindly operation of long pacific intercourse, have done to humanize the aspect of these latter days, we are far from sure whether upon the displacement of certain guards and barriers of

[1] T. Chalmers, "The Influence of Christianity in Augmenting the Mercantile Virtues", *Works*, vi, p. 51.
[2] T.Chalmers, "The Advantages of Christian Knowledge to the Lower Orders of Society", *Works*, vi, pp. 253–5.
[3] W. L. Mathieson, op. cit. pp. 141–60.
[4] T. C. Smout, *A History of the Scottish People, 1560–1830*, pp. 447.

security, the slumbering ferocities of men might not again announce their existence, and break out, as before, into open and declared violence."[1] He called on the upper classes to set an example, for their neglect of morals would, to put the matter at the lowest level, react upon themselves.[2] City magnates who failed to attend church themselves could hardly complain that the "multitude who pour forth upon our outskirts to the riot and extravagance of holiday" disturbed the Sabbath peace of their country mansions, and if business went on at the Royal Exchange with drawn blinds as the only concession to Sabbatarians it was little to be wondered at if "the reading rooms of sedition and infidelity are now open every Sabbath".[3] There existed now in Scotland a missionary need as urgent as any overseas. "When we are commanded to go into all the world and preach the Gospel to every creature, our imagination stretches forth beyond the limits of Christendom, and we advert not to the millions who are within these limits . . . yet who have never heard the Gospel of Jesus Christ."[4] His remedies were therefore education and evangelism. "The great instrument for thus elevating the poor is that Gospel of Jesus Christ which may be preached unto the poor . . . Jesus Christ died, the just for the unjust, to bring us unto God. This is a truth which, when all the world shall receive it, all the world shall be renovated."[5]

When he came to Glasgow, Chalmers had been plunged into a new industrial Scotland and a life of which he had no previous inkling. He was appalled, and rightly so, at what he saw, but his response was limited. He was drawn to those whom he understood. He had boundless pity for the poor, but little understanding. The craftsman's standards and interests, his pride of work, traditions of group action, his intellectual independence, and exposure to the harsh pressure of unemployment, vile housing, and sudden illness were things of which he was little aware. In his eyes irreligion was the source of all their ills.[6] Education and charity had much to do for them, but the preaching of the Gospel was

[1] T. Chalmers, "Importance of Civil Government", *Works*, vi, p. 345.
[2] T. Chalmers, "Vitiating Influence of the Higher Upon the Lower Orders of Society", *Works*, vi, p. 177.
[3] T. Chalmers, "Importance of Civil Government", *Works*, vi, pp. 366–7.
[4] T. Chalmers, "On the Duty of Christianizing our Home Population", *Works*, vi, p. 269.   [5] Ibid. vi, p. 260.
[6] T. Chalmers, "Importance of Civil Government", *Works*, vi, p. 367.

the fundamental cure, and his conception of the Gospel was now an individualistic one which failed to win the politically conscious members of the working class.[1] The evangelical message was thus the first element in his preaching, but the problems of the new society came a close second, and a third was the relationship between the Christian revelation and the advances of contemporary science, particularly in astronomy and geology.

The main achievements of eighteenth-century Scotland in Science had been medical,[2] for the most part. The College of Physicians in Edinburgh was incorporated in 1681; the old College of Surgeons got a royal charter in 1694, and a grant from the Town Council of unclaimed dead bodies. The anatomical theatre was opened in 1697. Thus a great medical school began to arise. William Cullen, the Monros, father, son, and grandson, the Gregorys, John and William Hunter and their nephew, Matthew Baillie, all contributed to the progress of medical knowledge. Closely associated with medicine was chemistry, where the name of Joseph Black, Professor of Chemistry, first at Glasgow and then at Edinburgh, is "assured of a place among the greatest men of science both as a chemist and as a physicist".[3] Already there existed, especially at Glasgow, that close and fruitful link, so alien to the academic aloofness of the two English universities at that time, which helped Scotland to take a lead in the Industrial Revolution, and which was to be exemplified supremely in the work of James Watt. The scientific staff at the Scottish universities were continually alert to the practical potentialities of their research. But the branch of science to which Scotland contributed most as the eighteenth century came to an end was geology, and this evoked widespread interest among enquiring lay minds, not only for its practical applications in mining, but for its implications as to the origins of the universe. "The truths of Geology," thought the young Hugh Miller,[4] "appear destined to exercise in the future no inconsiderable influence on natural theology."

The modern study of the subject largely derives from the work of James Hutton. The son of an Edinburgh doctor, he studied medicine at Edinburgh, Paris, and Leyden, where he graduated

[1] L. J. Saunders, *Scottish Democracy, 1815–1840*, pp. 210–11.
[2] J. Mackintosh, *The History of Civilization in Scotland*, iv, pp. 291ff.
[3] A. G. Clement and R. H. S. Robertson, *Scotland's Scientific Heritage*, p. 35.
[4] H. Miller, *My Schools and Schoolmasters*, p. 184 (xvii).

M.D. Having inherited the family estate in Berwickshire from which his name came, he set himself to improve its value by studying agriculture; this drew him to the study of geology. At Leyden he had heard the teaching of Werner of Freiburg that the changes in the earth's structure were due to great upheavals or catastrophes, but Hutton recognized that the stratification of rocks and the embedding of fossils were processes continually happening in seas, rivers, and lakes. The igneous rocks of the Bass Rock and Arthur's Seat might owe their origin to volcanic action in primitive times, but the sedimentary rocks had been laid down by the process still continuing in the mudflats of the estuary of the Forth. He thus renewed the forgotten observations of Leonardo da Vinci. The formation of the earth was to be explained in terms of natural forces. "No powers are to be employed that are not natural to the globe, no action to be admitted except those of which we know the principle." His *Theory of the Earth*, published in 1785, set forth the continual remoulding of the earth's surface by natural agents over long periods, but it was not till John Playfair, Professor of Mathematics at Edinburgh, published his *Illustrations of the Huttonian Theory* in 1802 that his work gained the ear of the public. A second Scot, Sir Charles Lyell,[1] whose long life saw a transformation in the study of the earth, marshalled the evidence for the cumulative effects of natural causes in his *Principles of Geology*, published between 1830 and 1833. From palaeontology Lyell went on to study archaeology and his best-known work, *The Antiquity of Man*, published in 1863, was to set before the reader his arguments for the early appearance of man on the earth and his general agreement with the teaching of Charles Darwin on the origin of species.

Lyell's work still lay in the future, but already the Scottish mind was aware that the study of the natural sciences was pointing to conclusions, as yet not clearly defined, which would be hard to reconcile with the traditional account of the creation as found in Genesis. What geology was teaching in Scotland was being related to the work of the French pioneers in zoology and biology, and thus raising the question of the fixity of species and of man's place in nature. Buffon[2] and Linnaeus[3] had retained their

[1] W. C. Dampier, *History of Science*, pp. 270–1.

[2] N. Hampson, *The Enlightenment*, p. 227.

[3] John Dillenberger, *Protestant Thought and Natural Science*, p. 217.

belief in a static environment and the fixity of species, but the question of some half recognized and ill defined theory of evolution was on the threshold of scientific thought. Lamarck had dismissed the idea that a series of catastrophes had been responsible for the disappearance of extinct species, and had ventured to think that all creatures could be ordered into a single pattern of development, but differentiated as they adapted themselves to their environment. This implied that the development took place through long periods of time. The French Protestant, Cuvier, accepted the concept of geological ages, but still adhered to the fixity of species. The Fathers of the Church had not always been prepared to accept the creation narratives in Genesis at face value,[1] but Protestant thought had long done so. These new ways of thought seriously questioned the reliability of the Mosaic account of creation. Even had it not been so, a fundamental change in the human outlook[2] was implied, for the universe was now to be presented, not in terms of instantaneous creation and of fixity, but of historical process. This was an important step in the development of the modern mind, and one not easily made.

Here again Chalmers took the lead in expressing the thoughts of his contemporaries even if his achievements hardly equalled his courage. He was aware that the work of such men as Laplace and Cuvier raised problems for conventional theology, but his mind, at first, was set in a thoroughly conservative mould. "We feel vastly little either of confidence or satisfaction," he wrote,[3] "in any of these theories. It is a mere contest of probabilities, and an actual and well established testimony should be paramount to them all. We hold the testimony of Moses to supersede all this work of conjecture." "The recorded testimony of those who were present or nearer than ourselves to the facts in question, we hold to be a likelier path to the information we are in quest of, than the inferences of a distant posterity upon the geological phenomena around them. . . . You must pronounce upon the testimony of Moses on appropriate evidence. It is the testimony of a witness nearer than yourselves to the events in question; and if it be a sound testimony, it carries along with it the testimony of a Being Who was something more than an actual spectator of the creation.

[1] Origen, *De Principiis*, iv, p. 16.
[2] Herbert Butterfield, *The Origins of Modern Science*, p. 203.
[3] T. Chalmers, "Cuvier's Theory of the Earth", *Works*, xii, p. 353.

He was both spectator and agent."[1] But the mind of Chalmers gradually passed beyond this muddle of bad logic.

It was in the field of astronomy that he became acutely aware that questions unknown to men before were arising in his own generation, that the non-Christian answers to these questions were themselves questionable, and that Christian answers might not only be equally valid but, in fact, the only true answer. In his *Astronomical Discourses* which he preached to crowded[2] congregations in the Tron Kirk on Thursdays he stated his conviction that the difficulties posed for Christian faith sprang, not out of the discoveries of Sir Isaac Newton, but out of assumptions made from them. Newton's cosmology, he maintained, had no direct and necessary implications for history or philosophy. Unfortunately at this point he went on to defend Newton's unseasonable ventures into theology in his *Commentary on Revelation*. It is easy to understand why Pascal had appealed to Chalmers, for each was aware that a Christian faith which regarded man and his globe as the centre of the universe was outdated, and the words of Pascal,[3] "The eternal silence of these infinite spaces terrifies me," might have been those of the Scottish divine. It was not so much the discovery of Copernicus that the earth was not the centre of the universe as the untold worlds revealed by the telescope which appeared to be in conflict with the faith. Chalmers was aware of the argument by analogy that since other planets revolved around other suns other men might also live upon these unknown spheres. He was aware of the arguments of Fontenelle[4] and others, and he was not prepared to close his mind on the subject. Infidels could not be permitted to assume that the Christian faith was for this planet only. "The assertion is, that Christianity is set up for the exclusive benefit of our minute and solitary world. The argument is, that God would not lavish such a quantity of attention on so insignificant a field. . . . How do infidels know that Christianity is set up for the single benefit of this earth and its inhabitants? How are they able to tell us, that if you go to other planets, the person and religion of Jesus are

[1] Ibid. xii, pp. 361–2.

[2] For an account of Chalmers' oratory and the effect it created, cf. Lord Cockburn, *Memorials of His Time*, pp. 238–9.

[3] Pascal, *Pensées*, p. 61.

[4] Fontenelle, *The Plurality of Worlds*.

there unknown to them? We challenge them to the proof of this announcement."

The problem of the opponents of the faith, as Chalmers saw it, was that they found it impossible to believe in God's providential care and love for each man in the light of the infinite vastness of the universe. He retorted that if the telescope revealed the vastness of space the microscope equally revealed the incredible order existing in the minutest details of creation which man could know. "By the one I am told that the Almighty is now at work in regions more distant than geometry has ever measured, and among worlds more manifold than numbers have ever reached. But, by the other, I am also told that with a mind to comprehend the whole, in the vast compass of its generality, He has also a mind to concentrate a close and separate attention on each and on all of its particulars; and that the same God, Who sends forth an upholding influence among the orbs and the movements of astronomy, can fill the recesses of every single atom with the intimacy of His presence, and travel, in all the greatness of His unimpaired attributes, upon every one spot and corner of the universe He has formed."[1] "The more we know of the extent of nature," he says elsewhere in a passage which, if read aloud, tells something of the fascination which his oratory possessed at the time and of the reason for its later neglect, "should we not have the loftier conception of Him Who sits in high authority over the concerns of so wide a universe? But is it not adding to the bright catalogue of His other attributes to say, that, while the magnitude does not overpower Him, minuteness cannot escape Him, and variety cannot bewilder Him; and that, at the very time while the mind of the Deity is abroad over the vastness of creation, there is not one particle of matter, there is not one single world in that expanse which teems with them, and that His eye does not discern as constantly, and His hand does not guide as unerringly, and His Spirit does not watch and care for as vigilantly, as if it formed the one and exclusive object of His attention?"[2]

To think otherwise was to reduce God to human terms, and to suppose that human limitations applied to Him. Chalmers thus repudiated natural theology as it had been accepted among the Moderates, the argument pointed out in the seventeenth century

[1] T. Chalmers, *Astronomical Discourses*, p. 82.   [2] Ibid. pp. 74-5.

by John Wilkins and expressed by Paley, in which belief in God and providence were justified without appeal to Scripture or revelation. Instead he saw it as a precursor of revelation, setting the question, and awaiting the Christian answer. "It can state the difficulty, but cannot unriddle the difficulty — having just as much knowledge as to enunciate the problem, but not so much as might lead to the solution of the problem. There must be a measure of light, we do allow; but, like the lurid gleam of a volcano, it is not a light which guides, but which bewilders and terrifies. It prompts the question, but cannot frame or furnish the reply. Natural theology may see as much as shall draw forth the anxious interrogation, 'What shall I do to be saved?' The answer to this comes from a higher theology."[1]

Much of the population of Glasgow had once been crowded within the bounds of the old medieval city. Eight parish churches served this area. But when Chalmers came to Glasgow the city had spread far beyond these bounds, into the Barony parish which surrounded it, and into the Gorbals on the south bank of the Clyde. As the Church still maintained the fiction that she represented the population within each parish, no effective method of numbering her actual adherents existed, but the system of charging seat rents enabled a guess to be made at the numbers of those claiming some association with her, even though their participation was only nominal. When Chalmers went to St John's he found that only 2,930 out of its 10,304 parishioners had even this connection. In the Barony parish, where one church and three chapels served a population of 51,861, things were even worse. Chalmers was ready to make generous acknowledgment of the work done by the Seceders. "Let no petty jealousies," he wrote, "interfere with the acknowledgements due to men who have done so much to retard the process of moral deterioration." But even with their aid, less than one-fifth of the population could be held to have some Church connection. In the Goosedubs, a lane off the Stockwell, where the inner city conditions were worse than in the Barony, only 109 out of 945 had a Church connection, and in one part of the Bridgegate only 7 out of 209.[2] Chalmers

[1] T. Chalmers, *The Bridgewater Treatises on the Power, Wisdom, and Goodness of God as Manifested in Creation.*
[2] T. Chalmers, "Christian and Civic Economy of Large Towns", *Works*, xiv, pp. 124–7.

immediately concluded that numbers were so vast that parish ministers and kirk sessions could not provide proper pastoral oversight.[1] He had scarcely settled in the Tron Kirk when he decided that the problems were insoluble on the existing parochial basis, and that the number of parishes required to be tripled. "Nothing but the multiplication of our Established Churches with the subdivision of parishes and the allocation to each parish of its own church, together with a pure and popular exercise of the right of patronage, will ever bring us back again to a sound and wholesome state of the body politic."[2] These last words are significant. Chalmers wished to revert to what he regarded as the older social system of Scotland, but it did not occur to him that the new industrialism and the economics on which it was based — and which he himself accepted — made this an anachronism. He put pressure on the magistrates to provide for an extension of the parochial system. It is plain that he was not alone, but that the Town Council was anything but enthusiastic. However, they made a concession to his demands. Glasgow had ten parishes; Chalmers urged that it needed thirty; but the council was willing to provide only two more. He had been inducted to the Tron Kirk on 21 July 1815; in April 1817 the council agreed to found the new parish of St John's in the Gallowgate; on 5 June 1818 he was elected its minister and on 3 July he was admitted.[3] The new church was, in effect, a preaching hall in the style of the Gothic Revival known in Scotland as Heritors' Gothic. It was, Chalmers[4] said, "capable of accommodating 1,640", but this number was reached only by some legal fiction, for the true seating was less than half.

At the time of his coming the parish had 10,304 inhabitants, but the formation of St James's parish a year later reduced it to 8,294. It consisted of tenements of the poorer class, even if they were not so degraded or overcrowded as the filthy lanes between the Saltmarket and the Stockwell, and there were still open spaces. But if it was more free of the worst slums than some other parts of the city, it was uniformly poor. Only twenty families were

[1] T. Chalmers, "Christian and Civic Economy of Large Towns", *Works*, xiv, pp. 99–100.

[2] W. Hanna, *Memoirs of the Life and Writings of Thomas Chalmers*, ii, p. 264.

[3] *Fasti*, II, p. 30.

[4] T. Chalmers, "Speech before the Assembly of 1822", *Works*, xvi, p. 145.

counted other than working class.[1] Chalmers was not the man to allow one idea to dominate his mind at a time, but it is plain that when he came to St John's his uppermost thought was the control of pauperism. On 3 August 1819 he wrote to the Lord Provost to state his intentions. The poor in Scotland were divided into the "ordinary" or disabled poor, of whom a roll was kept, and the "occasional" or sick but otherwise able-bodied poor. Only the former were entitled to relief. In Glasgow this was done out of the General Session funds and, if need be, by the Town Hospital. Chalmers proposed that his parish should opt out of this system and — with the exception of widespread distress due to sudden trade depressions — be responsible for its own poor. His kirk session would systematically control poor relief out of their church collections. It was anticipated that there would be a surplus, and he asked permission to devote this to parochial schools. Paupers from other parishes were not to be aided, and in turn St John's promised not to burden others.[2]

The active participation of the laity in parish work was essential to his pattern of poor relief as to every other side of church work. The parish was divided into twenty-five "proportions" or subdivisions, each having about 400 persons or 60 to 100 households. To each of these units an elder was attached for spiritual oversight and evangelism. Each also had its Sabbath School, staffed by voluntary teachers, in addition to the four schools in the parish,[3] whose teachers had their salaries paid out of the collections. Each also had its deacon, who was responsible for poor relief. This last office had fallen into disuse in the Scottish Church, but Chalmers held that the duties of elder and deacon could not competently be fulfilled by one man.[4] Since the stipend of the minister, the costs of the building, and other basic needs were met by the Town Council, which recouped itself, as far as possible, out of seat rents, all collections at the church door were available for poor relief. Collections at the morning service raised £450 annually and those at the evening service, where the poor attended, came to £80. The first sum was applied to the burdens

[1] Ibid. xvi, pp. 217–20.   [2] Ibid. xvi, pp. 164–7.

[3] T. Chalmers, "General Appendix on Pauperism", Works, xvi, pp. 184, 199.

[4] T. Chalmers, "Christian and Civic Economy of Large Towns", Works, xvi, pp. 253–63.

of relief taken over from the old system, while the second was available for the new plans. Out of it all the new cases were met and after two and a half years a surplus of £65 had been accumulated.[1] Chalmers himself made claims for this system which were far too high, and he has been ill served by biographers whose idolatry permitted them to see no flaw in the work of their hero; but, so far as the relief of poverty was concerned, it had sad limitations.

What Chalmers set out to end was not poverty, but pauperism, i.e. the support of the poor by charitable contributions. In an older Scotland the poor had been sustained, not so much by kirk session doles, as by the bonds of family and local life. All this was now changed in industrial areas. In the older parish a family had consisted not merely of parents and children, but of the far flung relationships created where marriages had been confined within the same district since past the memory of man. Industrial families, by contrast, consisted of the one household, and had lost touch with other relations. In addition, members of a small community had known the others all their lives whereas in Glasgow residents in the same street, or even the same tenement, could be utter strangers. Chalmers proposed to reawaken in these areas the ancient spirit of local kindness of the country parish and so to destroy the need for appeal to public funds. The poor would help the poor out of Christian charity and goodwill and each would bear one another's burdens. Up to a point this certainly succeeded, for applications for kirk session aid steadily declined, but there is another side to the matter and it was this side which must have been most evident to Chalmers' parishioners. He relates with a strange guilessness cases where the new system seemed to have brought satisfactory results. A weaver who, "though he had a pension of sixpence a day", was in trouble because of typhus in his family. "Our confidence was in the sympathies and kind offices of the immediate neighbourhood; and we felt quite assured that any interference of ours might have checked or superseded these. . . . An outcry, however, was raised against us — and we felt compelled . . . to investigate, as far as we could, the amount of supplies that had been rendered, and actually found that it exceeded, at least, ten times the whole sum that would have been allowed." A man under sentence of transportation left a child,

[1] T. Chalmers, "General Appendix on Pauperism", *Works*, xvi, pp. 172–4.

for whom an application was made. It was discovered, however, that the man had a small pension which could be arrested and that a grandmother was prepared to take the child.[1]

Chalmers looked back to the kindly society of the country parish where each helped the other, but in practice he had also assimilated the outlook of Adam Smith that nothing supplies so good an incentive to work as an empty stomach. He saw Christian charity as the act of individuals alone and had no conception that the magnitude of the problem before him required that the community as such should also show that charity. "Legal charity," he said, "is injurious." Private charity, on the other hand, brought rich and poor into personal contact, lessened class feelings, and promoted a tranquil society. The root of poverty, he held, was in defect of character rather than in the harsh nature of a competitive society.[2] Comfort depended on character. "We have long thought that by a legal provision of indigence, two principles of our moral nature have been confounded . . . humanity and justice. . . . It is right that justice should be enforced by law, but compassion ought to have been left free." Pauperism, in the sense that any man had a right to maintenance by society, was "a thing not to be regulated, but destroyed".[3] In all this Chalmers had surrendered himself, as had his age generally, to the economic teachings of Adam Smith, and all his benevolence, like that of Stevenson MacGill in prison reform, John Dunlop in temperance, and Henry Duncan of Ruthwell in savings banks, was directed towards succouring the victims of a harsh society while leaving unquestioned those principles on which that society was constructed.

Chalmers did not remain long at St John's once his experiment was fairly launched. On 14 November 1823 he entered on new duties as Professor of Moral Philosophy at St Andrews, and in 1828 he moved to the chair of Divinity at Edinburgh,[4] for despite his interest in economics he retained the Scottish conviction that those who form the intellects of men govern their destinies. He was satisfied that his system was working well under his successor at St John's,[5] but in 1837 it was brought to an end,[6] not for the

---

[1] Ibid. xvi, pp. 189–91.
[2] T. Chalmers, "Christian and Economic Polity of a Nation", *Works*, xiv, v.
[3] Ibid. xiv, ix.   [4] H. Watt, op. cit. pp. 70, 82.
[5] T. Chalmers, "General Appendix on Pauperism", *Works*, xvi, pp. 344–5.
[6] Ibid. xvi, pp. 422–34.

reasons which he was disposed to give, but because the voluntary charity of individuals was totally incapable of solving the problems of an industrial and competitive society. It was the work of critics such as — to quote Thomas Carlyle[1] — "the brave and humane Dr Alison" and legislation such as the Poor Law (Amendment) Act[2] of 1845 which dealt with the problem of poverty, so far as it ever was dealt with in Victorian Scotland, and a part of that remedy lay in the removal of poor relief from the spheres of the Church and private benevolence. Possibly Chalmers left a legacy to Victorian Scotland in his harsh distinction between the deserving and the undeserving poor or it may be, as so often, that he merely sensed the mood of the new age and expressed it. At any rate, the Scotland of the nineteenth century followed him in the conviction that the undeserving poor should "feel the weight of those severities which are intended by the God of Nature to follow in the train of idleness, improvidence, and vice",[3] a conviction drawn, not from the New Testament, but from the gospel according to Adam Smith.

His experience in the city predisposed Chalmers in favour of management and against organized labour even had Adam Smith not taught him so. He suggested that after a strike an employer might "signalize the ringleaders of the opposition by a determined exclusion of them, and that he might readmit the rest on less favourable terms than before", and even that a master might recoup any possible losses by deducting them from the wages of those he re-employed. Here, indeed, was the pattern for the Victorian industrialist, evangelical and philanthropic, but hard-faced to his workmen. The acceptance of Adam Smith's economics was all too evident, and thus commenced that rift between the self-conscious working-class groups and the Evangelical leadership of the Church which was to continue into the days of Chartism and the Disruption, and beyond.[4] This is rather a sad judgment to pass on the work of a man who, in an age of crisis, essayed so much and so gallantly. He saw that the Scottish Church was entering a new age, for which she was ill equipped. His

---

[1] Thomas Carlyle, *Past and Present*, p. 3. W. Hanna, op. cit. iv, pp. 196–204.   [2] T. Ferguson, *The Dawn of Scottish Social Welfare*, p. 195.

[3] T. Chalmers, "Sufficiency of the Parochial System without a Poor Rate", *Works*, xxi, p. 175.

[4] L. J. Saunders, *Scottish Democracy, 1815–1840*, pp. 220–1.

exuberance and panache deceive the reader into thinking that he was alone in his day, but Chalmers was very much a man of his time. What he did in spectacular fashion, others were doing in less striking ways. He shared their merits, and can hardly be held responsible for their defects.

Chalmers' best legacy to the Victorian Church from his Glasgow days was his determination to apply the parish system to town life and to provide the laity with an active place within it. Even here, ironically, the first part was largely destroyed by the Disruption of which he was a leader. It was left to one who stood outside the Christian faith, Robert Owen, to do what Chalmers might have done, to question the economic foundations and to envisage a more ideal pattern of society rather than tinker with the ills of industrialism. This was not the first time that a Scot had envisaged the good society in purely secular terms, but it was contrary to the ethos of the older Scotland. At the time, the Union of 1707 had not seemed a total surrender of the country's independence since so much of her life was little affected by parliament and controlled by local institutions, of which the Church was chief. But now the Church of Scotland, which once had represented the whole nation, had sunk to a position not so very different from that of a private religious society, despite its legal standing. The pressure for reform was steadily being turned into secular channels and, in particular, into a demand for burgh and parliamentary reform. Discontent with the Union of the Parliaments, which had smouldered all through the eighteenth century, died away. Industry and commerce saw little future in an independent Scotland which had lost the great markets of England and her foreign dependencies, and nationalism was at a low ebb. In deference to Scottish opinion William of Orange had reigned in Scotland without the attachment of any number to his name, but William IV was proclaimed by that style and no one was troubled. Not till the government at Westminster persistently refused to pay heed to the demands for reform in the Church were the full effects of the Union of 1707 to be seen.

Owen, a social critic at the opposite extreme from Chalmers, had come to Manchester from Wales in 1786 and in 1791, at the early age of twenty, had set up for himself as a master cotton spinner.[1] He succeeded David Dale in the management of the

[1] Margaret Cole, *Robert Owen of New Lanark*, p. 21.

mills at New Lanark and in 1799 married his daughter. Until his retirement from New Lanark in 1829 he was both a successful business man and a model employer. Between 1799 and 1813 the value of the mills increased from £60,000 to £114,000; and over the years 1809 to 1813 the profits were £160,000.[1] Owen thus inherited his father-in-law's capacity for making money, but while Dale had combined this with evangelicalism, Owen, who was an atheist, combined it with a passion for social reform. He intended not to be "a manager of cotton mills . . . but to change the condition of the people". No man of his time was so acute a critic of the new industrialism or foresaw so many developments which, in time to come, would remedy its ills, but Owen was something of an egotist who lacked the ability to convince other people. "Like you," he wrote to his fellow industrialists, "I am a manufacturer for pecuniary profit. But having for so many years acted on principles the reverse in many respects of those in which you have been instructed, and having found my procedure beneficial to others and to myself, even in a pecuniary point of view, I am anxious to explain such valuable principles, that you and those under your influence may equally partake of their advantages."[2]

Environment and education determined character, he held, and anything could be made of children rightly brought up. He reorganized the school of New Lanark down to the smallest detail. Cobbett, who visited there in 1832, was shocked to find that small boys, wearing the kilt, were taught to dance with girls.[3] Owen had held that Scots wore too many clothes. Owen envisaged the establishment of a new pattern of society on a basis not unlike that of an Israeli kibbutz. The size of each community was to be controlled and related to its agricultural background. Food was to be bought in bulk and cooked communally, and children were to be brought up together. This would provide better meals and housing than were known to the poor who were "surrounded by every object of discomfort and disgust, in the cellars and garrets of the most unhealthy courts, alleys, and lanes in . . . Edinburgh and Glasgow".[4]

Owen had a streak of genius and a touch of lunacy. His name

---

[1] V. A. C. Gatrell, *A New View of Society*, Introduction, p. 40.
[2] R. Owen, *A New View of Society*, p. 94.
[3] William Cobbett, *Tour in Scotland*, pp. 209–10.
[4] R. Owen, *Report to the County of Lanark*, p. 240.

might have been written on the page of history as plainly as that
of Karl Marx, but it was not to be, for he was an odd mixture of
prescience and futility. The mind which had so firm a grip on
business lost its control in the field of ideas where all he scattered
broadcast was allowed to run to seed. His life covered a long span,
and the present writer in other days has talked with men whose
families recalled the unsuccessful experiment in Communism at
Orbiston in Lanarkshire which had been run by the disciples of
the son-in-law of David Dale. Owen was the first advocate, in
this country, of town planning, green belts, and the control of
industrial growth; he urged the need to care for employees and
provide high wages; unlike Chalmers, he held that the care of
the poor was a national responsibility; and all the time, in his
own mills, he was as much the master and business man as David
Dale. Unfortunately he lacked the ability to persuade ordinary
people, and as he got older he got odder. In America[1] and at
Harmony Hall in Hampshire he launched out on experiments in
"Communism with a human face". While Chalmers looked back,
Owen anticipated what was to come, but his actual social achievements in Scotland were, if possible, less than those of Chalmers.
His significance for Scotland lies in the fact that as the industrial
revolution destroyed the older restraints of society he offered
a totally secular pattern of common life and that this lead was to
be accepted in time by the political leaders of the working class.
It was in a journal which he ran that the word *socialism* first
appeared in English in 1827.

[1] J. F. C. Harrison, *Robert Owen and the Owenites in Britain and America.*

CHAPTER NINE

The Gathering Storm (I)

Chalmers had not stayed long at St John's. His early departure was due to his volatile personality, but it might as well have been due to frustration. His work had been, in a sense, the last great attempt to apply the older social structure to the problems of a new age, and his success had not been as great as he flattered himself that it had been. The ancient legal basis of Scottish corporate life was inadequate to meet the tasks awaiting it, parliament in distant London was uninterested in adapting it or in freeing the Church from its restraints, and already the growing radicalism was seeking a solution in parliamentary reform. Meantime the Church was shackled in any attempt to meet her social obligations in poor relief and education, to enlarge her parochial system as the distribution of population changed, or to accommodate herself to new thought.

With the departure of Chalmers from Glasgow in 1823 interest in a solution of the problem of poverty in the midst of plenty waned, though the burden still had to be carried. Instead the Church became increasingly aware of the question of her own nature and mission in a non-Christian environment, and of the need to convert men to the faith. Evangelical movements like those of the Haldanes and the missionary societies now being formed were scarcely consistent with scholastic Calvinism, with its doctrine of the elect, for whom alone Christ died. "If it were not true that Christ died for the heathen," asked James Morison,[1] "pray, what gospel is the missionary to preach when he lands on a foreign shore? Is he to tell them that God loved a few men scattered somewhere or other throughout the world, and that therefore, for aught that he could know, there may happen to be

[1] James Morison, *The Extent of the Propitiation*, p. 156. The missionary was Robert Moffat.

some of these favoured ones among them, and for these Christ died. . . . Men need not go to heathen lands with the doctrine of a limited atonement in their creed; or, if they go with it, they must hide it, and preach in a manner practically contradictory to it. One of the greatest missionaries of modern times . . . when asked by me what he preached to his poor Africans, replied, that it was a maxim with him and his true yoke-fellows to tell all and sundry that Christ died for them.''

A formal acceptance, at least, of the doctrines of the Westminster Confession had long been required within the Church, but from the time of John Glass onwards small groups had left her membership because of dissent. Henry Davidson[1] of Galashiels and Gabriel Wilson of Maxton had done so about 1735, though a generous Presbytery had taken no action against them. James Smith[2] of Newburn and his neighbour Robert Ferrier of Largo, the founders of the Old Scots Independents, did so in 1768, and John Barclay,[3] the founder of the Bereans, in 1772, but with all charity it cannot be said that these counted for much in the national life. Greater numbers followed the Haldanes, and when they became Baptists the growing cause of Congregationalism found a leader in Greville Ewing,[4] who had resigned from the ministry of the Church of Scotland. He combined an evangelistic outlook with a concern for foreign missions and was the editor of the first missionary magazine to be published in Scotland.

Inside the National Church there had been a change of outlook since the Assembly of 1796 refused support for missions. When the East India Company had to renew its charter in 1813 the Assembly lodged a petition that provision should be made for missionary work. The Rev. James Bryce, who had gone to India as a chaplain to Scotsmen there, came home and presented to the Assembly of 1824 a memorial urging that the Church should sponsor missionary work in India, particularly among the educated classes.[5] In a secondary respect, this was a new venture, since, oddly enough, the Church had never till now envisaged any

---

[1] *Fasti*, I, pp. 550–1, 557.

[2] *Fasti*, II, pp. 447, 453. D. Beaton, "The Old Scots Independents", *SCHS*, III, pp. 135ff.

[3] John Campbell, "The Berean Church", *SCHS*, VI, pp. 138ff.

[4] *Fasti*, I, p. 80.

[5] Elizabeth G. K. Hewat, *Vision and Achievement, 1796–1956*, p. 34.

religious activity on other than a congregational and parochial basis. A collection for foreign missions was authorized; out of over 900 parish churches and 55 "chapels of ease", which supplemented the parochial system in certain self-contained industrial communities, only 59 churches and 16 chapels contributed, raising £937 13s 9d in all. The fact that the chapels of ease, more recently founded and saddled with financial responsibilities which parish churches did not have, proportionately made a much better response, is a pointer to where evangelical sympathies were strongest. Until now Scottish missionary work had been done through the societies. A school at Kingston in Jamaica had been founded in 1800 by the Rev. George Bethune,[1] but had struggled against many difficulties since it was associated with the agitation against slavery. Anglican, Baptist, Methodist, and Moravian missionaries were all active in the island, and the Scottish contribution was still a small one, but with the coming of George Blyth in 1824 and Hope Waddell in 1829 it began to increase. By 1836 the annual report of the Scottish Missionary Society could tell that it had now eight stations and six churches in Jamaica.

The best-known of Scottish missionaries at the time, Robert Moffat, born at Ormiston in East Lothian in 1795, had found his vocation when working as a gardener in England, and had gone out to South Africa under the auspices of the London Missionary Society. Settled on an oasis on the verge of the Kalahari Desert, Moffat taught his converts to work the soil by irrigation. He mastered the Tswana language, reduced it to writing, and by 1857 had not merely translated the whole Bible but had himself seen it through the press at Kuruman. This is to anticipate, but Moffat had already started his African work in 1826.[2]

It was now the turn of the Church of Scotland to send out its first missionary, and in August 1829 Alexander Duff was ordained in St George's, Edinburgh, for service in India. Donald Mitchell, the first Scottish missionary in India, had arrived in Bombay as an agent of the Missionary Society in 1823 and during the nine short months before his death — few early missionaries survived long — he had founded ten schools. Four missionaries followed who pursued the same line of approach so that by 1827 they had

[1] Elizabeth G. K. Hewat, op. cit. p. 14.
[2] K. S. Latourette, *History of the Expansion of Christianity*, v, p. 345.

80 schools with 3,000 pupils. Up to date there were no converts, but with the coming of John Wilson in 1829 conversions began and in 1831 an Indian congregation, numbering only eight at first, commenced in his house at Ambroli.[1] In 1832 he founded at Bombay what was later to be Wilson College.

So far Scottish missionary work had owed most of its support — though by no means all — to the Seceders, but Duff came as a representative of the National Church. A man of original mind, he began by surveying the achievement — or lack of it — up to date. With the notable exception of Carey's work at Serampore, Protestant missionaries had largely been occupied in preaching and organizing elementary schools. The few converts won had mainly been from the lower castes. Arriving in Calcutta at the end of May 1830 Duff resolved, against his instructions, to settle in the city and to found a school which would attract the sons of upper-class Hindus. He abandoned the possibility of using Sanskrit or Bengali as the medium of communication and decided that English must be the basis of higher education in India. In this he had the support of Raja Rām Mohun Roy, the founder of Brāhmo Samāj, and of the future Lord Macaulay, who at that time was a legal member of the Governor's Council in Calcutta.[2] Macaulay's intention, of which the first part alone came to fruition, was to create an intellectual élite, at home in Western languages and science, and from this beginning to extend education through all classes.

Duff began with five boys, but soon had 200. Between August 1832 and April 1833 four young men were baptized; there was a hostile reaction but the work of the school was not hindered. Converts were not many; in 18 years he had 33, but all were men of standing and potential influence. In 1835 Wilson and his colleagues in Bombay who had learned from Duff's example, transferred from the Missionary Society to the Church of Scotland. Wilson's wife had started girls' schools in Bombay, and at Poona, where James Mitchell had been working since 1834, Mrs Mitchell, the first woman missionary other than the wife of a missionary, founded others. At Madras the impetus for missionary work came from Scots in the business community who brought out

[1] E. G. K. Hewat, op. cit. pp. 43-4.
[2] S. Neill, *A History of Christian Missions*, p. 274. Macaulay was the grandson of John Macaulay, minister of Cardross.

John Anderson in 1837. In May 1839 Anderson transferred to Conjeveeram, leaving a new arrival, Robert Johnston, to continue his work in Madras.[1] Missionary work continually increased, in the numbers of staff and converts, and in interest and support in Scotland.

The entry of the Church into the foreign mission field was the work of an enthusiastic and forceful minority which succeeded in persuading the Church to sponsor its cause despite the lethargy of the majority. A similar situation was to be found — though later events were to show that here the basis of popular support was very much wider — in the endeavour to modify the ancient parochial structure of the Church to deal with a rapidly growing population. Since Webster's census in 1755 the population had grown from 1,265,380 to 2,364,386 in 1831. Every county shared in the increase, and as yet the Highlands and the Borders showed no decline. Elsewhere the increase was phenomenal. Lanarkshire had grown from 81,726 to 316,819, and Renfrew from 26,645 to 133,443.[2] In counties like Kincardine or Kirkcudbright the increase mattered little as it consisted in the limited growth of existing communities, but the uncontrolled increase of population in the industrial belt involved the creation of new centres of population. Growth in the cities had made the parochial system a mere pretence, and in the countryside new villages, based on the new industries, had sprung up in places far removed from their parish church. These self-contained little communities, cut off through lack of transport and centred round a mill or coal pit instead of the familiar centres of social life, the church and the school, threatened to become heathen.

Faced with this, some presbyteries had approved the building and endowing of what were called "chapels of ease", created, as was industry, by private enterprise. But many in the ruling circles of the Church looked with disfavour on these new congregations, and not altogether without reason, since they diverted church collections from the support of the poor, and could be misused as an excuse to avoid the services of an unpopular minister. As one party in the Church wished the authorization of these chapels, so another wished their regulation, and after long debate the Assembly of 1798 enacted that no chapel should

---

[1] E. G. K. Hewat, op. cit. pp. 53, 83–4.
[2] J. G. Kyd, *Scottish Population Statistics*, SHS, pp. 82–3.

be recognized until the Presbytery of the bounds obtained full
and detailed information and submitted it to the Assembly for
approval.[1] Regulations were drafted for the qualifications of
ministers appointed, the provision of stipend, and the use of
collections. In particular all such congregations were excluded
from a share in the government of the Church by the refusal of a
place in Presbytery to their ministers and by the subjection of
their congregations to the oversight of the sessions of the existing parishes. Among the first to obtain recognition in this way
were the chapels built in Glasgow to serve Gaelic-speaking immigrants, and Airdrie,[2] formerly no more than a small weaving
village in New Monkland parish, but now commencing unprecedented development because of coal mining and blast furnaces.
Chapels like these served the new industrial areas, so different
from the old countryside of Scotland or the comfortable new
suburbs of the bourgeoisie, as the coal bings, coke ovens, and
mineral railways spread across the blackened landscape. They
inherited a harsh tradition, for the old Scottish miners had lived
a life apart, bound to servitude by an Act of Parliament of 1606,
given a limited opportunity of freedom by an Act of 1 July 1775,
but not fully freed until 1799.[3] This was particularly the case with
the older coalfields of Fife and the Lothians, but less so in
Ayrshire and Lanarkshire where mining had not so long a history,
numbers were smaller and standards were higher so that the
names of miners may be found in the lists of subscribers to religious books. Women and children worked in the pits under
conditions which, as the evidence given before Thomas Tancred
and R. H. Franks, the Scottish Commissioners for the parliamentary enquiry of 1840, testifies, were unspeakably bad.[4]

    In addition the provision for chapels of ease enabled some to
avoid separation from the National Church, and the former
congregation of Thomas Gillespie led the way by obeying his
dying wish that they would return to the Church of Scotland.
But the growth of chapels was by no means as rapid as the needs
of the time required. By 1826, 27 had been recognized. In addition
42 were being built in the highlands and islands as a result of a

---

[1] *AGA*, 1798, v, Abridgement, 23 May, Sess. 6.
[2] H. Hamilton, *Industrial Revolution in Scotland*, pp. 185, 200.
[3] R. Page Arnot, *The History of the Scottish Miners from the Earliest Times*, pp.
3–13.   [4] Ibid. pp. 18–31.

parliamentary grant of 1824. Compared with the grant voted to the Church of England, the grant to the Church of Scotland was contemptibly small. Thomas Telford produced an economical design which was used, with variations, for all. One such, Iona Parish Church,[1] remained intact until 1939. It had a pulpit in the middle of a long wall, a communion table running the length of the church, box pews beside the pulpit, and three or four long pews beyond the table. Though complaint has been made about the changes of 1939 the standard of workmanship was so miserable as not to merit preservation. Edinburgh Town Council provided the New Town with monumental churches, and Thomas Chalmers persuaded Glasgow to provide two much poorer churches, but all the time the need increased at a greater rate. As Chalmers frequently observed, the parish had lost its unity in the cities, where church members joined any congregation they chose, where the Seceders looked only to their own congregations, and where the old parish churches could no longer adequately fulfil their function of pastoral care and evangelism for every resident within their bounds. Until now the provision of parish churches had always been the responsibility of the community, and so in 1828 the Assembly[2] agreed that a committee be appointed "to represent the evils resulting from the inadequate state of church accommodation in many of the large towns, manufacturing villages, and populous parishes of the country, and without delay to take such measures as to them may seem best calculated, by bringing the subject under the notice of the government, or otherwise, to procure ultimately a remedy for so alarming an evil". For some years the committee, under a lethargic convener, did nothing about it, but the matter was too important to be swept under the carpet in this manner.

All the problems of the Church in pastoral care and poor relief were repeated in education. Here again the national tradition had run its course, virtually unaffected by the Union of 1707, not because education had been safeguarded under the Treaty as had the Church and the Law, but because of the happy indifference of parliament. Schools were still the responsibility of the local community and its representatives in Church and State under the

---

[1] G. Hay, *Architecture of Scottish Post-Reformation Churches 1560-1843*, pp. 118, 181.

[2] *AGA*, 1828, Monday 26 May, Sess. 4.

Act of 1696.[1] Heritors and sessions in country parishes, councils and sessions in burghs, were under obligation to provide schools and support teachers. The First Book of Discipline of 1560 may long have remained a devout imagination, but its comprehensive plan for universal education on a national basis, which aimed at the development of Christian manhood and good citizenship, had formed the ideal of Scottish schooling. "Knox," said Thomas Carlyle[2] in his Rectorial Address to Edinburgh University, "was heard by Scotland, the people heard him and believed him to the marrow of their bones; they took all his doctrine to heart, and they defied principalities and powers to move them from it." Whatever else may be doubtful in this characteristically rhetorical statement, the relevance to education is correct. It both reflected and created the essentially democratic quality of Scottish life, the inherent equality and disregard of wealth and title, and the respect for intellectual achievement, which have distinguished the country from her southern neighbour.

Education was valued for its own sake and for the formation of personality, rather than for any future professional use or profit. It was neither compulsory nor free but in the older Scottish society — except in isolated and outlying parts — the lack of it was regarded with some shame as the mark of the socially depressed and irresponsible. Scotland knew nothing of the wide gulf existing in England between village schools and the great public schools. Her educational system was egalitarian. All the children of a parish, rich or poor, took it for granted that they would be schooled together, and on the whole the standard of scholarship in village and burgh schools was comparable. Speaking at a dinner in 1825, Lord Brougham[3] observed, "A public school like the old High School of Edinburgh is invaluable, and for what is it so? It is because men of the highest and lowest rank in society send their children to be educated together." One of his own fellow pupils had been the son of a nobleman, while others came from the poorest homes in the Cowgate. "There they were, sitting side by side, giving and taking places from each other, without the slightest impression on the part of my noble friends of any superiority on their part to the other boys, or any ideas of

[1] *APS*, x, p. 63.
[2] T. Carlyle, *Rectorial Address to the University of Edinburgh*.
[3] W. Steven, *History of the High School of Edinburgh*, p. 212.

inferiority on the part of the other boys to them; and this is my reason for preferring the old High School of Edinburgh to other and what may be termed more patrician schools, however well regulated and conducted."

The result was a community of values marked by self respect, independence, and intellectual and moral effort.[1] While family connections were always of value, so that even the independently minded David Hume commenced his autobiography by telling that he came from a good family, entry into the professional and business groups was more open to the working people than in any other country of Europe. Whatever his background, the "lad o' pairts" might hope to pass from school to the university, where nothing in the least resembling the social character of the two English universities was found, and so to enter the ministry, medicine, or the law. But here again the nineteenth century brought changes. Rural and industrial changes took away the old equality of opportunity. The children of the poor left school early to work in the fields or the factory. Many others had no schooling at all. Teachers, whose salaries were still controlled by the long outdated Act of 1696, were miserably underpaid and their standards declined. National pride in education continued long after it had ceased to have any warrant, until the country could be described as a "half educated nation".[2]

This was an understatement. In the Highlands 30 per cent of the population of Perth and Argyll[3] were illiterate, and in the Outer Hebrides and the more inaccessible parishes of the western seaboard the proportion rose to 70 per cent. In parts of Glasgow, such as Calton and Milend, the conditions were as bad.[4] To deal with this the Assembly of 1824 set up an Education Committee[5] which opened just over a hundred new schools in its first quarter of a century. In Glasgow an Infant School Society had been active since 1826 and in 1827 David Stow opened the Glasgow Model School for instruction in teaching. Aided by a government grant, the Glasgow Church Building Society had built 18 schools by 1840 and had 8 more building or projected. In 1837 the Assembly Committee opened a pioneer college for teacher training, and

---

[1] L. J. Saunders, *Scottish Democracy 1815–1840*, p. 242.
[2] George Lewis, *Scotland a Half Educated Nation*.
[3] L. J. Saunders, op. cit. pp. 262–3.   [4] Ibid. p. 276.
[5] *AGA*, 1824, Thursday 27 May, Sess. 7.

an Assembly deliverance of the same year showed that the Church
had every intention of retaining control of education at all
levels though, so far as the universities were concerned, this was
now an anachronism.

A different reaction came from the newly moneyed classes who
were reluctant to see their children share the company and
accent of the working class and wished to have them admitted
to the prestigious universities of England. In 1824 Edinburgh
Academy was opened to serve the wealthy areas of the New
Town. It was expensive by the standards of the time, for it
charged three guineas a quarter while the High School charged
only half a guinea. The Vicar of Lampeter[1] was brought north
to be its rector and other teachers were recruited from England.
Apart from the fact that it was a day school and not a boarding
school it was modelled on the English exemplar and it was
immediately and correctly accused[2] of being a school for the
wealthy and inconsistent with the Scottish tradition. Sir Walter
Scott, whose son had been tutored by the new Rector in his
student days at Oxford, made the opening speech on 1 October
1824. "The observation of Dr Johnson," he said,[3] "was well
known, that in learning, Scotland resembled a besieged city,
where every man had a mouthful, but no man a bellyfull. It
might be said, in answer to this, that it was better education should
be divided into mouthfuls, than served up at the banquet of some
favoured individuals, while the great mass were left to starve.
But, sturdy Scotsman as he was, he was no more attached to
Scotland than to truth; it must be admitted, that there was some
foundation for the Doctor's remark. The Directors were anxious
to wipe off this reproach, and for this purpose had made every
provision in their power." In other words, the traditional
Scottish philosophy of education was abandoned, and the new
school cultivated the study of Greek to prepare its pupils for
Oxford and Cambridge. This example was copied by other
schools, particularly in Edinburgh, where it was accepted by the
Town Council that in matters of education there was much to be
said for having one law for the rich and one for the poor.

[1] G. E. Davie, *The Democratic Intellect*, p. 26.
[2] L. J. Saunders, op. cit. p. 365.
[3] J. G. Lockhart, *Life of Sir Walter Scott*, p. 526; cf. *Peter's Letters to His Kinsfolk*, i, p. 202.

Johnson's comment marked the difference between the Scottish and the English universities. Scottish universities were not places of privilege. Their fees and living expenses were low and could be met — with a struggle — by students from middle-class homes and even by the sons of working-class[1] homes who "cultivated literature on a little oatmeal". Duncan Dewar[2] was born on 6 March 1801, the son of a crofter on Loch Tay two miles above Kenmore. In the late autumn of 1819 he set out for St Andrews University to begin his studies for the ministry. Rising early in the morning he set out on foot to walk to Perth across the hills by way of Amulree and Logie-Almond, a distance of 25 miles as the crow flies. There he collected his baggage which had been sent ahead by carrier, boarded the steamer which left at noon for Dundee, crossed the Tay by ferry to Newport, and walked the eleven miles to St Andrews as the night came on. At St Andrews he studied Latin and Greek in his first year, the senior class in each in his second year, as well as Logic and the first class in Mathematics. In his third year he studied Moral Philosophy, the second class in Mathematics, and Geography, and also went back to the senior Latin and Greek classes, but without paying a fee. In the fourth year he studied Natural Philosophy. Normally the fee for each class was a guinea and a half, but in Geography it was only half a guinea. His annual expenses at college came to about £16, and part of this was recouped from a bursary, while in the summer he supported himself by tutoring. The range of the subjects he studied in his Arts course was somewhat wider than the class list might suggest, for Economics and History were included in the work of other classes.

Dewar was typical of Scottish students in his background, his economy, and his studies. Students often came to the university as young as fourteen or fifteen. They chose their classes with or without the intention of graduating, lived unsupervised in lodgings, and made their own arrangements for study. What they earned in the summer often enabled the poorest to work his way through college. The most important feature in the curriculum was the range of studies, which usually covered languages, mathematics, science, and philosophy, but it was the last named which dominated all. During the eighteen-twenties there were

[1] Thomas Guthrie, *Autobiography*, p. 34.
[2] Peter R. Scott Lang, *Duncan Dewar's Accounts*, pp. 49ff.

about 600 divinity students[1] at the four universities, most of them
doing a four-year course, but the degree of attendance at classes
was variable in the extreme. Systematic Theology, Hebrew, and
Church History had provided the course until the University
Visitors of 1826 urged the addition of chairs of Biblical Criticism.

Dewar's course was typical of Scottish students again, in that
his specialized professional training was preceded by the degree
in Arts with its general character. Early specialization was dis-
couraged, or rather, it had been, for there was now a growing and
influential group of Scots who were alienated from the working
class, disliked the Scottish speech and traditions, and regarded
England as the model to be copied. They distrusted the general
character of the Arts course in Scotland and its domination by
philosophy, and wished instead to raise the entrance age by improving the schools, and so to make the university course a
specialized one.[2] The basic course of a Scottish student combined
the classics, philosophy, and the exact sciences, experimental and
mathematical, whereas in England the student had the choice of
two specialized courses, the one mainly classical, and the other
mainly mathematical. "We do not in this part of the kingdom,"
wrote George Jardine,[3] Professor of Logic at Glasgow, "attach
to classical learning that high and almost exclusive degree of
importance which is ascribed to it elsewhere, thinking it of
greater consequence to the student to receive instruction in the
elements of science both physical and mental, than to acquire even
the most accurate knowledge of the ancient tongues, when all
that is most valuable in them may, it is thought, be obtained
without so great a sacrifice of time and labour." In other words,
Jardine admitted that the good student in England far excelled
his Scottish counterpart in detailed scholarship in classics or
mathematics, as the case might be. "Dalziel," wrote Lord Cockburn[4] of his old Professor of Greek at Edinburgh and the University's historian, "used to agree with those who say that it is
partly owing to its Presbyterianism that Scotland is less classical
than Episcopal England. Sydney Smith asserted that he had over-
heard the Professor muttering one dark night on the street to

[1] L. J. Saunders, op. cit. pp. 350ff.
[2] G. E. Davie, op. cit. p. 5.
[3] George Jardine, *Outlines of a Philosophical Education*, quoted in G. E.
Davie, op. cit. p. 10.   [4] Lord Cockburn, *Memorials of His Time*, p. 18.

himself, 'If it had not been for that confounded Solemn League and Covenant, we would have made as good longs and shorts as they.'" On the other hand, Jardine would have claimed that the average Scottish student had a philosophical background which affected his general outlook, taught him to look for general principles, and to apply his mathematics and science to life and to society.

It was this last factor which had created the fertile link in technology between the Scottish universities — and Glasgow especially — and the commercial community; but it was the philosophical background which had created the ferment in Scottish thought in the eighteenth century. "It is apparent that these errors[1] could only originate and grow amongst a people of a metaphysical turn of mind, and of sequestered habits of life; when they began to be published in the Church of the South Britons . . . the British clergy would not receive them; but yet could not reply to them, being more inclined to visible symbols of truth, and less to abstract conceptions. It is curious to perceive the strong and striking characteristics of the Scotch and English churches, thus early revealing themselves." This comment of Edward Irving on the rise of Pelagianism may not have much value as history, but it is an accurate evaluation of the mental habits created by the Scottish and English universities of his time.

[1] Edward Irving, "Historical View of the Church of Scotland", *Works*, i, p. 556.

CHAPTER TEN

The Gathering Storm (II):
Theology

After long years of comparative backwardness Scotland distinguished itself during the eighteenth century in practically every field of intellectual life or technical ability then available. It has been observed that the one exception to this was theology; and the reason is plain. The fact that any explicit deviation from the accepted pattern of theology in the Westminster Confession excluded a man from the ministry was responsible for the total absence of any constructive thought by the clergy in what should have been their distinctive field. Paradoxically, it was at the very time that the Royal Commission of 1826 began to challenge the Scottish university system that theology began to break free and to respond to its metaphysical background.

This phenomenon in the Scottish Church does not stand alone, for a storm of religious controversy was to appear in England and Ireland also. To radicals like William Cobbett the English Church seemed no more than a lethargic and over-endowed institution, and the prevailing dullness gave no hint of the forces within it which were soon to affect men so diverse as John Henry Newman and his brother, Francis, the one to enter the Roman Church and the other, first to be one of the founders of the Christian Brethren, and later to abandon the Christian faith. In Ireland the counterpart was the controversy between 1827 and 1830, the two sides headed by Henry Cooke and Henry Montgomery, over the refusal of the Arians among the Irish Presbyterians to subscribe to the Westminster Confession.[1] In Scotland controversy centred round three men, Thomas Erskine, Edward Irving, and John McLeod Campbell, and the matters of debate were the

[1] J. M. Barkley, *A Short History of the Presbyterian Church in Ireland*, pp. 45–8.

Person of Christ, the nature and scope of the atonement, election, eternal punishment, and the gifts of the Holy Spirit.

The most significant figure in Scottish theological thought in the quarter of a century preceding the Disruption—and perhaps in the nineteenth century—was a layman, Thomas Erskine of Linlathen. Though he had a wide circle of influential friends Erskine was an unobtrusive man, and since his death he has been generally neglected. Born in 1788, the son of an Edinburgh Writer to the Signet, he was a descendant of the Regent Mar, and a nephew to Dr John Erskine, Robertson's successor in Greyfriars and the one-time leader of the Evangelicals.[1] In 1810 he became a member of the Faculty of Advocates, but when he succeeded to the family estate on the death of his brother in 1816 he retired from the law. Between 1820 and 1837 he published *Remarks on the Internal Evidence for the Truth of Revealed Religion, An Essay on Faith, The Unconditional Freeness of the Gospel, The Brazen Serpent,* and *The Doctrine of Election,* as well as a few essays. At this point he almost ceased to write, but when he died in 1870 he left behind him a few papers which were published as *The Spiritual Order.* Erskine's writings were not systematic or orderly, but they formed a new venture in the Scotland of the time.

Though the historians of his Church have, by and large, ignored the fact,[2] Erskine was a Scottish Episcopalian by birth and upbringing.[3] Consequently his family background was one that rejected the national Calvinism. For many years every man ordained to the Scottish ministry was required to disclaim "all Popish, Arian, Socinian, Arminian, and Bourignian errors". The obscure lady whose name was thus bracketed with those of greater heretics was an eccentric daughter of the seventeenth-century Roman Church who shared something of the principles of the Quakers and Pietists. From the Low Countries her heresies, so-called, spread to Scotland and in 1701 the General Assembly[4] condemned not only her but also Dr George Garden of Aberdeen, an Episcopalian minister who had been led astray by her writings. He had described her book as "representing the great end of Christianity, which is, to bring us back to the love of God and

---

[1] Thomas Erskine, i, *Letters,* pp. 1–10.
[2] cf. G. Grub, *Ecclesiastical History of Scotland.* F. Goldie, *Short History of the Episcopal Church in Scotland.*
[3] Thomas Erskine, *Letters,* ii, p. 381.   [4] *AGA,* 1701, x, xi.

charity". Among his errors had been the repudiation of the doctrine of election, the assertion that "there must be in man some infinite quality whereby he may unite himself to God", teaching that Christ had taken on Himself the nature of fallen man, and much else besides. Later Assemblies saw fit to repeat the condemnation,[1] but the Scottish Bishops did not and their clergy had considerable theological liberty. Erskine inherited such thoughts, and though he respected Calvinism he did not share it. When he commented that all the most deeply devout men he had known had been brought up as Calvinists he was asked how he could reconcile this with his opposition to Calvinism. "In this way", he replied. "Calvinism makes God and the thought of him all in all, and makes the creature almost as nothing before Him. So it engenders a deep reverence, a profound humility and self-abasement, which are the true beginnings of all religion. It exalts God infinitely above the creature. In this Calvinism is true and great, and I honour it. What I cannot accept is its conception of God as One in Whom power is the paramount attribute, to which a loving righteousness is made quite subordinate, and its restriction of the love of God in a way which seems to me not righteousness but partiality."[2] Despite this tribute to the reverence created by Calvinism, Erskine was strongly critical of the manner in which the Scottish Church had so largely substituted theological discussion for prayer and adoration, making doctrinal conformity the criterion of Christian life. His gardener at Linlathen had been something of an amateur theologian. One day, speaking of the men he had known, he observed, "And then there was Mr Campbell of the Row; he was a very gude man, but then he divairged [diverged]." "As if," said Erskine, "after that there was no more to be said for him."

Erskine thus regarded faith as far more than the acceptance of certain doctrines or events. Though he lived long enough to resent the questioning of the historical reliability of Scripture by Renan and Bishop Colenso,[3] Erskine, unlike the eighteenth-century Apologists, was not so much concerned with the defence of the historical origins of the faith as with its vindication

[1] *AGA*, 1709, xii; 1710, ix.
[2] J. C. Shairp, *Reminiscence of Thomas Erskine*. Thomas Erskine, op. cit. ii, p. 369.
[3] Ibid. ii, pp. 211, 375.

through its conformity to men's spiritual needs. More than the mere title of one of his books indicates his obligations to Soame Jenyns,[1] a most uncharacteristic son of the eighteenth century whose apologetics brought down the contempt of Dr Johnson. "Many persons,"[2] Erskine wrote, "in their speculations on Christianity, never get further than the miracles which were wrought in confirmation of its divine authority. Those who reject them are called infidels, and those who admit them are called believers; and yet, after all, there may be little difference between them. A belief of the miracles narrated in the New Testament does not constitute the faith of a Christian." By faith Erskine meant a spiritual condition which showed that a man had responded to the love of God. "There is one thing," he wrote, "which I have long felt to be a great defect in our popular theologies, the want of distinguishing between faith, as meaning filial trust in God—the faith which Jesus Christ Himself had and lived by—and faith as meaning belief in what Jesus Christ was, and did, and suffered."[3]

Again, while the thought of the Scottish Church in the early nineteenth century was coming to be as individualistic as the economics and social thought of the age, Erskine thought in terms of the community of mankind. He returned to the Scriptural thought of Christ as the Second Adam, the Head of a new and redeemed humanity. Consequently he repudiated the Calvinist version of the atonement which goes back to St Anselm and which saw Christ's death as the price paid to satisfy the demands of divine justice. "The humanly devised doctrine of substitution has come in place of, and has cast out, the true doctrine of the headship of Christ. . . . Christ died for every man, as the Head of every man—not by any fiction of law, not in a conventional way—but in reality as the head of the whole mass of human nature which, although composed of many members, is one thing—one body—in every part of which the head is truly present. . . . He did not suffer the punishment of sin, as the doctrine of substitution supposes, to dispense with our suffering it, but to change the character of our suffering, from an unsanctified and unsanctifying suffering, into a sanctified and sanctifying suffering. The work

[1] S. Jenyns, *A View of the Internal Evidence of the Christian Religion.*
[2] T. Erskine, *Internal Evidence for the truth of Revealed Religion*, p. 184.
[3] T. Erskine, *Letters*, ii, p. 249; cf. *The Spiritual Order*, p. 113.

of Christ is thus the source of life. It was a work which no creature could have done—a work which none but He could have done—a work without which no man could have been saved. . . ."[1]

"I believe," he wrote to a correspondent,[2] "that Christ is in every man, and that it is His suffering voice which speaks in the conscience of every man. I believe that He is thus suffering for every man, the just for the unjust, that He may bring us back to God. I believe thus that the recorded history of our Lord in the Gospels is the outward and objective manifestation of a great subjective truth which is going on, and which will go on until every soul of man is brought back to God. And I am sure that the sorrow which holy love feels for sin is the true and essential and divine medicine for sin."

This carried with it a repudiation of what could be, but was not always, taught within the Scottish Church on eternal punishment. "What good will it do you in hell," asked a preacher[3] in a parish not far distant from Erskine's home, "that you knew all the sciences in the world—all the events of history, and all the busy politics of your little day? Do you know that your very knowledge will be turned into an instrument of torture in hell? . . . The place in hell is quite ready for every unconverted soul. . . . As when a man retires at night to his sleeping-room, so a place in hell is quite ready for every Christless person. . . . The fires are all quite ready and fully lighted and burning." Erskine's deep conviction of the limitless power of the love of God made him revolt against such teaching. "Faith in the eternity of punishment is as hurtful a dogma as the Real Presence or Transubstantiation, interfering woefully with all trust in God. I have been lately struck with the direct contradiction of that faith in the 11th chapter of Romans. I am surprised that anyone can resist it. . . ."[4] Though this was written in his latter years, it states a conviction very early formed.

In 1834 Hugh Craig, an elder of the High Kirk of Kilmarnock, and a member of the Presbytery of Irvine, was deposed from the office of ruling elder because, at a meeting in Kilmarnock at

[1] T. Erskine, *The Brazen Serpent*, pp. 34–58.
[2] T. Erskine, *Letters*, ii, pp. 84–5.
[3] H. F. Henderson, *Erskine of Linlathen*, p. 76.
[4] T. Erskine, op. cit. ii, p. 238.

which he took the chair, a petition had been made to the government asking for separation of Church and State.[1] Hugh Craig later published a pamphlet entitled *The Final Salvation of all Men from Sin*, and Erskine, who had received a copy from a friend, wrote to the author[2] saying, "The principles contained in it are those with which I have *long* concurred and sympathised. . . . It is surely most unreasonable to suppose that God should change His manner of dealing with us, as soon as we quit this world, and that if we have resisted, up to that moment, His gracious endeavour to teach us righteousness, He should at once abandon that purpose for which He created and redeemed us, and give us up to the everlasting bondage of sin. Do we not feel that such a supposition is too horrible—that it is most dishonouring to Him Who has said, 'I will never leave thee nor forsake thee', and, 'The mountains shall depart, and the hills be removed, but My kindness shall not depart from thee, neither shall the covenant of My peace be removed, saith the Lord Who hath mercy on thee'?" This, it is plain, had been the mind of the Moderates in the eighteenth century, but they had been obliged to maintain a discreet silence. Erskine did not. As a layman he could be ignored up to a point, but his clerical friends could not hope to be as outspoken and yet escape.

As though this was not enough, there was one further point at which Erskine challenged not merely the doctrine of Calvinism, but its whole temper. From 1827 until 1830 a group of some fifty persons had been meeting in the house of Henry Drummond at Albury to study the prophetic books of the Bible, and although Erskine, like McLeod Campbell, soon had his reservations, he was early attracted to this group. Out of these Albury conferences came, in time, the Catholic Apostolic Church. Those taking part were deeply concerned with the expectation of the Second Coming of Christ in the near future, and with the gifts of the Holy Spirit as seen at Pentecost, speaking with tongues, and the gift of spiritual healing. Simultaneously these phenomena began to appear in Scotland. One Sunday late in March 1830 as Mary Campbell[3] of Row on the Gairloch, an habitual invalid, lay on her sofa, she broke out into speaking in an unknown tongue

[1] *AGA*, 1834, Abridgement, Thursday 29 May, Sess. 8, p. 55.
[2] T. Erskine, op. cit. ii, p. 238.
[3] T. Erskine, op. cit. i, pp. 175–85, 392–3.

and continued so for an hour. Across the Clyde at Port Glasgow two shipbuilding brothers, James and George Macdonald, had the same gift. Visiting his sister Margaret, who was desperately ill, one of the brothers took her by the hand and said, "Arise and stand upright." She did so, and was well. They wrote to Mary Campbell and the same happened to her. Erskine, two of whose friends, Robert Story and McLeod Campbell, were ministers on the Gairloch, came to see for himself, was convinced — for the time being — and wrote his tract, *On the Gifts of the Holy Spirit*, at the close of 1830. Mary Campbell declared that she was speaking in Turkish or the language of the Pelew Islands, but the surviving specimens are only gibberish.[1] At a later time Erskine retracted his conviction that these happenings were identical with those recorded in Acts, but he added,[2] "I still continue to think, that to any one whose expectations are formed by, and founded on, the declaration of the New Testament, the disappearance of these gifts from the Church must be a greater difficulty than their re-appearance could be."

Scotland has never given Erskine the attention he deserves and his books, especially *The Brazen Serpent*, are now almost unobtainable. He broke with Calvinism, though not with Christian orthodoxy, even if the Church at the time was of a different opinion. As an Episcopalian layman Erskine was beyond the reach of the Church courts, but their full wrath descended upon his clerical sympathizers. Of these, the most spectacular was Edward Irving. Ill equipped in patristics, Irving became aware, through references which he had picked up at second hand, that many of the thoughts of Erskine and of himself were not heretical, but had been expressed by men of great standing in the Church in the days before theology became ossified; and he was anxious to demonstrate support not merely from the older documents of the Scottish Church[3] but also from the wider Church. He picked up quotations from Tertullian, Ambrose, Jerome, and Hooker to vindicate his orthodoxy.[4] Yet it was not through study of the Fathers, but out of his reading of the Bible and meditation upon

[1] A. L. Drummond, *Edward Irving and His Circle*, pp. 143–70.
[2] T. Erskine, op. cit. i, p. 408.
[3] E. Irving, *Orthodox and Catholic Doctrine of our Lord's Human Nature*, pp. 35–54.
[4] E. Irving, *Extracts from Divines on the Humanity of Christ*, pp. 4–12.

it that Erskine had returned to what had been taught on the nature and work of Christ by St Gregory Nazianzen and St John Damascene,[1] St Thomas Aquinas,[2] and Richard Hooker.[3]

Edward Irving, as spectacular as Erskine was unassuming, was born at Annan in 1792. Leaving Edinburgh University in 1809 he taught, first in Haddington, and then in Kirkcaldy, and so commenced his lifelong involvement with the troubled marriage of Jane Welsh and Thomas Carlyle.[4] Irving had been licensed as a probationer in 1815, but no parish came his way, and in October 1819 he became assistant to Chalmers in St John's until, in July 1822, he was ordained as minister of the Caledonian Church in London. This was little more than the chapel of the Caledonian Orphanage, with a congregation of barely fifty. Irving was a commanding figure whose classical good looks were if anything made more commanding by what Carlyle described as a villainous squint. In London, no longer overshadowed by Chalmers, Irvine suddenly made his mark. He had a strong and melodious voice, deep and passionate earnestness, an air of prophetic authority, and a gift of oratory which even an unsympathetic modern reader of his sermons at times can sense. Behind the flow of words, the listener was aware, there was an attempt to restate the conventional doctrines of the faith in relevant and vivid terms. He had been carried away by the tide of Romanticism. Chalmers, taken by Irving to listen to Coleridge in 1827, was less impressionable. "His conversation, which flowed in a mighty unremitting stream, is most astonishing, but, I must confess, to me is still unintelligible. I caught occasional glimpses of what he would be at, but mainly he was very far out of all sight and all sympathy. I hold it, however, a great acquisition to have become acquainted with him. You know that Irving sits at his feet, and drinks in the inspiration of every syllable that falls from him. There is a secret and to me as yet unintelligible communion of spirit betwixt them, on the ground of a certain German mysticism and transcendental lake-poetry which I am not yet up to. Gordon says it is all unintelligible nonsense, and I am sure a plain Fife man as uncle

---

[1] R. S. Franks, *The Work of Christ*, p. 661.
[2] Thomas Aquinas, *Compendium Theologiae*, pp. 208-13. In Thomas Gilby. *St Thomas Aquinas: Theological Texts*, pp. 512-21. *Summa Theol.* 3a, 7, 1-9.
[3] Richard Hooker, *Law of Ecclesiastical Polity*, v, li-liv. Irving read Hooker.
[4] T. Carlyle, *Reminiscences*, i, p. 74; ii, pp. 1-220.

'Tammas', had he been alive, would have pronounced it the greatest *buff* he had ever heard in his life."[1] For a brief spell, encouraged by a stray reference to Irving in the House of Commons, the fashionable world flocked to hear him, and in 1827 a new church was opened for him in Regent Square. But already his popularity was on the wane. Chalmers timed one of his prayers and found that it lasted forty minutes. The crowds no longer thronged his church and criticisms of his growing eccentricity were widespread.

Irving had become absorbed in millennialism, and was soon to be associated with the "speaking with tongues". He had started to take part in the Albury conferences and thus had become infected with the absorption in prophecy and the Second Coming. "There is no question, nor ever has been, nor even can be, concerning Christ's personal reappearance in human form upon the earth; although I perceive the faith of the Protestant Churches to be so withered by absolute infidelity, or by intellectual demonstration, which is the egg of infidelity, that they start when you say that Christ will appear again in personal and bodily presence upon the earth. . . . Before I had insight given to me into this mystery, I had never found it treated as a personal act of Christ, or rightful act of His mediatorial office; but as a personal thing to us, a whip to scourge our lethargy, a spell to break our sleep, a thunder note to awaken our terrors; treated as a metaphysical part of the metaphysical idea of moral responsibility, rather than as the grand demonstration of the power and majesty of the humbled son of God, the grand act of the justification of Christ's injuries and injuries of His suffering Church upon those who have done them wrong. And I am sure the Judgement has become a dead letter in our creed and in our preaching, from being thus abstracted away from the personal and bodily presence of Christ the Judge."[2]

Irving had long been friendly with Robert Story of Rosneath, and in May 1828 when he came north to Edinburgh to preach a series of lectures on the Book of the Revelation at the surprising but characteristic hour of 6 a.m. he met John McLeod Campbell of Row. The two men discussed assurance of faith and the belief

---

[1] W. Hanna, *Memoirs of the Life and Writings of Thomas Chalmers*, iii, p. 160.
[2] E. Irving, *Preliminary Discourse to the Coming of Messiah in Glory and Majesty*, p. 45.

that Christ died for all men and not, as the Confession taught, for the elect only.[1] Next Sunday Irving preached for Story at Rosneath and on the following three Sundays of the month Campbell, who had found a kindred spirit in Irving, preached for him at Regent Square. Through this friendship with Campbell and Story, Irving learned of the new phenomena at Rosneath and Port Glasgow, and his emotional temperament was immediately fascinated. Prophecy, speaking with tongues, and the gift of spiritual healing were for him the signs that a new apostolic age was about to dawn. When he returned to Regent Square, full of this news, the tongues appeared there also. Confusion broke out at almost every service until his office-bearers, having failed to persuade their minister to halt the interruptions, had him ejected from the church by the Presbytery.

The first sign of a reaction was a refusal of the Assembly to receive the nomination of Irving as its Assembly elder by the burgh of Annan,[2] since, as a London minister, he was not entitled. Irving's intimate friend, Hugh Baillie MacLean, had been minister in the Scots Kirk at London Wall since 1827 when Irving delivered his ordination charge. In the spring of 1830 MacLean was presented to the parish of Dreghorn, but his induction was frustrated by a petition from parishioners accusing him of heterodoxy on the doctrine of our Lord's human nature. His case came to the Assembly, which sent it back to the Presbytery for detailed hearing.[3] Through the previous winter there had been murmurs in his parish and Presbytery about the teachings of McLeod Campbell, and he noted that a shorthand writer was regularly taking down his sermons.[4] His Presbytery held that he had taught "the doctrine of universal atonement and pardon through the death of Christ, and also the doctrine that assurance is of the essence of faith and necessary to salvation", and he was surprised to see that the charge awakened far more emotion than did the denial of the divinity of Christ, even in those outside the Church.[5]

An appeal was made to the Assembly, which noted that the

[1] John McLeod Campbell, *Memorials*, i, pp. 51-4.
[2] *AGA*, 1829, Abridgement, p. 35.
[3] *AGA*, 1830, pp. 41-3.
[4] John McLeod Campbell, *Reminiscences and Reflections*, p. 31.
[5] Campbell, *Memorials*, i, p. 67.

doctrines attributed to McLeod Campbell had been condemned by an act of 1720 and were contrary to Scripture, and commanded the Presbytery to make a full hearing.[1] In September he was informed that the Presbytery had found the charges correct and that he was to be deposed from the ministry.[2] On Tuesday 24 May 1831 the Assembly heard the case. No less than 500 pages of printed evidence were laid before the Commissioners, and long after midnight Dr Cook, the leader of the Moderates, moved Campbell's deposition. The Rev. Lewis Rose of Nigg unsuccessfully moved the milder sentence of a temporary suspension. Campbell's father then spoke in his son's defence. He presented a petition signed by nine-tenths of his son's parishioners. "You have heard him this day in his own defence," he said, "and he has told you that he just preaches that 'God so loved the world that He gave His only-begotten Son, that whosoever believeth on Him should not perish, but have everlasting life,' and with regard to universal pardon, he has told you that he just means by it that sinners may come to God through Jesus Christ as to a reconciled Father. Now I am sure there is none among us all who has anything to say against this. And with regard to Assurance, what he says is no more than this—that a sceptic is no Christian,—that doubting God is not believing him. And he has told you that he abhors what are called the Antinomian doctrines of the 'Marrow', and I can say that I never heard any preacher more earnestly and powerfully recommending holiness of heart and life. . . . I bow to any decision to which you may think it right to come. Moderator, I am not afraid for my son; though his brethren cast him out, the Master Whom he serves will not forsake him; and while I live, I will never be ashamed to be the father of so holy and blameless a son."[3] By 119 votes to 6 the Assembly then found McLeod Campbell guilty and deposed him from the ministry. He returned to Row for a last visit and on a Sunday evening at the end of July he preached to 6,000 hearers in the New Churchyard at Greenock.

Next day the Assembly deposed Hugh Baillie McLean[4] and

---

[1] *AGA*, 1830, pp. 43–4; cf. *AGA*, 1720, v.
[2] Campbell, *Memorials*, i, pp. 71–2.   [3] *Reminiscences and Reflections*, pp. 37–9.
[4] *AGA*, 1831, Abridgement, pp. 47–8; cf. Warrand Carlile, "On the Human Nature of Christ" (*The Morning Watch*, ix), *Letter to John Rodman, M.D.*, pp. 26–34, for a full statement of his teaching by H. B. McLean.

on Friday A. J. Scott[1] of Paisley, a licentiate who had voluntarily admitted that he could not accept the confession and who, in 1850, became the first Principal of Owen's College,[2] which later developed into the University of Manchester. Every year new men were deposed. In 1832 William Dow of Tongland was deposed for repudiating the Confession.[3] Next the Assembly heard the case of his brother David, Assistant Minister at Kirkpatrick Irongray. In this instance someone had erred in procedure, so the Assembly, "as this cause involves a subject of great and urgent importance", instructed the Presbytery to hear it at the next meeting. David Dow's resignation was accepted on 7 August 1832; he was deposed from the ministry and went to the Cape of Good Hope where he became a farmer.[4] On 28 May the Assembly heard a report on Edward Irving and decided that he should appear before the Presbytery of Annan,[5] which deposed him on 13 March 1833.[6] The Assembly of 1833 noted that his Presbytery had deposed Patrick Buttar, the minister of Abertarff, "for avowing and maintaining sentiments contrary to the Word of God and the standards of this Church".[7] While the Assembly was sitting it was reported[8] that on 13 May, on the Monday after Communion in Trinity College Church, Walter Tait, the minister, had permitted a Mr Carlyle — who had acted as Counsel for McLeod Campbell — to break out into speaking with tongues at the thanksgiving service "as a manifestation of the Spirit". This was referred to the Presbytery of Edinburgh, which deposed him on 22 October. By now a high pitch of excitement had been aroused both in the membership and leadership of the Church; the Assembly of 1834 ordered the deposition of Hugh Craig, a Kilmarnock elder,[9] and was relieved to find that expressions used by Dr Ritchie of St Andrews in his "Lectures on Romans" had no heretical intent. In 1841 Thomas Wright[10] of Borthwick was deposed for "denying the doctrine that Jesus Christ freely gave

[1] *AGA*, 1831, Abridgement, pp. 52–3.
[2] Campbell, *Memorials*, i, p. 224.
[3] *AGA*, 1831, Abridgement, pp. 39–40.
[4] *Fasti*, i, p. 594.   [5] *AGA*, 1832, Abridgement, p. 48.
[6] A. L. Drummond, op. cit.   [7] *AGA*, 1833, Abridgement, p. 41.
[8] *AGA*, 1833, Abridgement, p. 47. *Fasti*, i, p. 33.
[9] *AGA*, 1834, Abridgement, pp. 55, 54; cf. supra, p. 198.
[10] *AGA*, 1841, Abridgement, pp. 34–8. J. Bryce, *The Church of Scotland, 1833–1843*, i, p. 87.

Himself a voluntary sacrifice unto death for sin, and that by His death He made a proper and real satisfaction to His Father on behalf of His people". However accurately they were represented, all these were associated with the teachings for which McLeod Campbell and Edward Irving were condemned.

Nothing comparable with this series of depositions existed in the history of the Scottish Church since the fury of the seventeenth century. *The Marrow of Modern Divinity* had been condemned, but the men who defended it had been left in their charges. Alexander Ferguson and William McGill had not been penalized, and even John Simson had been comparatively mildly treated. Indeed the whole temper of the eighteenth-century Church had been tolerant, as well it might be when most of its leading clergy found it best to maintain a discreet silence on doctrinal matters. The Seceders were themselves responsible for their breach with the Church and the nearest parallel to these events is the case of Thomas Gillespie, who was penalized for a breach of discipline rather than of doctrine. Those who now suffered showed much the same spirit as Gillespie. Irving's health was deteriorating and his personality was breaking down. He died on 4 December 1834 and was buried in the lower church beneath the choir of Glasgow Cathedral. As the mourners retired there remained by the grave-side a handful of young women, dressed in white, waiting for him to rise again.[1] In Victorian times he was commemorated by a stained glass window, not inappropriately, of John the Baptist. His life had been, in the words of H. R. Mackintosh,[2] "one of the greatest and saddest of the century". McLeod Campbell conducted a congregation in Glasgow, but retained both respect and affection for the Church which rejected him. He had no intention of founding a denomination and when he was invited to join the Catholic Apostolic Church, which had originated out of the Albury conferences and the work of Irving, he declined, unlike Walter Tait, who was ordained by two apostles of the new Church as the angel of their Edinburgh congregation.[3] Erskine of Linlathen, like McLeod Campbell, dissociated himself from the Catholic Apostolic Church,[4] but Mary Campbell, who had been Irving's

---

[1] A. L. Drummond, *Edward Irving and His Circle*, pp. 227–8.
[2] H. R. Mackintosh, *The Person of Jesus Christ*, p. 276 .
[3] Campbell, *Memorials*, i, pp. 102–3.
[4] T. Erskine, *Letters*, i. pp. 228–9.

evil genius, married an Edinburgh clerk who came to Gairloch to hear her speaking with tongues and, with him,[1] went south to join the new Church. No one has paid much attention to her. This is a serious underestimate, for whether they care to admit it or not she is responsible for the modern Pentecostal movements. From the United States and Canada Pentecostalist missionaries have worked in Asia, Africa, and South America. At times in the mission field their willingness to compete with other bodies has created painful tensions, but they have had "a special gift for making the Christian message audible where human misery is at its worst".[2] They are especially strong in Chile, Brazil, and East Africa, and their success among the depressed and downtrodden raises the question of whether the conventional churches have not lost something which was inherent in the Church of the New Testament.

Irving and McLeod Campbell at different times appealed to Thomas Chalmers, but Chalmers, who might have done so much, did nothing to aid them. His mind, for all its great qualities, was essentially that of a conservative, while they, despite the conservative form of words used by Campbell especially, had sensed the atmosphere of a generation to which the traditional language of the Confession meant nothing. "I would not despair of the times," said Irving,[3] "if I saw preaching beginning to resume the character which it had at the Reformation, and adding whatever other weapons out of the armoury the Lord may give us for the fearful odds that are now against us. But I do despair when I behold ingenious reasonings, loose declamations, and other forms of man's wayward mind, substituted in place of the royal ordinance of preaching, and the plentiful demonstration of Christ's glorious person." But the Church was tied to the Confession so that when William Dow was condemned his appeal to the Bible was disallowed on the grounds that the Confession was authoritative in the Church.[4] "That thou doest, do quickly," said an unidentified voice as Chalmers was about to declare Dow's deposition from the moderator's chair, but the Church was not altogether to be condemned for its verdict on Irving. Apart from his eccentricities

[1] A. L. Drummond, op. cit. pp. 148–51.
[2] S. Neill, *A History of Christian Missions*, p. 460.
[3] E. Irving, *Preliminary Discourse to the Coming of the Messiah in Glory and Majesty*, p. 84.   [4] T. Erskine, *Letters*, i, p. 191.

—which were not part of the charge but which alienated men — his verbosity led to a certain obscurity or ambiguity as to his teaching.

Irvine was charged with holding "the sinfulness of Christ's humanity", but as H. R. Mackintosh observes,[1] the charge is unjust. Irving was so deeply impressed with the reality of the Incarnation that he had to affirm that it was the nature of fallen man which Christ took upon Himself. "If He were not a man, but only the apparition of a man, a superior being who for a certain end and purpose had clothed Himself with human form; if He had not a reasonable soul, the consequences cannot be denied. His human feelings and affections were but an assumed fiction to carry the end which His mission had in view; and His sufferings and His death were a phantasmagoria played off before the eyes of men, but by no means entering into the vitals of human sympathy, nor proceeding from the communion and love of human kind, nor answering any end of comforting human suffering, and interceding for human weakness."[2]

"Whenever I attribute sinful properties and dispositions and inclinations to our Lord's human nature," he explained,[3] "I am speaking of it considered as apart from Him, in itself; I am defining the qualities of that *nature* which he took upon him. . . . To understand the work which He did, you must understand the materials with which He did it. The work which He did was to reconcile, sanctify, quicken, and glorify this nature of ours, which is full of sin, and death, and rebellion, and dishonour unto God. The most part of those who are opposed to the truth agree in this; but differ from us in maintaining that the substance of human nature underwent a change in the miraculous conception. We maintain that it underwent no change, but was full of fellow-ship and community with us all His life long, and was not changed but by the resurrection. We hold that it received a Holy Ghost life, a regenerate life, in the conception; in kind the same which we receive in regeneration; but in measure greater, because of His perfect faith; which perfect faith He was enabled to give by being a Divine Person, one of substance with the Father. The thing, therefore, which we maintain is, that as Adam was the

[1] H. R. Mackintosh, *The Person of Jesus Christ*, p. 276.
[2] E. Irving, *Doctrine of the Incarnation Opened*, p. 118.
[3] E. Irving, *Orthodox and Catholic Doctrine of our Lord's Human Nature*, vii–viii.

perfect man of creation, Jesus was the perfect man of regeneration; perfect in holiness, by being perfect in faith; perfect in faith, though all the created universe strove to alienate Him from God; and prevailing to believe in the Father, against the universe, through the Divinity of His person. . . . His union with the Father by faith stood good against the whole creation, and prevailed to draw creation out of the hands of its oppressors back again, and to reconcile it to God." Or again,[1] "I believe that my Lord did come down, and toil and sweat, and travail, in exceeding great sorrow in this mass of temptation with which I and every sinful man are oppressed . . . and bearing it all upon His shoulders, in that very state into which God put it after Adam had sinned . . . by His faith and patience did earn for Himself the name of 'the man of sorrows' and 'the author and finisher of our nature'." Through most of the nineteenth century Scottish theologians paid more heed to the defects in Irving's doctrines[2] rather than his profound insights, but his work has had a more favourable response in this century[3] though the diffuseness of his writings has limited the interest in them.

McLeod Campbell's great book, *The Nature of the Atonement*, was not published till a quarter of a century after his deposition; in the meantime his thought had developed greatly, but it had not substantially altered. He still thought on the same lines. Rightly described[4] as "Scotland's greatest contribution to theology", it is, unfortunately, by no means an easy book to read, and if this is partly due to intricate thought, it is also the consequence of a heavy prose style. "Man, you have a queer way of putting things," his father[5] once said to him, and this is demonstrated both in *The Nature of the Atonement* and in *Thoughts on Revelation*. He wrote most clearly in his letters. He had been condemned for teaching that Christ died for all men and that assurance was of the essence of faith, but as Irving was led on to consider the doctrine of the person of Christ so Campbell was led to consider that of the atonement. Like F. D. Maurice, he was deeply indebted to Erskine. But, unlike *The Brazen Serpent*, *The Nature of the Atone-*

[1] E. Irving, op. cit. pp. 2-3.
[2] A. B. Bruce, *The Humiliation of Christ*, pp. 252-7.
[3] D. M. Baillie, *God Was in Christ*, pp. 14-20.
[4] J. H. S. Burleigh, *A Church History of Scotland*, p. 332.
[5] Edgar P. Dickie, *The Nature of the Atonement*, xx.

ment was systematically arranged, and he was able to relate his thoughts to those of earlier theologians and, in particular, to those of Martin Luther, as found in his *Commentary on Romans*. It seems he did not know Abelard, whose thought was so like his own.

Campbell discussed, critically, if not unsympathetically, the theory of the atonement as it had been taught by Calvinists. He could not accept the doctrine that Christ died only for the elect and not for all men. "That cannot be the true conception of the nature of the atonement which implies that Christ died only for an election from among men."[1] And he found no satisfaction in the way in which Chalmers, in his *Institutes of Theology*, hedged at this point. He was deeply dissatisfied with those penal theories in which Calvinists like Ralph Wardlaw[2] had discussed the doctrine in legal terms. By contrast, he set out to consider it, not in the light of the divine justice, but in terms of God's love. In all He did, Christ had fulfilled the will of His Father. "Lo, I come to do Thy will" was therefore to be the keynote of the doctrine. Therefore, loving the Father with all His being, the Saviour loved His brethern as Himself. Unlike the elder brother in the parable, he longed to say, "My brother was dead, and is alive again." At this point Campbell found a point of contact with, and also one of departure from, Principal Edwards, considered as an exponent of Calvinism. "Principal Edwards . . . dwells on His love to those for whom He was to intercede, because of which He felt so identified with them that what touched them touched Him. . . . There is something which surely commends itself to us in this recognition of love. . . . May we not go further? . . . seeing love *to all men* as that law of love under which Christ was, must we not both wonder and regret, that his deeply interesting thoughts in this region did not lead Edwards to see, that by the very law of the spirit of the life that was in Christ Jesus He must needs come under the burden of the sins of all men?"[3]

What Christ suffered is not to be seen in physical pain alone, but in the grief which holy love bore for the sins of men. "I refer[4] to what has been urged by some as a reason for holding that the sufferings of Christ were penal, viz. that otherwise there is no explanation of the sufferings of one Who was without sin, as

[1] J. McLeod Campbell, *The Nature of the Atonement*, pp. 59–60.
[2] Ibid. p. 91.   [3] Ibid. pp. 124–6.   [4] Ibid. p. 140.

endured under the righteous government of God. Do we never see suffering that we must explain on some other principle than this? Surely the tears of holy sorrow shed over the sins of others . . . shed before God in prayer . . . are not to be conceived of as having been penal. But the fact is, that the truth that God grieves over our sins, is not so soon received into the heart as that God punishes sin, — and yet, the faith that He so grieves is infinitely more important, as having power to work holiness in us, than the faith that He so punishes, however important." The coming of sin into the world brought sorrow, not to the sinful only, but also to the holy and loving. That such suffering as that of Christ should have existed in the universe and in One Who was holy and sinless raised a question which could not be answered adequately by any penal theory. Christ's suffering was vicarious, an atonement for the sins of men as distinct from a punishment of them. His sufferings were not merely human, but divine; God's will was revealed in them, and not merely in connection with them; and it was God's love as much as His righteousness that was present.

What Christ was and did in His incarnate life revealed the hidden capacities of humanity. "Not for his own sake but for our sakes did the Son of God reveal the hidden capacity of good that is in man by putting forth in humanity the power of the law of the spirit of His own life — the life of sonship."[1] He Who was perfect offered Himself to God the Father that His brethren might share that fellowship with the Father which was His own; and what God accepted for men in Christ is also what God has given to us in Christ. All Scriptural words such as "a way into the holiest", "reconciliation", and "peace with God" were "to be seen in the light of our spiritual relation to the Father of our spirits which demands for them a spiritual, as distinguished from a mere legal meaning". Similarly justification by faith must have "a spiritual and self-evidencing character". "The Amen of faith, — the being reconciled to God, — peace with God through our Lord Jesus Christ, — these, in meekness and lowliness, are known in the light of the atonement. For that light of eternal life harmonises us with itself and so with God; and in it it is impossible to trust in self . . . impossible to doubt that God is just in being the justifier of him that believeth in Jesus."[2]

[1] J. McLeod Campbell, *The Nature of the Atonement*, p. 168.
[2] Ibid. pp. 225–6.

The forgiveness of the sins of men and their hope of eternal life depended upon the atonement given in the death of Christ, but the ultimate ground of all is the great love of God in Christ, a love so strong that it cannot fail to attain its end. To stop at the atonement, and not to ascend to this divine love, is to misunderstand all. "It has been truly said, that men have perverted creation, and instead of using it as a glass through which to see God, have turned it into a veil to hide God. I believe the greater work of redemption has been the subject of a similar perversion. It is the commendation of the light in which Christ's doing of the Father's will, Christ's declaring of the Father's name, has now been contemplated, that, as I have said, it ever raises the mind to the Eternal Will, the Unchanging Name.[1] Christ in His love had done for men what in their best moments they might have sought to do but could not, and His confession and repentance on our behalf entered into every soul that believed on Him and brought men to eternal life. Any abbreviation or summary of this complex book is bound to be unsatisfactory. McLeod Campbell avoided any breach with his brethren so far as he could, and served, without pay, as pastor of his little congregation in Blackfriars Street in Glasgow until the time came when the Church which had deposed him paid a belated tribute to him. He had been telling in Scotland, though without any indebtedness, what Schleiermacher had said in Germany, but whereas Schleiermacher had done so on more philosophical lines, Campbell had been more Scriptural in thinking of God as Father and of fellowship with Him as the life of sonship. He had expressed with unusual power and wonderful sympathy[2] the thought that Christ in divine love had offered to the Father a full repentance on behalf of His brethren for the sins of the world.

It was not merely the thinking of Irving, McLeod Campbell, and their friends, which was significant, but the vindictiveness with which they were hounded down. Something had happened within the Church, so that there arose a readiness to question the long established documents of Calvinism and, at the same time, a readiness to defend them. Until his death in 1827 Sir Henry Moncrieff[3] of St Cuthbert's had been the acknowledged leader of the Popular, or Evangelical, Party within the Church. It was he

---

[1] Ibid. pp. 333–4.   [2] R. S. Franks, op. cit. p. 672.
[3] *Fasti*, I, p. 122.

who took the chair at the public dinner in Edinburgh which celebrated the defeat of the old Moderates in the dispute over Professor Leslie's appointment.[1] He was a man of aristocratic authority and magnanimity. "His air," says Lockhart,[2] is decidedly that of a man of birth and station — he holds himself with the true mien of a dignitary — and looks (under favour) when surrounded by his adherents, very much like a Lord Bishop receiving the bows of his country curates at a visitation . . . Nobody can look upon the Baronet without perceiving that nature meant him to be a ruler, not a subject . . . . Had he come into Parliament, I have very little doubt his peculiar faculties would have made him as powerful a person there as he is here in the General Assembly of the Kirk." So long as Sir Henry led the Evangelical or Popular party, it was restrained by his personality. "Throughout his life," Lord Cockburn[3] wrote, "he was the oracle of the whole Church in matters not factious, and the steady champion of the popular side. In comparison with him every other Churchman who has appeared since I knew the world must withdraw. Nothing that I could say would express one-half of my affectionate and reverential admiration of this great man."

Under his régime the difference between Moderates and Evangelicals, long fading, became barely apparent, and in 1818 Sir Henry conceded publicly that patronage was "at last completely established". But this was only the lull before the storm. Andrew Thomson of St George's who, with Chalmers, led the Evangelicals after Sir Henry's death, was a man of a different temper. Like Chalmers, Thomson was an orator, a pioneer of social reform, and an advocate of popular education as well as being so strong a spokesman for the abolition of slavery that he alienated more moderate public men. Something of his flamboyant personality is preserved in the psalm tune, "St George's Edinburgh", which he composed. Probably it is an error to blame Thomson for the rising passion and uncompromising spirit with which ecclesiastical issues now came to be judged; his passion was not so much a cause as a sympton of rising temperatures. High blood pressure affected his personal conduct, but the increasingly controversial mood was not his alone, but probably arose from the greater

[1] Lord Cockburn, *Memorials of His Time*, p. 124.
[2] J. G. Lockhart, *Peter's Letters to His Kinsfolk*, iii, pp. 46–8.
[3] Lord Cockburn, op. cit. p. 139.

religious intensity of the time and the social changes which had brought to the forefront new classes, undisciplined by the spirit of the old Moderates.

In *The Edinburgh Christian Instructor*, of which he was editor, Thomson handled the controversies of the time with a touch of truculence, and he took a lead in the pursuit of Irving and McLeod Campbell. At the same time Thomas McCrie, writing from the standpoint of the most conservative Seceders, produced his *Life of Knox* in 1811 and his *Life of Melville* in 1819. They mark a new standard of scholarship in Scottish historiography, but they show an intransigence worthy of their subjects and a spirit which Thomson's journal cordially welcomed. Andrew Thomson suddenly dropped dead at his own doorstep in Melville Street in 1831. His controversies, says Lord Cockburn, were immediately forgiven. " A stranger would suppose that Thomson now had never an opponent. . . . His energy, courage, formidableness, and purity of objects, made him a great stay of the right cause; and had he had moderation to keep himself more clear of personal conflict, his influence would have been boundless."[1] He had leant the weight of his personality and his pen to the pursuit of the heretics. The note of intransigence and conflict was not to die with him.

In the decade before the Disruption there was a change in the whole nature of society. Lord Cockburn regarded it with mixed feelings. He acknowledged those respects in which change was for the good. "In some respects," he said,[2] comparing the end of the eighteenth century with the decade before the Disruption, "there was far more coarseness in the formal age than in the free one. Two vices especially, which have long been banished from all respectable society, were very prevalent, if not universal, among the whole upper ranks — swearing and drunkenness. Nothing was more common than for gentlemen who had dined with ladies, and meant to rejoin them, to get drunk. Swearing was thought the right, and the mark, of a gentleman. And, tried by this test, nobody, who had not seen them, could now be made to believe how many gentlemen there were. Not that people were worse tempered then than now. They were only coarser in their manners. . . . The naval chaplain justified his cursing the sailors, because it made them listen to him; and Braxfield apologised to a lady whom

[1] Lord Cockburn, *Journal*, i, p. 4.
[2] Lord Cockburn *Memorials of His Time*, pp. 26–7.

he damned at whist for bad play by declaring that he had mistaken her for his wife."

This has been interpreted as due to the growing strength of the Evangelicals within the Church, and it is largely true, but it is also the case that the Evangelicals themselves were no longer quite what had once been meant by that name. They were changing. One element in this was the growing reaction against the steady increase of the Roman Catholic immigrants, which can be seen in a flood of writings such as Nathaniel Paterson's *The Dangerous Nature of Popery*, and the series of weekly pamphlets issued by William McGavin under the name of *The Protestant*, Popery had been the traditional bugbear of Scottish Protestantism, but this stream of pamphlets is a sign of mounting ill feeling.

Similarly there was a marked growth of sabbatarianism. James Wright of Maybole reflected the outlook of the Moderates of his youth when he hinted to his farming congregation that as the harvest was in a sorry state and the Sunday was warm and dry, it would be a work of necessity and no sin if they went to work in the fields after the service.[1] But even as early as 1807 the outlook had changed, and he was cited before his Presbytery. The Assembly of[2] 1826 called on the fishermen of St Cyrus to let down their stake nets on the Sabbath, an action with which all anglers would sympathize, but not done for that reason. In 1831 John MacMaster, a probationer, was deposed, not merely because he had eloped with a lady, but for "the gross profanation" of having done so "under cloud of night" on the Sabbath.[3] At the opening of the Assembly of 1834 the Moderator, Dr Stirling, had a private interview with the Lord High Commissioner, Lord Belhaven, and was relieved to hear that His Majesty had graciously acceded to the request of the Assembly Committee on Sabbath Profanation,[4] and had decided to discontinue the dinners which His Grace had formerly been giving on Sundays. "There is no contrast between those old days and the present that strikes me so strongly as that suggested by the differences in religious observances; not so much by the world in general, as by deeply religious people. . . . I could mention many practices of our old pious which would horrify

[1] *Fasti*, ii, pp. 126–7.   [2] *AGA*, 1826, Abridgement, p. 41.
[3] *AGA*, 1831, Abridgement, p. 53.
[4] Abridgement. Commission of Assembly, 1831, p. 51. *AGA*, 1834, Abridgement, pp. 44, 46–7.

modern zealots. The principles and feelings of the persons commonly called evangelical, were the same then that they are now; the external acts by which these feelings and principles were formerly expressed, were materially different. In nothing do these differences appear more strikingly than in matters connected with the observance of Sunday. Hearing what is often confidently prescribed now as the only proper mode of keeping the Christian Sabbath, and then recollecting how it was recently kept by Christian men, ought to teach us charity in the enforcement of observances which, to a certain extent, are necessarily matters of opinion."[1]

But the most important factor in the changing temper of the Church was an increasing dogmatism. In the eighteenth century it had been the Seceders who stood most closely to the Westminster Confession while the Evangelicals had followed the lead of the men who found in *The Marrow of Modern Divinity* teachings akin to those of McLeod Campbell; but now the Evangelicals were becoming more rigid in doctrine. Calvinism has long been the *bête noire* of a school of Scottish writers. So far as this dislike has historical as distinct from psychological origins, it is a resentment against the school of popular piety which steadily gained in strength and assertiveness in the years before the Disruption. Robert Murray McCheyne,[2] who died as a young man on the eve of the Disruption, had more of the older evangelical tradition which went back to the Cambuslang Revival; but in the Highlands a more austerely doctrinal pattern of faith was increasing every year in strength. Until now the Highlands had counted for as little in the Scottish Church as they did — if truth be told — in affairs of State, but now a distinctive Highland piety, strictly Calvinist, was being formed.

When Donald Sage[3] came south to his first meeting of the Assembly he looked on the old Moderates as being on the side of "the Prince of this world", and John Kennedy's memoir of his beloved father's ministry in Killearnan[4] from 1814 onwards is the story of how a parish experienced a great quickening of its Christian faith, but it is an account which makes plain that this took

[1] Lord Cockburn, *Memorials of His Time*, p. 35.
[2] Andrew A. Bonar, *Memoir and Remains of R. M. McCheyne.*
[3] D. Sage, *Memorabilia Domestica*, p. 375.
[4] John Kennedy, *The Days of the Fathers in Ross-shire*, pp. 149–238.

place in the pattern which later was that of the Free Church. Lord Cockburn tells how public sympathy within the membership of the Church drifted away from the last representatives of the Moderates. Of Dr John Inglis[1] of Old Greyfriars he writes, "He was one of many men who have been wasted by being cast on an unworthy scene. The powerful qualities which Inglis threw away in attempting to repress the popular spirit of our Church, would have raised him high in any department of public life. Deducting eloquence and the graces, he was a first-rate preacher. The fanatical taste of the age, however, diminished his hearers, till at last his church was nearly empty. Yet the almost bare walls heard as good, if not better, everyday sermons, than were preached in any church in Scotland, except by Chalmers."

There are signs in contemporary writing that this renaissance of dogmatic Calvinism alienated some Scots of the time even more than it did Lord Cockburn. Thomas Carlyle, like Edward Irving, had worshipped as a boy in the Secession Church at Ecclefechan, but despite his rhetoric about its "tongues of authentic flame from Heaven",[2] he gave up his early thoughts of entering the ministry, and his mind travelled far from the faith. Scott as *Redgauntlet*, *Old Mortality*, and *The Heart of Midlothian* show thoroughly understood the Covenanting tradition, and the mind of the old-fashioned devout countryman; but he himself stood outside the tradition both by ancestry and conviction. In contrast, his son-in-law, J. G. Lockhart, not merely stood outside the tradition, but totally failed to understand it. He had been born in a manse and knew all about the forms of church life in Scotland, but his psychological novel, *Adam Blair*, shows that this was the limit of his understanding. Based on the story of George Adam,[3] minister of Cathcart from 1738 till 1759, it was given a romantic character and a mawkish sentimentality far removed from the bluntness of religious life in an eighteenth-century parish. It exhibits "the morbid side of contemporary morality"[4] which provided a good market for Victorian novelists, but it bears no relation to the working faith found in the Scottish Church. Lord Cockburn,[5] who knew his Scotland better, told of the older

---

[1] Lord Cockburn, op. cit. p. 138.
[2] Thomas Carlyle, *Reminiscences*, ii, p. 15.   [3] *Fasti*, ii, 61.
[4] David Craig, *Some Passages in the Life of Mr Adam Blair*, xvi.
[5] Lord Cockburn, op. cit. p. 56.

generation that" though they were not merely decorous in matters of religion, but really pious, they would have been deemed irreligious now. Gay-hearted and utterly devoid of every tincture of fanaticism, the very freedom and cheerfulness of their conversation and views on sacred subjects would have excited the horror of those who give the tone on these matters at present."

But the most startling question mark against the renascent Calvinism of the time is James Hogg's brilliant and fantastic novel, *The Private Memoirs and Confessions of a Justified Sinner*. Scott knew the working people of Scotland, but Hogg was one of their number. He and his forebears came from the country where "Annan, Tweed, and Clyde, A' rise out of ae hillside". These bare hills, which separate other people, are a place where the herds, who walk the high tops, meet and talk at the marches. Here, in the seventeenth century Episcopalian and Presbyterian spheres of influence met. Hogg came from the Episcopalian side of the hills where it was possible for a man to observe[1] that it was a pity that Psalm 109 "should ever have been admitted into Christian psalmody, being so averse to all its mild and benevolent principles"; but he knew both worlds of thought.

Apart from being an unusual experimental form of novel, the *Confessions of a Justified Sinner* is an essay in morbid psychology. It is concerned with the two sons of the Lady Dalcastle, one her husband's son and the other, apparently, "the crazy minister's son from Glasgow".[2] Whatever interpretation is to be placed upon this masterpiece it is plain that Hogg, though ready enough to distinguish it from what Calvin[3] taught, had no love for contemporary Scottish Calvinism. The central character of the novel, Robert Wringhim — unless that place belongs to Gil-Martin or Satan – was an exponent, or caricature, of the teaching ascribed to Antinomista in *The Marrow of Modern Divinity*. From childhood he had been brought up to debate theology. " 'Now, madam,' added I, 'My question to you is, What is Ineffectual Calling?' 'Ineffectual Calling? There is no such thing, Robert,' said she. 'But there is, madam,' said I, 'and that answer proves how much you say these fundamental precepts by rote.' . . . 'What a wonderful boy he is!' said my mother. 'I'm feared he's to be a conceited gowk,' said old Barnet, the minister's man."[4]

[1] James Hogg, *The Private Memoirs and Confessions of a Justified Sinner*, ed. John Garey, 1969, p. 32.   [2] Ibid. p. 23.   [3] Ibid. p. 2.   [4] Ibid. p. 99.

Wringhim held to "the doctrine of the double decree", of some predestinated to eternal life, and others to damnation. "I found it more congenial to my nature to be cutting off sinners with the sword, than to be haranguing them from the pulpit, striving to produce an effect, which God, by His act of absolute predestination, had forever rendered impracticable. The more I pondered on these things, the more I saw the folly and inconsistency of ministers, in spending their lives, striving and remonstrating with sinners, in order to induce them to do that which they had it not in their power to do. Seeing that God from all eternity decided the fate of every individual that was to be born of woman, how vain was it in man to endeavour to save whom their Maker had, by an unchangeable decree, doomed to destruction."[1] The counterpart to this was an indifference to morals. "I could not but despise the man in my heart who laid such a stress upon morals leaving grace out of the question."[2] No sins committed could lead to the condemnation of the elect. "None of us knows what is pre-ordained, but whatever is pre-ordained we *must* do, and none of these things will be laid to our charge."[3] "That I was a great, a transcendent sinner, I confess. But still, I had hopes of forgiveness, because I never sinned from principle, but accident . . . the grace of repentance being withheld from me, I regarded myself as in no degree accountable for the failure. . . . Upon the whole, I think, I had not then broken, that is, absolutely broken, above four out of the ten commandments; but for all that, I had more sense than to regard either my good works, or my evil deeds, as in the smallest degree influencing the eternal decrees of God concerning me, either with regard to my acceptance or reprobation. I depended entirely on the bounty of free grace, holding all the righteousness of man as filthy rags, and believing in the momentous and magnificent truth, that the more heavily laden with transgressions, the more welcome was the believer at the throne of grace."[4] Here, once again, is the note of resentment against the direction of religious thought to which the strongest party in the Scottish Church was turning.

The theology which Hogg caricatured had been at its strongest among the Seceders but even here, as has been observed, the seeds

[1] James Hogg, *The Private Memoirs and Confessions of a Justified Sinner*, ed. John Garey, 1969, pp. 122–3.
[2] Ibid. p. 221.   [3] Ibid. p. 126.   [4] Ibid. pp. 113–14.

of liberal thought were working. In the spring of 1839 James Morison[1] was sent to preach to a struggling little Seceder congregation in the Cabrach on the borders of Aberdeenshire and Banffshire. On his way north he read Charles Finney's *Revivals of Religion* and next Sunday, moved by what he had read, he laid aside his manuscript and preached from the heart. He regarded this as the time and place of his new birth. Next autumn he was called to the congregation of Clerk's Lane in Kilmarnock, but the service of ordination was delayed for an hour while the Presbytery debated the orthodoxy of a tract, *What Must I Do To Be Saved?* which he had written. But the agitation against him continued, for Morison was preaching a gospel of universal salvation; on 2 March 1841 the Presbytery began his trial and in June the Synod — the highest court of the United Secession Church — declared him no longer a minister; but Morison had the support of his congregation, and together they formed an Independent congregation. Robert Morison,[2] his father, the minister of the Secession congregation in Bathgate, upheld his son and in 1842 he, too, was expelled. With two other ministers, one evangelist, and thirteen elders they formed themselves into the Evangelical Union in May 1843. Morison apparently owed nothing to Erskine, Irving or McLeod Campbell, but he belonged to the old evangelical tradition which had expressed itself again in Robert Murray McCheyne and the revival of 1839–40. He set out his teaching in a little book, *The Extent of the Propitiation*, in 1841, and it found a wide circle of readers. "I do most firmly believe, O anxious sinner," he wrote,[3] "whomsoever you be, and whatsoever may have been your character, that all that Jesus did on Calvary He did for you." It taught the doctrine of universal redemption. "Jesus came into the world to save sinners. . . . The word *sinners* in this blessed passage is no crust that conceals beneath it the word *the elect*. It is an honest word . . . . It is as great as the world. What word is more universal than *sinner*?"[4] There had been a revolt against Calvinism in what had been its strongest citadel.

[1] R. Small, *Congregations of the United Presbyterian Church from 1753 to 1900*, i, p. 117; ii, pp. 288–91. Harry Escott, *A History of Scottish Congregationalism*, pp. 116–21.

[2] R. Small, op. cit. i, pp. 602–3.

[3] J. Morison, *The Extent of the Propitiation*, p. 11.

[4] Ibid. pp. 60–1.

CHAPTER ELEVEN

The Ten Years' Conflict

The time had gone when the Church of Scotland could be regarded more or less as the nation in its spiritual aspect. The
alienation of the industrial masses, the growth of a sizeable
Roman Catholic minority, and, above all, the steady increase of
the Seceders in numbers and influence, had put an end to this. It
was only a matter of time before the Church's privileges should
be challenged. Since 1819 the Scottish middle class had lost its
fear of a working-class revolution, but the demand for a bourgeois
revolution, like that of 1830 in France, which would give the
middle class their due place, had steadily grown. In 1829 the bill
for Catholic Emancipation became law. Anti-Roman prejudice
was now even stronger than at the time of the riots of 1778 and
1779 but ministers were less ready to inflame it and, in the Church
of Scotland, Chalmers and Thomson in particular, less subject to
popular pressure than their Seceder brothers, gave emancipation
their public support.[1]

Simultaneously the country was involved in the great storm of
agitation for parliamentary reform,[2] and both these movements
stirred the Scottish Seceders and Radicals into action. In 1804
the Seceders had produced a new *Narrative and Testimony* modifying their acceptance of the Confession's statement on the relations
of Church and State,[3] a step which lost them Thomas McCrie. In
1824 John Ballantyne[4] preached and printed a sermon which
pressed the argument, now congenial to most Seceders, that an

---

[1] W. L. Mathieson, *Church and Reform in Scotland 1797–1843*, p. 282.
[2] E. L. Woodward, *The Age of Reform*, pp. 75–83.
[3] J. Cunningham, *The Church History of Scotland*, ii, p. 449. W. L. Mathieson,
op. cit. pp. 60–2.
[4] R. Small, *Congregations of the United Presbyterian Church from 1753 to 1900*,
i, p. 33.

Established Church was inconsistent with spiritual independence. Not much attention was paid to it, until he reprinted it in 1830. Meantime Andrew Marshall[1] of Kirkintilloch, who otherwise was one of the most conservative Seceders and a cantankerous man, had caught the changed public mind with a published sermon in which he argued that the Roman Catholic Church would now demand to be established in Ireland, and that the whole concept of a National Church was contrary to Scripture. Every member of the Church had a duty to support it, and the Church had a right to maintenance from them alone. So began what was called the "Voluntary Question".[2] Disaffected Protestants joined hands with Radicals who were indifferent or hostile to the Church, while Evangelicals like Chalmers and Thomson joined with Dr Inglis, the last of the Moderates, in defence of a National Church. Patrons of parishes had taken fright at the excesses of the French Revolution; they had been less indifferent to popular opinion and more ready to consult vacant congregations as to what kind of a minister they might wish. As a result the agitation against patronage had subsided, but this new controversy[3] co-incided with the obtaining of some measure of popular rights in the Reform Act of 1832 to stimulate a similar demand within the Church.

Lord Cockburn associated the rise of the Evangelical Party — which he described as "the Wild party" — with the events of 1830. "From the beginning of Principal Robertson's reign till about four years ago," he wrote[4] in 1838, "the Wild party was Whiggish, because the essence of the system introduced by him, and continued by his successors, was to repress the people, to uphold patronage even in its grossest abuses, and to discourage religious zeal. When the Whigs came into power, therefore, in 1830, there was a close alliance between them and this side of the Church. This, helped by other circumstances, gave them, who for above seventy years had always, except on a few detached oc-casions, been in a hopeless minority, the command of the Assembly, and led to the veto law, the admission of the ministers of the chapels of ease, and the suppression of the Moderate party;

---

[1] Ibid. pp. 151–4.
[2] David Woodside, *The Soul of a Scottish Church*, pp. 79–90.
[3] H. Watt, *Thomas Chalmers and the Disruption*, pp. 96–114.
[4] Lord Cockburn, *Journal*, i, p. 183.

being the three objects which the Wild had most ardently desired. But the Whigs soon found that they had raised a most impracticable power. It was imbued with fanaticism." But here Lord Cockburn was partly mistaken, for the Evangelical party was rising to power because of a change within the Church. Both those who defended and those who assailed the National Church were agreed that "the great tendency of the popular mind is towards those ministrations which breathe the spirit and inculcate the principles by which the Gospel is chiefly characterised",[1] and Evangelical churchmen had really no defence when it was answered that the preaching of Evangelical doctrine could never be sure so long as a patron could nominate whom he chose. They were to be obliged, first to advocate a curb on the exercise of patronage, and then to demand its abolition.

Had the National Church remained as somnolent as it once had seemed — to the Seceders — to be, there might have been less cause for animosity against a declining institution; but by now it was showing unexpected signs of vitality, and even its renascent Calvinism, which might not commend itself to a modern reader, was a sign of grace in Seceder eyes. The leakage of congregations into the Secession had halted. Worse still, the "Auld Kirk" had attractions for some who had gone out. In 1835 the Original Burgher Synod, instead of uniting with the other Seceders in the United Secession Church, wrote to ask the Clerk of Assembly if they might be received back into the Church of Scotland.[2] Their request was welcomed, and after the delay caused by procedure in church courts, they were received back in 1839.[3]

Unexpected changes in the National Church had made this possible. When a minister was nominated to a parish by the patron, it was customary for him to conduct worship in the church; a call then was signed by the congregation and presented to the Presbytery which, after sustaining the call, inducted the nominee. Under the Moderates the signing of the call, which had once been essential, ceased to be so, and after 1782, while it could not be dispensed with, it became a formality.[4] It must have seemed

---

[1] John Ballantyne, *A Comparison of Established and Dissenting Churches*, p. 173.
[2] *AGA*, 1835, Abridgement, p. 54.
[3] Ibid. 1838, Act XV; 1839, Act VIII.
[4] H. Watt, op. cit. pp. 115–19. Robert Buchanan, *The Ten Years' Conflict*, i, pp. 199–203.

ominous to men of the old régime when the Assembly of 1832, meeting in May just before the Reform Bill reached the statute book, elected Thomas Chalmers as Moderator. There was now to be a demand for popular rights in the Church as well as in the State. Overtures from three Synods and eight Presbyteries called for modification of the rights of patrons and for a reinstatement of the importance of the call. After long debate the Assembly refused by a majority of 46 to remit the subject to a committee.[1] In the course of the debate it had been said that the small number of overtures showed that there was little discontent; the Evangelicals, defeated for the time being, took the hint, and next year the Assembly received a larger number of overtures asking that it should be declared the law of the Church that no minister should be intruded into a congregation against the will of the congregation.

A time had been in Scotland when there was little chance that a local congregation would either wish to dissent from the laird's choice or be able to do so. That day had gone. The very fact that the laird chose him could damn a minister in the eyes of the congregation and their social and economic independence of the landowner was such that they could afford to speak their minds. The rights of patrons had never been held to be absolute. The selection and training of students lay entirely within the control of the church courts and it was only a probationer of the Church or one of her ministers who could be nominated. But what of the rights of congregations? The Act of 1690 abolishing patronage had recognized the right of congregations to object to a nominee, and that of the Presbytery to judge of the objections. Nor had the Act of 1712 explicitly denied these rights. Chalmers was confident that the Church had the power within herself to deal with the situation, for the status of the congregational call could, he held, be restored, as it had originally been impaired, by a series of decisions asserting it. But there were those who feared that this procedure would be too slow to meet the forces of dissent and that it would bring an unwanted conflict with the holders of patronage.[2] A different course was agreed upon. In the debate of

[1] Ibid. pp. 119-23. *AGA*, 1832, Abridgement, pp. 41-2. James Bryce, *The Church of Scotland 1833-1843*, i, pp. 14-15.

[2] W. L. Mathieson, op. cit. pp. 304-7. J. H. S. Burleigh, *A Church History of Scotland*, pp. 336-9.

1833 the minister of Portmoak[1] had reminded the Assembly of a call which had been signed only "by the patron's factor, who did not reside in the parish, by a labouring man from another parish, and by the kirk officer", but which yet had been sustained. Apart from dismissing such calls and requiring an adequate number of signatures, the Presbytery should assume the consent of the parishioners unless a majority expressed disapproval. "A majority of dissentient voices should lay a veto on every presentation." A motion by Chalmers to this effect was lost by twelve votes, and instead the Assembly approved one from the Moderate side which required that calls be not sustained only if the objections be found to be well grounded.[2] This retained a factor soon to be lost sight of, the right and duty of Presbyteries to adjudicate. A proposal to petition the King and Parliament against Patronage was also lost.

But the Church was now not merely preparing to meet popular demands; she was also to set about adapting her parochial basis to the needs of a changed Scotland. She now had 82 congregations[3] which had neither parishes of their own nor a place in the church courts. Of these, 40 were the churches recently erected in the Highlands and Islands under the Parliamentary Act of 1824, and the remainder were chapels of ease formed under the Assembly Act of 1798. These last were unendowed; and while they sometimes served districts with populations of 5,000 or 6,000, they lacked the rights of country parishes with only a twentieth of their population. Taken on the whole, their ministers and congregations were committed to the Evangelical party. At the Assembly of 1833 full rights were conceded to the parliamentary churches, but the case of the chapels of ease was referred to a committee.[4] It was argued from the Moderate side that to raise the chapels of ease to parochial status by an Act of Assembly alone was beyond the legal powers of the Church. Correct procedure required an approach to the government for legal action to divide parishes and the obtaining of endowment for the new charges.

[1] H. Watt, op. cit. p. 118.

[2] AGA, 1833, Abridgement, pp. 45–6, 49. J. Bryce, op. cit. i, pp. 15–18.

[3] W. L. Mathieson, op. cit. p. 290.

[4] AGA, 1833, Abridgement, pp. 40–1. R. H. Story, The Church of Scotland, iii, p. 781. Charges formed under this Act were classed as Quoad Sacra, i.e. parishes for church purposes only.

What these events foreshadowed came to pass in the Assembly of 1834. In the years after 1688 Carstares and his successors had, somewhat uncertainly at first but later with complete confidence, established their control of the Church as against those who claimed, not incorrectly, to represent the popular tradition of the Covenanters. But now, for the first time in the memory of man, the control of the Assembly had passed from the Moderates and was securely in the hands of their opponents. They immediately set about implementing their programme without foreseeing the conflicts into which it would lead them and, incidentally, extending their voting power in the Assembly.

The Assembly disregarded the scruples about its legal power and gave the chapels of ease parochial rights.[1] But it was the decision to restore the rights of congregations in the call of a minister which signalized the end of an era and the commencement of the long dispute which was to lead to the division of the Church. Chalmers was not present this year to argue the case but in his place Lord Moncrieff, a son of Sir Henry Moncrieff, put forward and carried by 184 votes to 139 a measure which incorporated Chalmers' earlier proposal for a congregational veto on an unwanted nominee. Instead of declaring that a call must contain an adequate number of signatures to be sustained, the new proposals required that the Church should assume the consent of parishioners unless a majority expressed dissent. Lord Moncrieff's motion declared that it was the fundamental law of the Church that no pastor should be intruded on any congregation contrary to the will of its people. If the majority of male heads of families, being members of the congregation and in full communion, should disapprove of the nominee, this should be accepted by the Presbytery as grounds for refusing to sustain the call.[2] The defeated counter-motion had required that specific objections should be stated in writing so that a Presbytery might cite the parties, hear them, and adjudicate.

This was a revolutionary decree, hastily and emotionally forced through by a party newly come to power after long years in opposition, with consequences all unforeseen. As so often happens,

[1] *AGA*, 1834, Act IX, Abridgement, pp. 55, 61. J. Bryce, op. cit. i, pp. 19–20. R. Buchanan, op. cit. i, pp. 269–90.

[2] *AGA*, 1834, Abridgement, pp. 52–4. R. Buchanan, op. cit. i, pp. 246–69. H. Watt, op. cit. pp. 129, 134.

this revolution took its own course into ways which its first protagonists had not intended, and the attempt to get a clear understanding of the events from 1834 until 1843 is complicated by the fact that all the contemporary witnesses are plagued with an anxiety to testify to the unfailing consistency and orthodoxy of their own party. Before attributing blame to any it is essential to remember that no continuation of the *status quo* was possible in the Scotland of that decade.

This controversy began out of the endeavour of a section of the Church to secure what it held to be the rights of congregations in the choice of a minister, but passed into a contest regarding the spiritual independence of the Church. In Scotland, of all places, theoretically this discussion should have taken place on a Scriptural basis, but, as W. L. Mathieson[1] sardonically says, "the oracle of inspiration, if not dumb on the question of ecclesiastical establishments, was — to say the least — exceedingly obscure". The trouble for the Evangelicals, as for the Covenanters, lay in the fact that the New Testament did not support their case, while the Moderates were troubled by the fact that the Old Testament did not support their case, just as it had not supported that of the seventeenth-century Royalists. Out of this problem came the rather desperate efforts of Dr Inglis to support his case by Old Testament exegesis.[2] Failing to find as clear a case here as they wished, the contestants turned to Scottish Church History and hoped to demonstrate that they stood on the same platform as the Reformers and Covenanters.[3] Propaganda for the Free Church carried pictures of martyrs being burned at the stake and of the signing of the National Covenant. To Robert Buchanan the eighteenth century was "the dark age of the Scottish Church" and the word *moderate* now became only a term of abuse.

As the controversy progressed an impression grew that it had always been one on behalf of popular rights. From the start there were elements seeking the abolition of patronage, but this was far from being the mind of the leaders. Chalmers, in particular, had strong prejudices against democracy. Patronage at the time was working well, and it is noticeable that the legal cases which arose out of the Veto Act proceeded, not on the initiative of

[1] W. L. Mathieson, op. cit. p. 286.
[2] John Inglis, *A Vindication of Ecclesiastical Establishments*, pp. 28–40.
[3] R. Buchanan, op. cit. i, pp. 1–189.

patrons, but of unyielding nominees. "Patrons had begun, very generally," says one of the least partisan writers[1] of the time, "to consult the reasonable wishes of the people; and this Christian and patriotic consideration on their part had not been unappreciated. The Church was lengthening her cords and strengthening her stakes. Intrusion of unacceptable ministers had become a memory of the past — a thing indeed forgotten, except when the zeal of partisanship found it convenient to recall it." Accordingly, the intention of those who sponsored the Veto Act was not the abolition of patronage, but the making of such a concession to popular demands as would be likely to extinguish any resentment of it.[2] "We propose this day," said Lord Moncrieff when moving the Veto Act in the Assembly, "to stem the force of excitement and agitation, which many of us think has been greatly increased by the rejection of this motion in two former Assemblies." "Lord Moncrieff," wrote one of his opponents,[3] "was most strenuously opposed to the abolition of patronage, and one main object which he, and the great mass of his supporters, had in view, was to avoid the necessity of such a result, by providing a check against the felt and practical evils of patronage, conceiving that if these once were removed, the speculative objections entertained by a few, as well as the clamours of the people, would speedily die away, and be no more heard of." It was with the utmost difficulty, he says, that the outright opponents of patronage could be brought to accept the Veto Act, "because they saw that, if once any such measure were brought into operation, they might bid adieu, for ever, to their favourite scheme of abolishing patronage".

From the time of the Assembly debate there were divided minds on the question of the legality of the Veto Act. One of the Judges of the Court of Session had moved it in the Assembly and Lord Brougham, though he later condemned it as Lord Chancellor, spoke of it at the time as wise and salutary; but, significantly, the President of the Court of Session, the Dean of the Faculty of Advocates, and the experienced leaders of the Moderates, Dr Mearns and Dr Cook, questioned its validity. No less than 105 members of Assembly, a phenomenal number,

[1] J. Bryce, op. cit. i, pp. 1–256.
[2] A. Turner, *The Scottish Secession of 1843*, p. 158.
[3] John Hamilton, *Remonstrance to the Members of the Legislature*, pp. 36–40.

entered their dissent. Before taking effect this decision had to be sent down to presbyteries under the Barrier Act, but the Evangelical majority in the Assembly was so impatient that it swept aside the large body of intelligent dissent, voted to make the Veto Act effective from that moment by means of an Interim Act pending approval by presbyteries, and drafted a long series of regulations for the guidance of the church courts in enforcing the new law. The Veto Act of 1834 abandoned the attempt to reinstate[1] the full importance of the call by substituting what seemed a simpler way of satisfying popular demands. Its weakness is obvious; it lay wide open to abuse by an obstinate group of malcontents and — quite apart from any question of its conformity with the law of Scotland — it dispensed with the presbyteries' right and duty to assess objections upon their merits; any popular outcry, whatever its character, could be the final arbiter.

This was intended to be the beginning of a revolution. Among those who supported it the enthusiasm was immense. "These proceedings," wrote the more cautious Lord Cockburn,[2] "have extinguished the old Moderate party. The fabric which it was Robertson's great glory to have reared, and the great object of all his successors in the management of our ecclesiastical affairs to preserve, and which seemed, like Toryism, to be deeply and irremovably founded, has disappeared. The working of the new system I cannot guarantee. It is full of danger certainly. I am only confident that it must be better than the old one." Almost equally significant, in a different way, was the decision to raise funds by public appeal for the building of new churches. The Moderate party, or what was left of it, heard all this without enthusiasm, not so much for the reasons attributed by their victorious opponents, as because they feared that it added yet another danger to the bond between Church and State.

From now on the Scottish Church — or at least a very important section within it — was so thoroughly obsessed by this internal struggle that one might suppose, from reading its historians, that nothing else was happening in Scotland. In point of fact, the Ten Years Conflict, as it was called, roughly coincided with the great new outburst of industrial expansion and all the

---

[1] W. Hanna, *Memoirs of the Life and Writings of Thomas Chalmers*, iii, p. 352.

[2] Lord Cockburn, op. cit. i, p. 61.

social problems which it involved. Between 1796 and 1828 the Scottish output of iron had increased by a little over 100 per cent, but between 1828 and 1838 the increase was over 500 per cent.[1] David Mushet had discovered the vast deposits of blackband ironstone in Old Monkland in 1801, but it remained almost unexploited until the invention of the hot blast by J. B. Neilson in 1828. An immense expansion of the industry now commenced, aided by the very low royalties which the landlords of the west of Scotland, failing to appreciate the new discovery, had demanded, and by the low wage rates secured by the importation of Highlanders and Irishmen who could be used to break strikes.[2] The first to use the hot blast was the Clyde Iron Works of Colin Dunlop, followed by the Calder Iron Works of William Dixon, the Shotts Iron Works, and the Gartsherrie Works of William Baird. Only the long-established Carron Company, profiting well from its highly specialized and successful products, delayed the use of the new process.[3] In 1836 the Dundyvan and Sumerlee Works were opened at Coatbridge and the Coltness Iron Works at Wishaw. In 1838 the Carnbroe Works were also opened there and in 1840 William Dixon opened "Dixon's Blazes" to the south of Gorbals.[4] In May 1841 there were no less than 64 blast furnaces at work in Lanarkshire and 8 more being built. Most of these were in or around Airdrie, Coatbridge, and Wishaw. In north Ayrshire, West Lothian, and Fife much the same was happening. The demand for coal multiplied, and railways were laid down for cheap transport. When the Glasgow to Garnkirk Railway was opened in 1831, with George Stephenson driving the first engine, the cost of carriage of coal to Glasgow in a short time fell from 3s 6d to 1s 3d per ton.[5] A stimulus was provided to the shipbuilding and engineering on the Clyde, and all the subsidiary industries. The new labour forces required housing around the coal pits and foundries. New villages sprang into existence and new towns like Coatbridge sprawled aimlessly across the landscape.

The Church by now was only too well aware of this situation. "Our attention has been drawn to many painful facts," said a

[1] H. Hamilton, *Industrial Revolution in Scotland*, p. 173.
[2] R. H. Campbell, *Scotland since 1707*.
[3] R. H. Campbell, *Carron Company*, p. 201.
[4] H. Hamilton, op. cit. p. 184.   [5] Ibid. p. 246,

pastoral letter of the Assembly[1] of 1835, "all of which must in a great measure be traced to neglect or remissness in the discharge of the great duties of our Christian stewardship. The result of all our inquiries impresses on us more and more the appalling consideration, that in all the most populous districts of the kingdom, multitudes are passing onward to eternity, in utter ignorance of the only way of salvation, and many thousands of children are growing up to manhood, without being brought up in the nurture and admonition of the Lord; and we dare not acquit ourselves of the guilt of having failed to provide the means which it might have been in the power of our hand to employ, for averting or removing these growing evils." It was stated in an Assembly resolution of 1838 that in Glasgow and Edinburgh alone there were 100,000 adults among the poorest classes who were totally estranged from the Christian faith.[2] Nor could it be claimed that all was well in the countryside. It was reported to the Assembly of 1836 that in the Presbytery of Uist there was a parish with a population of 3,000, all except two being professing Protestants, but where only 450 were known to attend church and where only 14 were communicants. The Lord's Supper had been celebrated only three times in this parish since 1825, but there was a neighbouring parish where it had been celebrated only once in that time, and another in which it had only once been celebrated since 1818.[3] A long endeavour to adapt the parochial structure of the Church to the changing situation went on simultaneously with the struggle for congregational rights.

In 1828 the Church had been disturbed about "the evils resulting from the inadequate state of Church accommodation in many of the large towns, manufacturing villages, and populous parishes of the country" and had formed an Assembly Committee[4] to bring the matter to the attention of the government. But this committee did nothing very much until the Assembly of 1833 added the name of Chalmers to its membership, and urged it to raise funds. Here was a notable point of departure from precedent. Formerly it had been inconceivable that churches should be built or maintained within the National Church on any basis other than the support of the community. To this the chapels

---

[1] *AGA*, 1835, p. 45.   [2] *AGA*, 1838, Abridgement, p. 43.
[3] *AGA*, 1836, Abridgement, p. 65.
[4] *AGA*, 1828, Abridgement, p. 36.

of ease had been the first exception. Now it was proposed to raise
funds by private contributions as had been done for Foreign
Missions.[1] Next year the committee was made permanent, all
ministers were instructed to take collections for it, and Chalmers
was appointed convener.[2] The Church Building Society of
Glasgow, formed by William Collins, the publisher, proposed to
build twenty new churches in the city and in their first year raised
£20,000. The Assembly committee followed this example but also
took the traditional line of seeking endowment for the new
churches from the government. For a little while[3] it seemed that
there would be a response, but the very prospect of this brought
a violent reaction from the Seceders.

An interminable wrangle then started, with no prospect of
agreement. From the start the Assembly's case was compromised
by the fact that it was urged upon totally wrong grounds. It was
argued that the existing churches did not provide seating accommodation for the people, whereas the true case was that
pastoral work was urgently needed in the overcrowded areas in
which the parish ministers could not cope with the demands
upon them. Two concepts of the Church were involved, but not
clearly stated. For the National Church the parish was a sphere
of responsibility and evangelism and the territorial base for a
congregation; to the Seceders a congregation was a group of committed worshippers drawn together without respect to parish
bounds. Unfortunately the situation was complicated by that
growing bitterness which has already been noted in Andrew
Thomson. The language of churchmen in controversy became
more and more acrid and uncharitable. Discourtesy and intransigence separated the contestants until any hope of compromise
or agreement had gone and the uncommitted spectator became
indifferent or contemptuous. First arising between the National
Church and the Seceders, this controversial spirit next appeared
in the debates between leaders of the two parties in the Church,
filtered down into the ranks of the members, and became almost
a permanent feature of the Scottish scene with the Disruption in
1843. For the better part of a century this animosity was only too
real a factor in Church life in Scotland. Because of it almost

[1] *AGA*, 1833, Abridgement, p. 53.
[2] *AGA*, 1834, Abridgement, pp. 53–4.
[3] W. L. Mathieson, op. cit. p. 294.

everything that was said or written by men about those who differed from them during the "Ten Years Conflict" must be heavily discounted. Even today when an adverse judgment is passed, the writer must search his own mind as to whether he has allowed the atmosphere of controversy to corrupt his own judgment. When all allowance is made for this, it does not seem unjust to attribute the opposition of the Seceders at this time to anything other than small-minded motives. It is easy to understand in the changed atmosphere of today why men should object to having payment made in their name to a Church in which they have no part, but until now the Seceders had never verged from the traditional Scottish position which saw the maintenance of the Church as a public responsibility. It was only the fact that new life was stirring in the National Church and that she was tackling her responsibilities which made them abandon their traditional ground. Faced with their violent opposition, the government, which was not over anxious in any case, withdrew support. From now on it turned a deaf ear to the Assembly's spokesmen.

Faced with the clamour from Scotland, in 1836 the government set up a Royal Commission on the facilities for worship in Scotland, and at this point the Church made its second error, even if a lesser one, by attacking the composition of the Commission, though not without reason. "This meeting of the Commission of the Assembly," wrote Lord Cockburn,[1] "was held chiefly for the purpose of abusing the late commission of inquiry into the statistics of the Church. The objection to it is, that of the six working and travelling commissioners, three are understood not to be friendly to the Establishment — a well-founded objection, which I regret the Government did not avoid. It has given great dissatisfaction to the Church, which as usual has spoiled a good cause by violence of language. The Dissenters should certainly have been represented in the commission, but the Establishment ought to have had a majority of those who were to travel and to collect the facts." But an enquiry on this basis was bound to prove unsatisfactory to the Church, and the outcome fully confirmed this, since it plainly showed that sittings in churches were far from being fully let or occupied. To the great

[1] Lord Cockburn, op. cit. i, p. 101. W. Hanna, op. cit. iii, pp. 471–87. *AGA*, 1835, Abridgement, pp. 77, 80–2.

indignation of Chalmers, his cause did not get unanimous support from the Church, for Dr Lee of Edinburgh represented before the Commission an indifference to parochial work and a satisfaction with the congregational nature of the Church not unlike that of the Seceders.

Defeated in his appeal to a remote government, Chalmers met with astonishing success in his appeal for popular support for Church Extension. At the close of his first year as convener he was able to report to the Assembly that over £66,000 had been raised and that no less than 64 churches had been or were being built.[1] In four years the committee raised £206,000 and built 187 churches, and in the seven years of Chalmers' convenership the totals reached £306,000 and 222 churches. The lesson could hardly be lost on any spectator when this was compared with the small results of the parliamentary act of 1824. Until this time the Church of Scotland had depended upon her endowments while congregational givings went to the poor. It was the appeal for Foreign Missions which first showed how great could be the response from its members for the needs of the Church. The endowments still remained, but between 1834 and 1839 the givings of congregations for the general work of the Church multiplied fourteen times.

When the Veto Act was passed in the Assembly of 1834 among the reasons of dissent was a detailed one from John Hope,[2] the Dean of the Faculty of Advocates, questioning the legal character of the Assembly's decision. Described by the Free Church historian as "the author of the Disruption" and by Henry Dundas as "that crocodile Hope",[3] he argued that whatever effect the veto could have it could not deprive the nominee of the right to the benefice, as distinct from the pastoral duties. Hope's dissent had not long to wait upon a legal test, and with this came the next stage in the intensification of the dispute.

At the close of 1834 the parish of Auchterarder fell vacant and the patron, the Earl of Kinnoul, presented Robert Young. Neither then nor thereafter was anything said against his character,[4] but Auchterarder was a district where the movement for the outright

---

[1] R. Buchanan, op. cit. i, pp. 302–3, 307.
[2] R. Buchanan, op. cit. i, p. 269.
[3] W. L. Mathieson, op. cit. p. 199.
[4] Fasti, ii, pp. 748–50.

abolition of patronage had been strong, so his call was immediately opposed merely because he was not the choice of the congregation. Only two parishioners signed the call, while 286 male heads of families out of 330 expressed disapproval. On an appeal from Young the Assembly of 1835 instructed the Presbytery to proceed in terms of the Veto Act, and accordingly they rejected the nominee. The Earl of Kinnoul stood aside from the dispute, but Young, who must have been a peculiarly strong-minded man, determined to carry the case to its limits. He consulted Hope, and on his advice obtained from the Court of Session an *act of declarator* that the Presbytery was bound to take him on trials and, if found qualified, to induct him. It was an appeal, from within the Church, to a civil court. On 8 March 1838 the court delivered its verdict by a majority of eight to five, Lord Moncrieff, the mover of the Veto Act in the Assembly, being among the minority. In effect, the Court of Session held that the Assembly had acted *ultra vires* and infringed the civil rights of patrons and presentees. In the course of the proceedings, to the great joy of the Seceders and the humiliation of the Evangelicals, the conception of the Church as an independent spiritual community had been repudiated; as a national establishment it drew its powers from Acts of Parliament and was "wholly of statutory jurisdiction". The fact that simultaneously the bicentenary of the Covenanting Assembly of 1638 was being celebrated, and that McCrie's lives of Knox and Melville were being widely read, only added fuel to the flames.

The Auchterarder case then went to the House of Lords, which again upheld Robert Young's claim[1] on 2 May 1839. Lord Brougham commented that the call of the people was no more essential than the arrival of the horse of the King's Champion at Westminster Hall at the coronation. "The House of Lords," wrote Lord Cockburn,[2] "has affirmed the judgement of the Court of Session in the case of Auchterarder. There never was a greater cause adjudged in the House of Lords on reasons more utterly unworthy of both. . . . The ignorance and contemptuous slightness of the judgement did great mischief. It irritated and justified the people of Scotland in believing that their Church was sacrificed to English prejudices. The successful party laments that the mere

[1] R. Buchanan, op. cit. i, pp. 421–33.
[2] Lord Cockburn, op. cit. i, pp. 225–6, 169.

affirmance is all it has gained. We shall soon see what the Church means to do." Elsewhere he observed, "Scotland won't hear the last of this Auchterarder case for the next century." For years the case drifted on through the church and civil courts since neither party was prepared to give way until Robert Young was inducted after the Disruption. "His congregation daily increased in numbers, and many of those who had been his bitter opponents became his warmest advisers and best friends. And at his death on 15 September 1865 the whole parish mourned for him with unfeigned sorrow." But that, as Kipling says, is another story.

It was now evident that the Dean of Faculty's dissent from the Act of 1834 had unexpectedly strong legal support. The Evangelical party, so recently come to power in the Assembly and launched on a career of reform, thus found itself confronted with an unforeseen obstacle in its hour of victory, for the government, which had refused to meet the demands for an extension of the parochial system, was equally indifferent to the demand for popular rights in congregations. More heed was paid to Lord Durham's report on Canadian troubles than to the deputations which came south from Scotland. As passions rose it was determined among the Evangelical majority in the Assembly not to compromise or to procrastinate but to state the dispute in terms of the fundamental nature of the Church as a spiritual community possessing her own internal discipline. While the jurisdiction of the civil courts in relation to the civil rights and emoluments of the Church and its ministers was admitted, the Church's spiritual oversight was claimed as her own responsibility. "The Lord Jesus Christ," said a resolution of the Assembly[1] of 1838, quoting the Westminster Confession, "as King and Head of the Church, hath therein appointed a government in the hands of Church officers distinct from the civil magistrate . . . which 'power ecclesiastical (in the words of the Second Book of Discipline) flows immediately from God, and the Mediator Jesus Christ, and is Spiritual, not having a temporal head on earth, but only Christ the only Spiritual King and Governor of His Kirk'; and they do farther resolve, that this spiritual jurisdiction, and the supremacy and sole headship of the Lord Jesus Christ, on which it depends, they will assert and at all hazards defend, by the help and blessing of that Great God Who, in the days of old, enabled their fathers,

[1] *AGA*, 1838, Abridgement, p. 45.

amid manifold persecutions, to maintain a testimony even to the death, for Christ's kingdom and crown; and finally that they will enforce submission to the same upon Office-bearers and Members of this Church, by the execution of her laws, in the exercise of the ecclesiastical authority wherewith they are invested." The prevailing excitement, the appeal to Scottish history and the Covenant in particular, the new intransigence, and the will to state differences in terms of high principle are all evident in this document.

Any account of the Scottish Church during these years which failed to make plain how widespread and intense was the passion caused by these events would be grossly misleading. One party to the dispute, at least, was convinced that it dealt with no small issues, but the nature of the Kingdom of God and the Church of Christ. Nor was this conviction confined to them, for it was shared by some of their opponents who were prepared to wait for legal redress, even though others were inclined to dismiss the Evangelicals as hairbrained enthusiasts carried away by oratory and fanaticism. From the crucial year of 1834 onwards a series of disputes broke out in vacant parishes, at Kilmarnock, Urr, Trinity Gask, Dreghorn, Dron, Eskdalemuir, and elsewhere, Auchterarder being only one of the best-known cases. From the fact that many ministers nominated by patrons gave up their parishes and went into the Free Church at the Disruption it seems clear that most patrons were quite ready to nominate Evangelicals where congregations so desired. But whatever may have been said to the contrary, the character or party of the nominee was not the point at issue in these disputes, for the bone of contention was the inherent right of the congregation to make its own choice; or so it was felt.

At Lethendy in the Presbytery of Dunkeld a probationer, Thomas Clark, was presented by the crown on 8 June 1835 as assistant and successor to the aging minister.[1] This had been done at the request of a substantial number of parishioners after he had preached in the church for some time. But by the time his call came before the Presbytery they had changed their minds, probably because they had detected the drunkenness with which he was later charged. He appealed, but in vain,[2] against the Presbytery's decision, in keeping with the Veto Act, not to sustain

---

[1] *Fasti*, II, pp. 805–6.   [2] *AGA*, 1836, Abridgement, pp. 84–5.

the call. In January 1837 the old minister died, so that there was
a regular vacancy. Two steps were now taken; Clark raised against
the Presbytery an action to be taken on trials for ordination and
claimed the stipend; and the crown, having accepted the Presbytery's action in this case, presented Andrew Kessen. As in the
Auchterarder case, there were long legal proceedings until the
Commission of Assembly took the audacious step of instructing
the Presbytery to defy the Court of Session, to induct Kessen to
the parish, and to discipline Clark.[1] A counter-motion, urging
delay and caution in view of the troubles at Auchterarder, was
dismissed. By the casting vote of its Moderator the Presbytery
agreed to ordain and induct Kessen and did so on 13 September
1838, despite a warning from the Dean of Faculty that by their
action they rendered themselves liable to imprisonment.[2] On
14 June 1839 the Presbytery had to appear at the bar of the Court
of Session. After considerable discussion and a very even division
of opinion among the judges[3] it was decided to rebuke them and
advise that a repetition of this offence by any other Presbytery
would lead to imprisonment. They were obliged to pay Clark
costs to the amount of £346.

Not merely was this a further stage of deterioration in that a
Presbytery had defied a ruling of the civil court and had been
disciplined, but in his rebuke the Lord President said, "As for
those ministers of the Church whose conscience cannot submit
to the law; so long as it remains the law, I am afraid nothing
remains for those ministers but to retire from the Established
Church. It is impossible that they should remain ministers of the
Established Church, and yet reject the law by which they became
an Established Church. That great and good man, Ebenezer
Erskine, a hundred years ago, did not so think . . . and as he did
not think that he could conscientiously submit to the law, he
withdrew from the Church and founded the Secession; but alas!
I see no remedy. Either they must submit to the law, or they must
retire from the Church."[4]

At Marnoch in Aberdeenshire a case, in some ways similar, but

[1] *AGA*, Commission, 1838, Abridgement, pp. 61–2.
[2] R. Buchanan, op. cit. ii, pp. 8–17. *AGA*, Commission, 1839, p. 59.
[3] Lord Cockburn, op. cit. i, pp. 233–4. D. K. Guthrie and C. J. Guthrie,
Autobiography and Memoir of Thomas Guthrie, D.D., p. 352.
[4] H. Watt, *Thomas Chalmers and the Disruption*, p. 190.

in one respect very different, arose in 1837 when the patron nominated to the charge John Edwards, formerly schoolmaster of Grange, and for the previous three years assistant to the older minister of Marnoch.[1] As he was opposed by the majority of male communicants his case also passed through the church courts and came to the Assembly on 25 May 1838, only to be lost again. The patron now nominated David Henry. In his turn Edwards appealed to the Court of Session which again found in his favour. But whereas there had been a majority in the Presbytery of Dunkeld prepared to defy the Court of Session, the Presbytery of Strathbogie, to which Marnoch belonged, had a majority of Moderates prepared to obey the Court and defy the Assembly.[2] Though the Commission of Assembly had suspended all members of the Presbytery who had not dissociated themselves from its actions the seven who constituted the majority ordained and inducted Edwards to the charge. It was 21 January 1841 when they did so. The snow lay deep on the ground but a crowd estimated to number 2,000 had gathered in and around the church. As the Presbytery began the service the congregation, almost to a man, rose out of their seats, lifted their Bibles from the pews, and went out in silence.[3] For this act of ecclesiastical insubordination they were deposed by the Assembly of 1841 on the motion of Chalmers. The ordination of Edwards was declared null and void and his licence withdrawn.[4] At this point the Assembly was startled to learn that a messenger-at-arms was at the door to serve an interdict upon the Moderator, Clerk, Procurator, and Law Agent of the Church. It delayed hearing this until the Lord High Commissioner, temporarily absent from the hall, could return. "In circumstances so peculiar and so critical," it resolved, "this Assembly is solemnly called to protest against this violent intrusion of the secular arm into the ecclesiastical province, and to represent this most alarming state of matters to the rulers and legislators of this great nation, on whom must rest the responsibility of upholding the Established Church in the full possession of all her scriptural and constitutional rights; that, with this view these resolutions ought to be transmitted to her Majesty the Queen in Council."

[1] *Fasti*, III, pp. 208–9.   [2] *AGA*, Commission, 1839, pp. 60–3.
[3] T. Brown, *Annals of the Disruption*, pp. 22–4.
[4] *AGA*, 1841, pp. 44, 46, 48–52.

Though muddled in his reference to Ebenezer Erskine, the Lord President had clearly pointed out in his comment on the Lethendy case the dilemma confronting ministers where a dispute arose. They must choose between the commands of the Church and those of the Law. As the situation worsened the Assembly of 1839 appointed a committee to consider "in what ways the privileges of the National Establishment, and the harmony between Church and State, may remain unimpaired, with instructions to confer with the Government of the country if they should see cause".[1] Armed with documents, the committee went south to interview Lord Melbourne, who gave them an assurance about the exercise of crown patronage — about one-third of that of all Scotland — but evaded their main purpose, a promise of change in the law. When he reported to the Commission of Assembly in August, Chalmers[2] still seems to have hoped for government action, but when none appeared the committee approached Lord Aberdeen in January 1840. He accepted the principle of non-intrusion up to a point, and here, it seems, there was some misunderstanding between him and Chalmers. On 5 April 1840 he introduced in the House of Lords[3] a bill "for removing doubts in the settlement of vacant parishes in Scotland".

It seemed for a moment that Lord Aberdeen's proposals would satisfy the Evangelicals. One who sympathized[4] with them but did not go out at the Disruption wrote later that, "having at the time the opportunity of frequent intercourse with many who had been zealous in defence of popular rights", he could assert that "many of those who afterwards opposed were, at the first, and while unbiassed by sinister interpretations, satisfied with its provisions, and hailed it as a measure which was to bring peace to a distracted Church". But Chalmers had come to a different opinion. Lord Aberdeen's bill required that the Presbytery should be able to assess and judge the objections offered, while Chalmers demanded that they should decide merely upon the fact that the congregation objected.[5] The writer quoted above tells how when the provisions of the bill became known in Glasgow he met a friend, who later became a minister of the Free Church, and the

[1] *AGA*, 1839, p. 40.   [2] J. Bryce, op. cit. i, pp. 160–1.
[3] A. Turner, op. cit. pp. 223–43. W. Hanna, op. cit. iv, pp. 151–74.
[4] A. Turner, op. cit. p. 233.
[5] W. Hanna, op. cit. iv, pp. 151–74.

two agreed that Lord Aberdeen's bill was satisfactory and that they should organize support for it. "We were just commencing when the orthodox interpretation arrived from the East. It was given by one who spoke with authority – by one whom both my friend and I respected. His interpretation did not alter my views. . . . It was otherwise, however, with my friend." On 10 July, in answer to a question from the Duke of Richmond, Lord Aberdeen[1] replied that "he had come to the conclusion, although very reluctantly, that it would not be expedient for him to press the third reading of the bill during the present session". Despite the argument of the Free Church spokesman that the abandonment of the bill was because of political reasons it is hard to believe that it was not due, in the first instance, to the attitude of Chalmers. It was at this juncture that first a few, and then others, began to detach themselves from the Evangelicals with whom, apart from questions of tactics, they had much in common and become known as the Middle Party.[2]

On 6 May 1841 the Duke of Argyll[3] again introduced a bill in the House of Lords akin to that of Lord Aberdeen, but extending the right of signing the veto from male heads of families to all male communicants aged 21 or over, and providing that the veto could be set aside if due to factiousness or prejudice alone. This was little more than a legalizing of the Veto Act of 1834 and the Moderate party therefore declined to accept it. A Modification proposed by Sir George Sinclair was rejected by Chalmers[4] so the Duke of Argyll's bill made no progress until 14 April 1842 when Mr Campbell of Monzie obtained leave to introduce it in the House of Commons. On 4 May, when the second reading was about to begin, a member of the Cabinet informed Mr Campbell that the government was seriously considering a measure of their own which was likely to satisfy the Church. The second reading was therefore delayed. From Sir James Graham, the Home Secretary, it was learned that the government proposals were substantially those of Lord Aberdeen. When Mr Campbell's[5] bill was

[1] R. Buchanan, op. cit. ii, p. 120.
[2] A. Turner, op. cit. pp. 241–3. J. F. Leishman, *Matthew Leishman of Govan*, pp. 106–64.
[3] R. Buchanan, op. cit. ii, p. 218. *AGA*, 1841, Abridgement, pp. 41–2.
[4] W. Hanna, op. cit. iv, pp. 237–43.
[5] R. Buchanan, op. cit. ii, pp. 338–43, 381–3. W. Hanna, op. cit. iv, p. 302.

reintroduced in June it had to be withdrawn on a newly raised point of procedure and the government failed to produce its own promised measure. Thus the crisis drew nearer.

When the Assembly[1] of 1842 met, with the Marquis of Bute as Lord High Commissioner, disputed commissions from both sides of the troubled Presbytery of Strathbogie and a string of disciplinary cases told of the distractions of the Church. At the Assembly of 1841 a motion calling for the abolition of patronage[2] had been defeated by no more than six votes and in 1842 opinion had so swung round that this time it was carried by 216 votes to 147. Patronage was declared to be a grievance which "has been attended with much injury to the cause of true religion in this Church and Kingdom, is the main cause of the difficulties in which the Church is at present involved, and ought to be abolished". A committee was appointed to prepare petitions on the subject to both Houses of Parliament, and an address to the Queen.[3] A declaration[4] "against the unconstitutional encroachments of the Civil Courts" was next read, and a counter motion calling for the repeal of the Veto Act, condemning the recent agitation, and recommending Lord Aberdeen's proposal was lost to it by 241 votes to 111.

On 24 May Dr Chalmers moved in the Assembly the adoption of the document known as "The Claim of Right".[5] This remarkable statement of the Church's case, drawn up mainly by Alexander Murray Dunlop,[6] a lawyer of strongly evangelical conviction, runs to almost 5,000 words. It declared that the position of the Church of Scotland, though guaranteed by the statutes of the realm, the constitution of the land, the Treaty of Union, and the oath of each successive sovereign had been threatened by that civil court to which the Church rightfully looked for protection. It declared that it was an essential doctrine of the Church that it had no head but the Lord Jesus Christ. Next came a résumé of the law of church and State in Scotland from the Reformation till the Treaty of Union, a denunciation of the Act of 1712 as an

[1] W. Hanna, op. cit. iv, pp. 291ff.

[2] AGA, 1841, pp. 39–40.

[3] AGA, 1842, XII, Abridgement, pp. 61–2.

[4] Ibid. pp. 62–3.

[5] W. Hanna, op. cit. iv, pp. 296, 299, 528–47. R. Buchanan, op. cit. ii, pp. 357–80.　　　　　　　　[6] Disruption Worthies, pp. 251–8.

infringement of the Treaty against which the Church had continually protested, and a summary of the more recent decisions of the Court of Session. By these last acts "the Court of Session, apparently not adverting to the oath taken by the Sovereign, from whom they hold their commissions, have exercised powers not conferred upon them by the constitution, but by it excluded from the province of any secular tribunal". Therefore, however much the Church valued her connection with the State, she claimed the right to possess her lawful liberties. She would not intrude ministers on unwilling congregations or carry on church government on the instructions of the Court of Session. She denounced the infringement of the Treaty of Union. All her actions, it was claimed, sprang from her determination to recognize Christ alone as the Head of the Church.

In January 1843 the Church was still further disturbed by an interdict obtained by the heritors of Stewarton against the admission of Mr Clelland, the Burgher minister at Stewarton, as a member of the Presbytery of Irvine as a result of the reunion of his church with the Church of Scotland.[1] This decision not merely displaced all the ministers of the former chapels of ease from their place in the church courts and removed the standing of their sessions, but it threw into doubt every decision of the Assembly since the fateful year of 1834. It made little difference. The die had already been cast. The Claim of Right[2] was a skilfully drafted document, too long and intricate to be mastered at a brief reading. Its adoption committed the Church to the Disruption which was about to come and it finally alienated the government from taking any action to prevent that event.

The Claim of Right had been transmitted — after a warning by the Lord High Commissioner that this did not imply acceptance— to the Queen, but as no acknowledgment had been received when the Commission[3] met in November 1842 the government was sent a reminder, and on 4 January Sir James Graham,[4] in an official reply which described the Claim as unreasonable, intimated that the government "could not advise her Majesty to acquiesce in

[1] W. L. Mathieson, op. cit. p. 364. R. Buchanan, op. cit. ii, pp. 403–12.
[2] For the text of the "Claim of Right" and other Disruption documents, cf. *Authorised Standards of the Free Church*, pp. 339–75.
[3] *AGA*, Commission, 1842–3, Abridgement, p. 64.
[4] A. Turner, op. cit. pp. 331–6.

these demands". As a last resort a petition was laid before the House of Commons by Fox Maule on 10 February, but on 8 March — after a two-day debate — the House declined give to it further consideration. By this time all hope of a negotiated settlement had gone.

CHAPTER TWELVE

The Disruption

All that now remained for the Evangelicals was to prepare for the day of parting and to muster the maximum support possible. Thirty-two of their leading ministers circularized all possible supporters to invite them to attend a Convention which was to be held in Edinburgh on the day following the November meeting of the Commission of Assembly.[1] A preparatory meeting was held on 17 November in St George's Church in Charlotte Square, not merely for divine worship but to warm the hearts of the faithful and to strengthen any faltering supporters. The men conducting the service were carefully chosen. Thomas Chalmers preached and a lesser known man, but one of tremendous influence among church people in the Highlands, Dr John McDonald[2] of Ferintosh, led the gathering in prayer. Known as the "Apostle of the North", he was a man whom the Evangelicals beyond the Great Glen, and in Ross-shire especially, could be expected to follow into the Free Church. Those present then adjourned to meet again in the Roxburgh Church, a small building in an obscure street. There were 465 ministers crowded into its limited accommodation. No minutes were kept and the proceedings were private. It was known, however, that careful procedural arrangements were made to permit representatives from each Synod to speak, and while each was encouraged to commit himself to the cause there was an endeavour to maintain unanimity. As a result a statement of the Church's grievances was signed by 423 ministers. A second statement then was prepared, the signatories to which undertook, if need be, to resign their offices and endowments and to enter the Free Church. Some added their names afterwards, but this time a smaller number of signatures was obtained, 354 out of the 465

[1] R. Buchanan, *The Ten Years' Conflict*, ii, p. 388.
[2] *Disruption Worthies*, pp. 49–54.

originally present, a difference, said the official apologist, due to the fact that many had had to go home.[1] A public meeting was held on 24 November in Lady Glenorchy's Church to make public the decisions of the Convention. An "Address to the People of Scotland" was drafted and printed, and a statement sent to the government.

From now onwards preparations for the coming division of the Church began to be made at congregational level. Committees were formed in parishes to make financial preparations, with the minister as chairman where he intended to join the Free Church. Minutes of their meetings were kept, and it will sometimes be found that these committee minute books have continued to be kept as the first volume of the kirk session minutes of the new congregation. From the start they are distinguished from the minutes of a parish kirk session by the fact that their main concern is the financial support of the congregation. This was the case at Prestonpans where an active minority of the congregation intended to follow the minister, W. B. Cunningham, into the Free Church. Ill-will naturally multiplied in the divided congregation as the day of the Disruption drew nearer and one Sunday, as Cunningham preached on the subject, Sir George Grant Suttie, the laird of Preston Grange, left his pew, hurried to the session house for paper, pen and ink and returned to take notes of the offending sermon. On the Monday he sent his estate joiner to the nearby parish church of Tranent to have two seats fitted up in the gallery there, one for himself, and the other for his tenants at Dolphington. There he worshipped until the Disruption, when he returned to Prestonpans. This congregation, like others, received weekly communications from the central committee, and adopted Dr Chalmers' proposals for a Sustentation Fund[2] to pay such stipend as was possible once they had abandoned their endowments. On 12 May 1843, before the Assembly met, they had arranged to worship for the time being in the malt barn of the local distillery, had received the gift of a site, and ordered plans for a church.[3]

[1] R. Buchanan, op. cit. ii, p. 397. W. Wilson, *Memorials of R. S. Candlish*, pp. 219–59. T. Brown states that the number of 354 was ultimately increased to 480 (*Annals of the Disruption*, pp. 52–3).

[2] W. Hanna, *Memoirs of the Life and Writings of Thomas Chalmers*, iv, pp. 551–71.   [3] MS. Kirk Session Records, Grange Church, Prestonpans.

But at this moment of crisis the Evangelical party, which had controlled the Assembly for a decade, felt uncertainty as to whether it could retain its grip.[1] The Evangelicals had been confident that they could muster a majority vote in the Assembly so that the Disruption would have the character of a rejection by the Church of the humiliations forced upon her by the State. Their party would then be seen as the Church in her new-found freedom and it would be open to them "to excommunicate those who remained in the Church as by law established".[2] The first blow to their hopes had been the refusal of the so-called "Middle Party", led by Leishman of Govan, sometimes known as "the Forty", but actually numbering 45, to accept the invitation to join the Convention. Instead they had held their own counter meeting in the Waterloo Hotel.[3] In addition, as the Evangelicals had run into unexpected legal difficulties, it had occurred to some of their opponents that their majority in the Assembly might be eroded by legal expedients. In January 1843 the decision in the Stewarton case meant that the ministers of all *Quoad Sacra* charges might be withheld from seats in the church courts. Of the 162 such ministers 91 went into the Free Church at the Disruption and many of the remaining 71 were held to be strongly sympathetic, so that this was a heavy loss.[4] Presbyteries were deeply divided and there were cases where two competing lists of commissioners[5] were sent up to the Assembly from different meetings, each claiming to be the Presbytery. In these alarming circumstances the Evangelicals decided to take no risks, to abandon this part of their policy, and to anticipate the constitution of the Assembly while their man was still in the chair.

On the day of the Assembly the Lord High Commissioner, once again the Marquis of Bute, held the customary levee at Holyroodhouse. An unusually large throng filled the throne room and jostled each other in the limited space before Lord Bute until the picture of King William[6] was dislodged and fell to the floor.

[1] A. Turner, *The Scottish Secession of 1843*, pp. 349–50. J. Bryce, *The Church of Scotland, 1833–1843*, ii, pp. 353–5. R. Buchanan, op. cit. ii, pp. 431–3.
[2] Donald MacLeod, *Memoir of Norman MacLeod*, p. 120. W. Wilson, *Memorials of R. S. Candlish*, p. 280.
[3] J. F. Leishman, *Matthew Leishman of Govan*, p. 153.
[4] A. Turner, op. cit. p. 360.
[5] H. Watt, *Thomas Chalmers and the Disruption*, pp. 288–9.
[6] W. Hanna, op. cit. iv, p. 336.

"There," said Mr Houieson Craufurd of Kilmarnock, "goes the Revolution Settlement." About 2.30 in the afternoon the sound of a military band told the crowd around St Andrew's Church in George Street, where the Assembly was to be held, that the service in the High Kirk of St Giles had ended and that the Commissioner was about to arrive. Thousands had been waiting for hours to see the outcome. Dr Welsh, the retiring moderator, took the opening prayer, but at this point, instead of constituting the Assembly as was customary, he avoided the danger of a vote by declaring that, because of the infringements of the Church's liberty, he protested against proceeding further. It was lawful for them to withdraw to a separate place of meeting and to separate from the Establishment; "and we now withdraw accordingly, humbly and solemnly acknowledging the hand of the Lord in the things which have come upon us, because of our manifold sins, and the sins of the Church and nation; but, at the same time, with assured conviction that we are not responsible for any consequences that may follow from this our enforced separation from an Establishment which we loved and prized, through interference with conscience, the dishonour done to Christ's crown, and the rejection of His sole and supreme authority as King in His Church." He then laid this protest, which had been signed by 203 commissioners, upon the table, turned and bowed to the Lord High Commissioner, and left the meeting.

Chalmers had been sitting, apparently lost in thought, but on this he collected himself, got up and followed Dr Welsh. Other leaders of the Evangelicals joined him and the whole party began steadily to file out of their seats till all one side of the building and some of the cross benches were empty. As they came out of the door of the church into George Street there had been no plan to form an orderly column, but the crowd so pressed upon them that they were obliged to walk in a column four deep. Almost a quarter of a mile long, the procession slowly made its way along George Street and down Hanover Street. The Lord Provost of Edinburgh walked down the hill with them and at Canonmills they were joined by the former Lord Provost of Glasgow and the Sheriff of Midlothian.[1]

At Canonmills the newly built Tanfield Hall — now part of the printing works of Morrison and Gibb — had been prepared for

[1] Lord Cockburn, *Journal*, ii, p. 26.

their coming. Between members of Assembly and the public some 3,000 persons were reckoned to be crowded into the hall when Dr Welsh opened the Assembly with prayer. He called for the election of Thomas Chalmers as Moderator, and as they stood to sing the opening psalm,

> O send Thy light forth and Thy truth,
> Let them be guides to me,
> And bring me to Thine holy hill,
> Ev'n where Thy dwellings be.

a ray of sunlight broke through the glass skylights which till now had been shadowed by storm clouds, and reminded many of Chalmers' text at the Convention, "Unto the upright there ariseth light in the darkness."[1]

David Octavius Hill had been commissioned to execute a painting of the great gathering at Tanfield Hall. Engravings of it were made and distributed all over the country so that every district might see the faces of its own ministers and elders side by side with the leaders of the cause in their hour of sacrifice and triumph. As a painter, the artist had few merits, but in his anxiety to obtain complete accuracy he took a long series of photographs of commissioners which constitute a landmark in the early history of photography. It is no disparagement of the fathers of the Free Church to say that this great event had been very well stage managed. They had taken an immense, if calculated, risk and they had no intention of letting their case pass by default. Their action stirred the public mind, and was intended to do so for the good of their cause. If the leaders of the Disruption may privately have been a little disappointed that the numbers of their clergy were not slightly greater, the number who went out into the Free Church was greater by far than those not directly involved in the struggle had ever anticipated.

"I know no parallel to it," wrote Lord Cockburn.[2] "Whatever may be thought of their cause, there can be no doubt or coldness in the admiration with which all candid men must applaud their heroism. They have abandoned that public station which was the ambition of their lives, and have descended from certainty to precariousness, and most of them from comfort to destitution,

---

[1] W. Hanna, op. cit. iv, pp. 335-41. Robert Buchanan, op. cit. ii, pp. 441-6.
[2] Lord Cockburn, op. cit. ii, p. 30.

solely for their principles. And the loss of the stipend is the least of it. The dismantling of the manse, the breaking up of all the objects to which the hearts and the habits of the family were attached, the shutting the gate for the last time of the little garden, the termination of all their interest in the humble but respectable kirk — even all these desolations, though they may excite the most immediate pangs, are not the calamities which the head of the house finds it hardest to sustain. It is the loss of station that is the deep and lasting sacrifice, the ceasing to be the most important man in the parish, the closing of the doors of the gentry against him and his family, the altered prospects of his children, the extinction of everything that the State had provided for the decent dignity of the manse and its inmates." He was even more impressed by the fact that 200 probationers abandoned the sudden prospect of desirable charges to join in the Free Church.

There are discrepancies about the number who took part in the procession to Canonmills, apparently because some men changed their minds on both sides on the opening day. According to Lord Cockburn[1] "193 members moved off, of whom 123 were ministers, and about 70 elders. Among these were many upon whose figures the public eye had been long accustomed to rest in reverence. They all withdrew slowly and regularly amidst perfect silence, till that side of the house was left nearly empty. They were joined outside by a large body of adherents, among whom were about 300 clergymen." The signatures of all concerned may be read in the documents of the Free Church. Chalmers' biographer[2] states that 470 ministers signed the deed of demission. A comprehensive analysis[3] published in 1844 gives the following figures.

The number of clergy in the Kirk of Scotland including the *Quoad Sacra* ministers was	1203
The number which adhered to the Church was	752
(This included 23 assistants and successors)	
The number which seceded was	451
(This included 17 assistants and successors)	
Thus showing a majority remaining in the Church of	301

[1] Ibid. ii, p. 21.
[2] W. Hanna, op. cit. iv, p. 341.   [3] A. Turner, op. cit. pp. 359–60.

There were in the Church

Quoad Sacra ministers amounting to	162
Of whom the number who went out was	71
So that of parish ministers remained	681
While of parish ministers seceded only	289
showing a majority remaining of	392

It thus appears that approximately one-third of the parish ministers of Scotland went out into the Free Church, and it has been calculated that had the vote been by presbyteries 60 would have had a majority for remaining while 18 would have voted to secede.

It had been the dream of the leaders of the Free Church that they might carry a majority vote in the Assembly of 1843, so that they could claim to act in the name of the Church rather than appear as dissenters. But even had the *Quoad Sacra* ministers been permitted to sit and vote, and had a majority been obtained in the Assembly for a breach between Church and State, it would still have been necessary, under the Barrier Act, for the decision to be sent down to the presbyteries; and there the Free Church case would have been lost by three votes to one.

There was hardly a parish in Scotland in which the Free Church was not represented by some determined members, but the number of enthusiasts varied greatly from place to place. Though the Free Church spokesmen constantly harked back to the Covenanting tradition, they got comparatively little support in some of the old Covenanting territory. Three ministers out of twenty joined the Free Church in the Presbytery of Dumfries, four out of eleven in Annan, none out of six in Langholm, one out of thirteen in Lochmaben, one out of nine in Penpont, and three out of fifteen in Kirkcudbright. In contrast to this, in the Synod of Ross five of the eight ministers in the Presbytery of the Chanonry entered the Free Church, ten out of fourteen in the Presbytery of Dingwall, while in the Presbytery of Tain only one of the ten ministers failed to do so. In Sutherland and Caithness similar conditions prevailed. The strength of the Free Church in these parts has been interpreted as an effect of the bitter resentment against the clearances, but it should be noted that this was the countryside where the evangelical movement and the influence of "the Men" — the lay leaders of evangelicalism in the Highlands — were at their strongest. The pages of Donald Sage in *Memor-*

abilia Domeſtica are sufficient to explain why the Free Church
won so strong a footing in his district. Fearn was the one parish
in the Presbytery of Tain where the minister did not join the
Free Church; but the evangelical party had been so strong in his
parish that when he was inducted in 1809 the Presbytery was
able to obtain access to the church only by calling upon the
Sheriff to defend them against the rioting parishioners.[1] The
numbers of members entering the Free Church — more difficult
to ascertain than those of ministers — must be regarded with
some scepticism, but they were very large and appear to cor-
respond roughly with the numbers of ministers for the districts
in question. Writing on the death of Thomas Chalmers in 1847
Lord Cockburn[2] said, "Even the Free Church, the last and greatest
actual change with which his name is connected, was neither his
work nor that of the clergy. It was the work of the people, who,
if every minister had stuck to his benefice, would only in greater
numbers have left the Establishment, which this fact would have
alienated them from the more. He did not send them through
the wilderness, but was only the pillar of fire that lighted them
after they were determined to go."

The statistics of the Disruption offer unexpected problems.
Vague estimates of the strength of the Free Church in its first
years are unreliable. Little groups of adherents were formed
wherever possible: some of these prospered, but others declined.
When allowance has been made, it seems that the Free Church
numbered some seven hundred congregations within a few months
of the Disruption, and even on 18 May 1843, the Day of the Disruption, 687 local associations had already been formed to promote its welfare. By Scottish standards the generosity of the
people of the Free Church was unprecedented. In the course of the
opening Assembly Chalmers said that, as the result of appeals
£232,347 had been given or promised, apart from local needs,
and at the close of the first year £366,719 had been raised
as compared with his estimated £300,000 required.[3] Through
the succeeding years this rate of giving was more or less maintained, and although so much was now needed for the demands of
congregations in Scotland the givings for the overseas work of
the Church also increased. The twelve Indian missionaries, and the

[1] *Fasti*, iii, p. 313.   [2] Lord Cockburn, op. cit. ii, p. 188.
                    [3] R. Buchanan, op. cit. ii, p. 465.

five Jewish missionaries stationed at Jassy, Budapest, Constantinople, and in Syria had all come over to the Free Church, as had the four South African missionaries of the Glasgow Missionary Society.[1] Within ten years the Free Church had grown to about 850 congregations, 760 served by ministers, and the remainder by probationers and laymen. For all these she had been building churches and manses. As though this was not enough, she set out to duplicate the schools run by the Church of Scotland, to provide Normal Schools and Training Colleges for teachers, and Divinity Colleges for her theological students. There was even a moment when she dreamed of providing her own universities. She had carried into her membership thousands of the most active and enthusiastic members of the Church of Scotland. Her achievements were so great that the reader can easily overlook her great weakness in the countryside, especially in the declining areas of the north, her problems in money and manpower in the attempt to establish herself as a second nationwide church, her weakness in work among the poor, and the astonishing recovery of the Church of Scotland, suddenly drained—as it seemed—of the most active of her ministers and members.

The young Free Church met with many hindrances and intense hostility from landed proprietors, but far from suffering from this, she drew popular sympathy from the obstacles put in her way. Many odd places were used for worship. At Garvald in East Lothian, at Bowden in Roxburghshire, Flisk in Fife, Cargill in Perthshire, and many other places, barns were used.[2] At Fort Augustus a maltbarn was used, at Keiss in Caithness a herring store, and at Campbeltown the distillery of John Grant & Co. In many places the Secession Churches offered the use of their buildings freely at hours other than those of their own services, and occasionally disused churches were available, but none of these expedients prevented a multitude of instances of hardship. At Symington in Ayrshire an abandoned public house was taken over, and for nine months the minister preached from an old door placed on two trestles. At Oyne in Aberdeenshire a large cartshed was used "which neither excluded the summer shower nor the winter's snow. It was pitiful during the winter of 1844 to see the old people sitting in this cold place of worship, and the snow drifting about them; and even the young people dismissed from

---

[1] T. Brown, op. cit. p. 813.   [2] Ibid. pp. 212ff.

their Bible classes on account of the cold."[1] At Canonbie the
Duke of Buccleuch, the sole proprietor of the parish, refused a
site for building. When the Free Church pitched a tent on some
moorland, a legal interdict was laid upon them, and from September 1843 until July 1844 the congregation worshipped on the
public highway. As the summer Communion approached the
Duke relented. "His Grace cannot bear," wrote his factor, "that
so holy an office should be desecrated by being unnecessarily
celebrated by the side of the public highway." The congregation
was then permitted to pitch a tent in a gravel pit, which remained
their place of worship until 1851. At Thornhill in Dumfries,
where the Duke similarly refused a site, an old woman gave her
cottage and its garden, and the church was built up to the irregular
outlines of the patch. At Durness in the far north the Duke of
Sutherland refused a site and there, as so often, the minister
preached in a gravel pit, sheltered from the weather by a small
canvas tent. " In it I was preaching on the said Sabbath of February. When about the middle of my sermon, which was in Gaelic,
there came on a snow shower, accompanied by a fierce blast
from the north. The consequence was that the cloth gave way—
it was rent from top to bottom. The people sat still, while a
few of their more active young men, expert at the furling of
sails from their intimacy with the sea, in fewer minutes than I
take to describe it, laid hold of the fluttering mass, and secured it
to the poles with its own cords. I then turned my back to the blast,
and having covered my head with a handkerchief, went on and
finished my discourse. The people crouched a little closer to each
other, and adjusted their cloaks and plaids, and then continued to
listen as if nothing had happened."[2] All over rural Scotland such
things took place. Landlords, out of touch with their people, had
supposed that a spell of difficulty would soon put an end to the
Free Church in their district, but the natural result was intensi-
fied loyalty and obstinacy, and a bitterness which endured for
generations.

Many stories were told of the ways in which sites were obtained.
At Methven a dog had rushed at Lord Lynedoch[3] as he returned
from shooting. He had immediately shot the dog and accidentally
wounded a child sitting at a cottage door. In compensation, he

[1] W. Ewing, *Annals of the Free Church*, ii, p. 40.
[2] T. Brown, op. cit. p. 240.   [3] Ibid. p. 272.

had given a plot of land to the child's father. At the time of the Disruption she was a pauper, but gave this ground for a Free Church. "She considered that in the province of God she had been honoured to do more for the Free Kirk than any one in that quarter, inasmuch as while 'others gae their siller to help to build it, she was shot to get a site for it'."

Country ministers who joined the Free Church suffered much hardship. All had to leave their manses, and there were many instances where landed proprietors made every effort to exclude them from decent housing. At Kilmallie until May 1844 Thomas Davidson had two or three apartments in Annat House, but after that "the only accommodation he could obtain was a hut twelve feet square and six feet high, and so open that it was neccessary by means of blankets and bedcovers to stop out the wind and rain. After this he got two small rooms in a Highland ferry house, and when a friend came to visit him, he was obliged to part with one of these, and his wife and children slept on the floor. Even this accommodation he was compelled to surrender . . . . In March 1847 he and his wife paid a visit to Glasgow, chiefly with a view of obtaining medical advice. Mrs Davidson's case was one in which medical skill was unavailing. She died in Glasgow, on 24th May, 'another victim' says her husband 'to the cruel oppression of the site-refusing proprietors of Scotland'."[1] Davidson himself preached at Kilmallie on the Sunday morning, then walked to Gairlochy to take a service in the afternoon, and then to Laggan between Loch Lochy and Loch Oich, where he took an evening service in an abandoned episcopal church. He stayed at Laggan for the night and on the Monday he walked the 21 miles back home to Kilmallie. In the towns and cities the Free Church ministers escaped these hardships and humiliations. They were rid of many burdens which they had carried in the Church of Scotland, and many of them suffered no financial loss whatever; but here again the country ministers suffered heavily. Their incomes, in many cases were cut to a third or a quarter of what they had been and, in addition, their former independence was lost. City congregations with strong middle-class leadership, might be determined to give their minister their own standard of living and one that would match the stipend of a parish minister, but the poorer country congregations, understandably, found it hard to see why, out of

[1] T. Brown, op. cit. p. 179.

their poverty, they should contribute to give a minister a higher standard of living than their own.

Reading the literature of the Scottish Church in the decade before the Disruption, one would have small cause to suppose that the mind of a large part of the Scottish public was absorbed, not with an ecclesiastical issue, but a political one. The People's Charter,[1] drawn up by the London Working Men's Association, contained six demands: for annual parliaments, universal male suffrage, equal electoral districts, the removal of the property qualification for Members of Parliament, a secret ballot, and the payment of Members. It won widespread support throughout Scotland, especially in the industrial areas. It drew its strength from the reaction to political methods after the collapse of trade unionism and the failure of the Reform Act of 1832 to grant voting rights to the working classes whose agitation had so largely contributed to its being passed. Alone among the clergy of the Church of Scotland, Patrick Brewster,[2] minister of the second charge of Paisley, actively associated himself with the cause. In September 1835 he attended a public dinner in Glasgow for Daniel O' Connell, and next day presided at a meeting in Paisley in his honour. For this he was admonished in the church courts. In May 1841 he was again prosecuted for preaching in the Christian Chartist Church in Great Hamilton Street in Glasgow on 18 April. The offence was augmented by a sermon in Paisley Abbey on 9 January 1842 which resulted in their commanding officer withdrawing the troops from his services. Brewster, who otherwise had sympathies with the Free Church case, was alienated from them by their political conservatism. "The door was quickly barred against me by their illustrious Moderator," he said, "whose opening speech – cheered to the echo – painfully convinced me that I should have less freedom in the FREE Church, than even within the pale of the Establishment." He referred to Chalmers' words, "There will be an utter absence of sympathy on your part with the demagogue and agitator of the day – so that in golden characters may be seen and read of all men this other inscription, that you are no anarchists." Brewster spoke for the Chartists[3]

[1] W. Ferguson, *Scotland; 1689 to the Present*, p. 304.
[2] S. Mechie, *The Church and Scottish Social Development*, pp. 100–18.
[3] W. H. Marwick, "Social Heretics in the Scottish Churches", *SCHS*, XI, pp. 229–31.

and for all the working-class radicals of Scotland when he said of the Poor Law, "The system in Scotland is one of fraud and injustice. It sets at defiance all law and right – all humanity and mercy." But he found no support among his brother clergy. It may be that the Free Church drew support from the Edinburgh Chartists who were dominated by fairly prosperous artisans, but she seems to have had little chance of support from the more Proletarian Chartists of Glasgow and the west. At a meeting of the Abbey congregation of Paisley on 6 June 1843 a resolution was passed which expressed sympathy with the Free Church "in their efforts to obtain for the people the choice of their ministers, and in the noble sacrifices they have recently made" but declaring that "as they have refused to recognise and claim the civil rights of a suffering and oppressed people . . . this congregation cannot unite or co-operate with them". It is evident that outside the industrial areas of Scotland the Free Church had canalized the resentment of the lower classes against the great landed proprietors into the channel of a religious dispute.

"It is perhaps idle to speculate now," wrote Lord Cockburn,[1] "on what might have been done to avert the irrecoverable step." Though he forgot this side of the matter in his sudden respect for the great sacrifices made by the Free Church clergy, there can be little doubt that an element in the Disruption was the intransigence and impatience of the leaders of the Evangelicals. Much might have been obtained had they been prepared to wait. On the other hand, Lord Cockburn was correct in laying the greater share of the blame upon the government. "I consider," he wrote, "it as nearly certain that these claims might have been adjusted, and even without much difficulty, if either the Whig or the Tory Government had interfered *sincerely and intelligently in due time*." But the Government had not been sufficiently interested in Scotland or the Scottish Church to do so. In Disraeli's *Lothair*,[2] written when he was an ex-premier of 66, Monsignore Berwick says, "We sent two of our best men into Scotland some time ago, and they have invented a new Church, called the United Presbyterians. John Knox himself was never more violent, or more mischievous. The United Presbyterians will do the business; they will render Scotland simply impossible to live in; and then, when the crisis arrives, the distracted and despairing millions will find refuge

---

[1] Lord Cockburn, op. cit. ii, p. 34.   [2] Disraeli, *Lothair*, ix.

in the bosom of their only mother." Disraeli's wit covers an ignorance of Scottish Church affairs and a contempt for them such as must have held the minds of Melbourne and Peel.

" The only real difficulty," if one may quote Lord Cockburn[1] again, " was as to the Church's claim of jurisdiction. . . . It is plain to me that the Church of Scotland had the jurisdiction, and that its practical exercise, as proved by immemorial experience, was quite safe. But the decision being otherwise, I do not see how the Government, relishing the decision, could do anything but adopt the law as delivered by the Court. Its error lay in relishing it. . . . And the failure of adjustment brought matters to this point — that Presbytery, as understood by the Church, was inconsistent with the genius of modern law. But this was a point which matters need never have reached. It did not occur till towards the close of the controversy, and if patronage had been timeously settled it would not have occurred at all." Matters had been intolerable for the Church when she was refused the right to adapt her parochial organization to a changed age or to administer her own spiritual discipline to her clergy, so that an establishment which had been created to maintain the Church became an instrument for throttling her.

But the matter goes further back. The Treaty of 1707 has been regarded as the union of the parliaments, but it was an unequal union since even in its years of activity after 1688 Parliament had never meant for Scotsmen what that institution meant for England. It was Parliament that had opposed Charles I in England, but it was the Kirk that had opposed him in Scotland. The central institutions of the Scottish State had always had a certain weakness and it was in the structure of local life that the nation was ordered and controlled. In their appeal to the nation the leaders of the Disruption continually harked back to Scottish history in defence of their actions, and not without cause, for they represented an element which had consistently been found in the country since the Reformation. Scotland had known two periods of post-Reformation Episcopacy, but in several ways these had scarcely interrupted the national tradition which the Stewart kings so resented. "Presbytery,"[2] King James VI was reported to have told the Hampton Court conference, " agreeth with a monarchy

[1] Lord Cockburn, op. cit. ii, p. 36.
[2] J. H. Burton, *History of Scotland*, v, pp. 427–8.

as well as God and the devil." Hard experience had taught him
that the authority of the crown in Scotland was but a limited one.
"I remember how they used the poor lady my mother in Scotland
and me in my minority. My lords the bishops," he said, "if once
you were out, and they in place, I know what would become of
my supremacy. No bishop, no king, as before I said." The First
Book of Discipline[1] had made plain the outlook of his opponents.
"To discipline," it said, "must all the Estates within this realm
be subject, as well the rulers as they that are ruled." And James
had learned from Andrew Melville that the Second[2] Book of
Discipline was not merely doctrinaire when it said, "As the
ministers and others of the ecclesiastical estate are subject to the
magistrate civil, so ought the person of the magistrate be subject
to the kirk spiritually, and in ecclesiastical government. . . . The
civil power is called the power of the sword, and the other the
power of the keys. . . . As ministers are subject to the judgement
and punishment of the magistrate in external things, if they offend:
so ought the magistrates to submit themselves to the discipline
of the kirk, if they transgress in matters of conscience and
religion." While the Stewart kings had twice suppressed[3] the
General Assembly, the central institution of Presbyterianism and
its most dangerous weapon, the local institutions, the kirk sessions
and presbyteries, had continued to function under the two
Episcopates. Later generations have regarded this as a theocracy,
but in contemporary eyes Scottish Presbyterianism in the seventeenth century had been a political movement akin to social
democracy, a revolutionary force opposed to strong central
government. Its spokesmen, John Knox, George Buchanan,
Andrew Melville, and Samuel Rutherford, were reckoned dangerous men. Presbyterianism, King Charles II told Lauderdale, " was
no religion for a gentleman".[4]

And it was this popular revolutionary force which King
William had been determined to unleash in Scotland no more
than was absolutely unavoidable. In some ways he had little
cause to be anxious, for the excesses of the Presbyterians in their

[1] First Book of Discipline, ix, iii.
[2] Second Book of Discipline, i.
[3] The second suppression took place under Cromwell in 1653, but Charles
II and James II never permitted an Assembly.
[4] Gilbert Burnet, *History of His Own Time*, i, p. 116.

time of power had alienated much national support, so that as the laity took their place in a Church nominally controlled by the Covenanting veterans they imposed their own temper on it. Under Carstares the Kirk, once fanatical, became Moderate, as King William had counselled. In 1834, as the fall of the Moderates from power in the Assembly was seen to be at hand, another royal letter, this time drafted by Lord Melbourne,[1] gave similar advice to the Assembly, but this time in vain. " We are satisfied that your proceedings will continue to be characterised by temper and calmness ... and that you will consider the grave and important questions which may be submitted to your decision in that true religious temper which is at once calm and fervent, and which is equally removed from indifference on the one hand and fanaticism on the other." Yet whether the temper of the Church had been moderate or fanatical the essentially democratic character of Presbyterian institutions and influence had never been forgotten or lost.

It was over the claims of the people against patronage that the Disruption took place, and this particular dispute ran back to the Act of Queen Anne in 1712 by which patronage was restored. It was intended, said Bishop Burnet,[2] "to weaken and undermine the establishment" of the Scottish Church. In the words of Lord Macaulay,[3] "The British Legislature violated the Articles of Union, and made a change in the constitution of the Church of Scotland. From that change has flowed almost all the dissent now existing in Scotland. . . . Year after year the General Assembly protested against the violation, but in vain; and from the Act of 1712 undoubtedly flowed every secession and schism that has taken place in the Church of Scotland." There can be no clearer evidence for the weakness of restored Presbyterianism in Scotland at the time than the fact that this Act, and the breach of the Treaty which it involved, was so quietly stomached. As we have seen, with time the annual protest of the Assembly against patronage became little more than a convention, or a sop thrown to the public, and in 1784 it disappeared altogether. Yet resistance to patronage never quite disappeared at popular level, so that from this came the steady leakage of the discontented into the Secession. Had there been a cultural unity within the nation, this might not have taken place, but the delicate balance of heritors and kirk sessions, on which Scottish Presbyterianism functioned, could not work when the mind of the upper classes was at variance with that of the working people. Throughout the eighteenth century the power of the older landed classes had steadily declined, and that of the new commercial and industrial classes had grown. Simultaneously, their minds had come to work on different lines.

The Act of 1712, as Bishop Burnet stated, had restored patronage in order to serve the interests of the Jacobite and Episcopalian gentry, but its original purpose had ceased to be relevant with the death of Queen Anne, the accession of a Hanoverian King to the throne, and the failure of the Rising of 1715; but the Act remained in force with this difference, that it now enabled patrons to nominate ministers with an outlook acceptable to themselves, but little to the liking of their congregations. Had the Scottish Church been partnered by a Scottish Parliament responsive to the national needs, not merely this Act, but all her relationships with the secular power might well have been modified from time to time as circumstances changed; but under the conditions which followed the Union of 1707 there was no hope of readjustment. The structure of the Scottish Church, as it were, became fossilized, tied to the conditions of the opening of the eighteenth century without hope of emendation. For this, the Westminster Confession, which the Church had bound upon her own back, was largely to blame, since it prevented open development of thought within the Church, but it was the remoteness and indifference of the civil power at London which effectively prevented any development of the structure of the Church to meet the requirements of a changing Scotland. She found herself involved in a vain effort to meet the Industrial Revolution with a parochial system little altered since medieval times.

Free Church propaganda so emphasized the dramatic importance of the Disruption that the natural reaction of many Scots is to discount it as a dispute within the Church, a storm in a teacup. There could be no greater error. What divided the Scottish Church in 1843 was an issue linked with the unceasing debate of Christendom on the relationship between the believing community and the secular world in which it is set. Apart from that, any judgment which underestimates the place of the Disruption

in Scottish history has failed to understand that the Church in
Post-Reformation Scotland was more than a purely religious
community. It was so integrated with the national life, so truly
established, that much of the structure of local government
operated through her. Education and social welfare were her
responsibility. Her discipline was a power in the land to be feared
— or respected. What the central government did long affected
the life of the ordinary citizen but little when compared with the
activities of the Kirk. In all these respects, she functioned through
the local community, depending on the intimacy of a life where
each man, up to a point, knew his neighbour. With the coming
of the Industrial Revolution this parochial structure became less
and less able to carry the burdens placed upon it. The shape of
society had been changed. In listening to the economics of Adam
Smith and in her new indifference to social and ethical considerations Scotland had committed herself to a new pattern of common
life uncontrolled by Christian considerations; and she paid the
price for this in an industrial development which devastated her
landscape and her social order in uninhibited exploitation. Even
the wealth which was its object and its sole reward was shared
only by a minority of her people.

With the coming of the nineteenth century most Scotsmen had
ceased to look for a solution of their urgent problems within the
traditional framework, and Chalmers' great effort in Glasgow
always had an element of anachronism within it. In the agitation
for the Reform Act the old Scottish system of local institutions
was tacitly abandoned in favour of a new insistence on the control
of national life by a central representative government. If the old
position of the Scottish clergy, the provision of a teind stipend
and their responsibility only to the courts of the Church, had
given them a highly desirable measure of independence in the
conduct of their duties, the nomination of ministers by men who
accurately reflected the public mind had been, along with the
powers of elders and heritors, a guarantee that the working of the
Church would be, not clerical, but popular. With the coming of
the Disruption in 1843 the old pattern of Scottish life was broken,
or at least a stage was reached in its decay, not merely because it
made sectarianism a factor in every parish, but because it made
inevitable the removal of education and the care of the poor from
the Church of the people and from local control. Of all those

elements in Scottish life which had prevented the assimilation of
the weaker partner to the Union of 1707, and had preserved the
distinctiveness of national life, the Church had been the strongest.
This was no longer so, and only at this point were some of the
results of the Union at last apparent. "In the early 'forties everything changed in Scotland at once," wrote Walter Elliot.[1] "The
distinctively Scottish tradition was broken. There came the Disruption. The Disruption was more than a quarrel about church
government. It was the fall of a régime. The democratic intel-
lectualism which had lasted for so many centuries was challenged
in its own house. It was challenged because it could not with
sufficient swiftness adapt itself to the conditions of the time."
From this came that provincialization of the country which so
strongly marked its life in Victorian times; those features of its
life which constituted "the peculiar institutional inheritance of
Scottish democracy" had been lost.[1]

One of the most significant comments on the Disruption from
a contemporary came from Professor J. F. Ferrier in reply to an
Essay on the Ecclesiastical History of Scotland by the Duke of Argyll.
"The General Assembly," Ferrier wrote, "is not an *ecclesiastical*
but is simply a *national* council." "Is this true?" he asked, and he
replied, "It contains so large an amount of truth . . . as to entitle
it to a very high place among the theories of our perplexing
constitution."[2] Ferrier's argument was that at the Reformation
the government of the Church had not been placed in the hands
of the clergy, for the radical distinction between clergy and laity
had been rejected by the Reformers. This was perfectly true and
there was abundant evidence to confirm it. Two solutions were
therefore open to the country. The clergy of the Reformed
Church might have been incorporated in the Estates of Scotland
in the place of the older Lords Spiritual. This, he says,[3] the clergy
resolutely refused, and on good grounds. Instead it was decided
that a new supreme council should be established for deliberation
on sacred affairs. Accordingly, this took place. "Our General
Assembly of the present day, however much it may have altered
its character, is the second and junior of these Scottish Houses of
Parliament." Seen from another angle, it was no other than the

[1] G. E. Davie, *The Democratic Intellect*, p. 287.
[2] J. F. Ferrier, *Observations on Church and State suggested by the Duke of Argyll's
Essay on the Ecclesiastical History of Scotland*, p. 6.   [3] Ibid. pp. 14–15.

first under a new face and a somewhat different organization. No
other theory, said Ferrier, would account for the extraordinary
power which the General Assembly had wielded. He did not
observe that the active participation of the Lord High Commissioner in the controversial debates of the Assemblies of the first
half of the eighteenth century, as distinct from his mere formal
and ceremonial presence in modern times, was consistent only
with the recognition of the Assembly as a constituent element in
the legislative structure of the nation.

While Ferrier's interpretation of the origins of the Assembly
was not that held by the Free Church and may sound surprising
to modern ears, it has had some support from modern scholarship. "It is certain," says Professor Gordon Donaldson,[1] "that in
some at least of the early Assemblies it is possible to discern the
same three estates which at that time formed the Scottish Parliament." Dr Duncan Shaw[2] points out that when it became only
too clear that there was no possibility of converting the Queen
to the Reformed faith, the Church gave up hope of her furthering
its cause and from this time onwards "it was deemed necessary
to have the Privy Council present to complete the membership
of the Assembly". Only after 1567 did the idealists in its ranks
begin to move away from the original concept of what a General
Assembly was to have been.[3]

On this historical foundation Ferrier argued that the General
Assembly had been entirely justified "in its late resolute resistance
to the decrees of the Court of Session" since "it stands by birth-
right on a level with the highest court in the realm". Similarly
the House of Lords had no judicial function to discharge in reference to the proceedings of the General Assembly any more than
it had to those of the House of Commons.[4] The General Assembly, he said, did not derive its spiritual authority from the
State, but possessed it *as the State*. "However much it may have
altered its character and complexion . . . this Assembly is the
eidolon at least, if not the veritable body of our old Scottish Parliament, deliberating on the affairs of the Church."[5] The error of the
Evangelical Party had been that when the Assembly found that

[1] G. Donaldson, *The Scottish Reformation*, p. 140.
[2] Duncan Shaw, *The General Assemblies of the Church of Scotland, 1560–1600*,
p. 41.   [3] Ibid. p. 47.
[4] J. F. Ferrier, op. cit. p. 21.   [5] Ibid. p. 37.

the Westminster Parliament was quite unwilling to entertain their case, the ministers "gave up their livings without waiting . . . to see whether they could be turned out. We do regard this as a most fatal blunder from a constitutional point of view. . . . They should have clung to their temporalities."[1]

In other words, Ferrier called, if somewhat late in the day, for the Assembly to take its stand on Scottish law and history and to speak for Scotland. But history is not concerned with what might have been. However correct he may have been from an historical point of view, it was no longer practicable for the Assembly to act so. Even had it been possible for her to speak with the backing of the nation, had there been no alienated classes in the industrial slums, no growing Roman Catholic minority, no recovery of the strength of the Scottish Episcopal Church among the landed gentry, no fringe of Seceders clamouring for a breach between Church and State and the ending of the Establishment, the Church was still divided within herself; Moderate and Evangelical had failed to listen to each other; and the Church could not speak with a single voice. And, in addition, Scotland's sense of nationhood has seldom been at a lower ebb.

"Many and heavy are the blows now daily dealt upon the poor Church — the direct result of the late measures of her friends for her protection," Lord Cockburn[2] wrote on 20 November 1843. For three centuries, it was said, and certainly since the Union, the bond between Church and State had been visible to every citizen of Edinburgh in the fact that the Provost and Magistrates had regularly walked in procession in their robes on Sunday mornings from the council chambers to the High Kirk of St Giles to worship, while the Judges of the Court of Session and of the Exchequer walked over in their robes from the court room. On the previous Thursday the Council had decided to do so no longer. "But it was inevitable; and those who produced the Free Church, and thereby doubled our Seceding population, have no right either to complain or to be surprised. Our Town Council of thirty-three has only nine churchmen in it, even our Provost being an Independent. . . . In a few years the weekly spectacle of centuries will be forgotten."

For almost a century and a half the Moderates had controlled the government of the Scottish Church, but by the time of the

[1] J. F. Ferrier, op. cit. p. 23.   [2] Lord Cockburn, op. cit. ii, pp. 55-6.

Disruption the word which King William had commended to the
Assembly of 1690 had become little more than a term of abuse.
"The time may come," Lord Cockburn wrote,[1] "when the reader
of Scottish history may ask what a *Moderate* was. My answer is
that, speaking generally, he was a Tory in politics, and in religion
not in the Scotch sense religious. But his Toryism had very little
purely political in it. It began (speaking only of clergymen) by an
early obsequiousness to an expectant patron, probably as a tutor
in his family, or in that of some of his friends. After obtaining his
living, in which the people were seldom thought of, and never
consulted, he naturally subsided into an admiration of the system
to which he owed his bread, and into a general sympathy with
the opinions and objects of the lairds, and into a fixed horror of
Dissenters and of the Wild, and of all who by popular zeal disturbed the slumber called his life. Thus his Toryism was not that
of direct political principle or party, but a mere passive devotion
to the gentry. But he was not necessarily irreligious. On the
contrary, he might be, and often was, a truly pious man; but he
had nothing of the Solemn League and Covenant about him, and
his clay was perfectly impervious to the deep and fervid spirit
which is the soul of modern religion. He had no personal dislike
to the people, who always found kindness at the manse; but he
had no taste for the people as desirous of either political or
religious advancement. It was this that destroyed them. They
believed that Principal Robertson was the Head of the Church,
and under this belief were prostrate before Toryism, and cold,
cold to all popular independence. In one respect alone most of
them were greatly superior to their Wild brethren. Socially speaking, they were better fellows. They lived more with the gentry,
and more in this world, and were more agreeable companions.
On the whole they were a decently respectable clergy. Their only
misfortune was that the people would not continue submissive
to their rulers, and lukewarm in their religion, and that, except
by being popular, their Church had nothing to stand upon,
neither wealth, nor rank, nor learning, nor power. And so as a
party they have evaporated. The structure which it cost Robertson so much trouble to rear, and his successors to preserve,
founded on no rock, has crumbled into dust."

[1] Ibid, ii, pp. 289–91.

Bibliography

Acts of the General Assembly. Edinburgh 1688–1843.

Acts of the Parliament of Scotland. Records Commission. Edinburgh 1824–75. 12 vols.

Allen, Robert. *The Principle of Non-Subscription to Creeds and Confessions of Faith as exemplified in Irish Presbyterian History*. MS. thesis, The Library, The Queen's University of Belfast.

Aquinas, Thomas. *Summa Contra Gentiles*. New York 1955.

Arnot, Hugo. *Criminal Trials in Scotland*. Edinburgh 1785.

Arnot, Robert Page. *The History of the Scottish Miners from the Earliest Times*. London 1955.

Authorised Standards of the Free Church. Edinburgh 1860.

Bagehot, Walter. *The English Constitution*. London 1878.

Baillie, Donald M. *God Was in Christ*. London 1958.

Ballantyne, John. *A Comparison of Established and Dissenting Churches*. Edinburgh 1830.

Barkley, John M. *A Short History of the Presbyterian Church in Ireland*. Belfast 1960.

Beaton, Donald. "The Marrow of Modern Divinity", *SCHS*, I. Edinburgh 1926.

"The Old Scots Independents", *SCHS*, III. Edinburgh 1929.

Becker, Carl Lotus. *The Heavenly City of the Eighteenth Century Philosophers*. Newhaven 1932.

Beckett, James Camlin. *Protestant Dissent in Ireland, 1687–1780*. London 1948.

Bengel, Johann Albrecht. *Gnomon Novi Testamenti*. London 1862.

Birnie, Arthur. *An Economic History of Europe, 1760–1930*. London 1935.

Blaikie, William G. *The Preachers of Scotland from the sixth to the nineteenth century*. Edinburgh 1888.

Blair, Hugh. *Lectures*. Halifax, Canada 1850.

Sermons. Edinburgh 1777–1801. 5 vols.

Blair, Robert. *The Grave*. London 1823.

Bonar, Andrew A. *Memoir and Remains of R. M. McCheyne*. Edinburgh 1886.

Bonar, James. *A Catalogue of the Library of Adam Smith*. London 1932.

Boston, Thomas. *Memoirs*. London 1908.

Boswell, James. *The Life of Samuel Johnson*. London 1906.

A Tour to the Hebrides. London 1936.

Bronowski, Jacob and Mazlish, Bruce. *The Western Intellectual Tradition*. London 1960.

Brown, Colin. *Philosophy and the Christian Faith*. London 1969.
Brown, Peter Hume. *History of Scotland*. Cambridge 1902. 3 vols.
Brown, Thomas. *Annals of the Disruption*. Edinburgh 1893.
Bruce, Alexander Balmain. *The Humiliation of Christ*. Edinburgh 1881.
Bryce, James. *The Church of Scotland, 1833–1843*. Edinburgh 1850. 2 vols.
Buchanan, Robert. *The Ten Years' Conflict*. Glasgow 1849. 2 vols.
Buckle, H. T. *History of Civilization in England*. London 1873.
Bulloch, James. "Conformists and Nonconformists", *Transactions of the East
    Lothian Antiquarian and Field Naturalists' Society*. VIII. Haddington 1960.
    "Ecclesiastical Intolerance", *History of Berwickshire Naturalists' Club*.
    XXXVI. Berwick 1964.
Burleigh, J. H. S. *A Church History of Scotland*. Oxford 1960.
Burnet, Gilbert. *History of His Own Time*. London 1818.
Burt, Edward. *Letters from the North of Scotland*. London 1759.
Burton, J. Hill. *History of Scotland*. Edinburgh 1897. 8 vols.
Butterfield, Herbert. *The Origins of Modern Science*. London 1949.

Calvin, John. *Institutes of the Christian Religion*.
"Cambuslang and Kilsyth Revivals, 1742, The. A Bibliography", *SCHS*, I.
    Edinburgh 1926.
Campbell, George. *A Dissertation on Miracles*. Edinburgh 1763.
Campbell, John. "The Berean Church", *SCHS*, VI. Edinburgh 1932.
Campbell, J. L. "The Irish Franciscan Mission to Scotland", *Franciscan
    College Annual*. 1952.
Campbell, John McLeod. *Memorials*. London 1877.
    Reminiscences and Reflections. London 1873.
    The Nature of the Atonement. London 1959.
Campbell, Roy Hutcheson. *Carron Company*. Edinburgh 1961.
    Scotland since 1707. Oxford 1965.
Carlile, Warrand. *On the Human Nature of Christ*. London 1831.
    Letter to John Rodman. Paisley 1831.
Carlyle, Alexander. *Autobiography*. London 1910.
Carlyle, Thomas. *Reminiscences*. London 1896.
    Past and Present. London 1896.
    Rectorial Address to the University of Edinburgh. London 1896.
Cater, Jeremy J. "The Making of Principal Robertson", *SHR*, XLIX. Aber-
    deen 1970.
Chalmers, Thomas. *Collected Works*. Glasgow 1838–42. 25 vols.
Chambers, Robert. *Domestic Annals of Scotland*. Edinburgh 1859. 3 vols.
Clark, Sir George. *The Later Stuarts*. Oxford 1955.
Clark, Ian D. "The Leslie Controversy", *SCHS*, XIV. Edinburgh 1962.
Cleland, James. *Annals of Glasgow*. Glasgow 1816. 2 vols.
Clement, A. G. and Robertson, R. H. S. *Scotland's Scientific Heritage*. Edin-
    burgh 1961.
Clerk of Penicuik, Sir John. *Memorials*. SHS, Edinburgh 1892.
Cobbett, William. *Tour in Scotland*. London 1833.
Cockburn, Lord. *Journal*. Edinburgh 1874. 2 vols.
    Memorials of His Time. Edinburgh 1856.

Cockburn of Ormiston, John. *Letters to His Gardener*. SHS, Edinburgh 1904.
Cole, Margaret. *Robert Owen of New Lanark*. London 1953.
Cooper, James. *Confessions of Faith and Formulas*. Glasgow 1907.
Craven, J. B. *Journals of Bishop Forbes*. London 1886.
Cunningham, John. *The Church History of Scotland*. Edinburgh 1882. 2 vols.

Daiches, David. *The Paradox of Scottish Culture*. London 1964.
Dampier, W. C. *History of Science*. Cambridge 1966.
Darragh, James. "The Catholic Population in Scotland", *Innes Review*, IV. Glasgow 1953.
Davie, G. E. *The Democratic Intellect*. Edinburgh 1961.
Dillenberger, John. *Protestant Thought and Natural Science*. London 1961.
Disraeli, Benjamin. *Lothair*. London 1927.
Disruption Worthies: a Memorial of 1843, ed. James A. Wylie. Edinburgh, n.d.
Donaldson, Gordon. *Scotland: Church and Nation through Sixteen Centuries*. London 1960.
   The Scottish Reformation. Cambridge 1960.
Dowden, John. *The Scottish Communion Office, 1764*. Oxford 1922.
Drummond, A. L. "Witherspoon of Gifford", *SCHS*, XII. Edinburgh 1958.
   Edward Irving and His Circle. London 1937.
   The Kirk and the Continent. Edinburgh 1956.
Dundee Textile Industry. SHS, Edinburgh 1969.
Dunlop, A. Ian. *William Carstares and the Kirk by Law Established*. Edinburgh 1967.
Durham, James. *Treatise Concerning Scandal*. Glasgow 1740.

Edgar, Andrew. *Old Church Life in Scotland*. Paisley 1886.
   "The Discipline of the Church of Scotland", in Robert H. Story, *The Church of Scotland*, V. London 1890.
Erskine, Ralph. *Works*. Glasgow 1764.
Erskine, Thomas. *Letters*, ed. W. Hanna. Edinburgh 1877–8 2 vols.
   The Spiritual Order. Edinburgh 1871.
   The Brazen Serpent. Edinburgh 1830.
   Internal Evidence for the Truth of Revealed Religion. Edinburgh 1820.
Escott, Harry. *A History of Scottish Congregationalism*. Glasgow 1960.
Ewing, W. *Annals of the Free Church*. Edinburgh 1941. 2 vols.

Fawcett, Arthur. *The Cambuslang Revival. The Scottish Evangelical Revival of the Eighteenth Century*. London 1971.
Ferguson, Adam. *Principles of Moral and Political Science*. Edinburgh 1792.
Ferguson, Thomas. *The Dawn of Scottish Social Welfare*. London 1948.
Ferguson, William. *Scotland: 1689 to the Present*. Edinburgh 1968.
   "Problems of the Established Church in the West Highlands", *SCHS*, XVII. Edinburgh 1972.
Ferrier, J. F. *Observations on Church and State suggested by the Duke of Argyll's Essay*. Edinburgh 1849.
Findlater, Thomas. MS. Library Catalogue, Newlands Kirk Session.
Fontenelle, Bernard de. *The Plurality of Worlds*. London 1695.

Foskett, R. "The Episcopate of Daniel Sandford, 1806–1830", *SCHS*, xv. Edinburgh 1966.
Foster, W. R. *Bishop and Presbytery, 1661–1688*. London 1958.
Franks, R. S. *The Work of Christ*. London 1962.

Galt, John. *Annals of the Parish*. Edinburgh 1895.
Gatrell, V. A. C. *A New View of Society*.
Gibbon, Edward. *Autobiography*. Everyman edition, London 1939.
Gilby, Thomas. *St Thomas Aquinas: Theological Texts*. Oxford 1855.
Goldie, F. *Short History of the Episcopal Church in Scotland*. London 1951.
Graham, Henry Grey. *The Social Life of Scotland in the Eighteenth Century*. London 1906.
Scottish Men of Letters in the Eighteenth Century. London 1901.
Graham, J. E. *The Poor Law of Scotland Previous to 1845*. Cupar and St Andrews 1924.
Gray, Malcolm. *The Highland Economy*. Edinburgh 1957.
Grub, George. *Ecclesiastical History of Scotland*. Edinburgh 1861. 4 vols.
Guthrie, D. K. and Guthrie. C. J. *Autobiography and Memoir of Thomas Guthrie, D.D.* London 1877.

Hamilton, Henry. *The Economic Evolution of Scotland*. London 1933.
The Industrial Revolution in Scotland. London 1966.
Economic History of Scotland in the Eighteenth Century. Oxford 1963.
Hamilton, John. *Remonstrance to the Members of the Legislature*. Edinburgh 1841.
Hampson, Norman. *The Enlightenment*. London 1968.
Handley, James E. *The Irish in Scotland*. Glasgow 1964.
Hanna, William. *Memoirs of the Life and Writings of Thomas Chalmers*. Edinburgh 1849–52.
Harrison, J. F. C. *Robert Owen and the Owenites in Britain and America*. London 1969.
Hay, George. *The Architecture of Scottish Post-Reformation Churches, 1560–1843*. Oxford 1957.
Hazard, Paul. *European Thought in the Eighteenth Century*. London 1965.
Henderson, H. F. *Erskine of Linlathen*. Edinburgh 1899.
Hewat, Elizabeth G. K. *Vision and Achievement, 1796–1956*. London 1956.
Hogg, James. *The Private Memoirs and Confessions of a Justified Sinner*, ed. John Garey. London 1969.
Hume, David. *Works*. Edinburgh 1825. 4 vols.
History of England. London 1802.
Hutcheson, Francis. *Inquiry Concerning Moral Good and Evil*. London 1726.
Hutchison, M. *The History of the Reformed Presbyterian Church in Scotland, 1680–1876*. Paisley 1893.

Inglis, John. *A Vindication of Ecclesiastical Establishments*. Edinburgh 1833.
Irving, Edward. *Collected Works*. London 1864–5. 5 vols.

Jenyns, Soame. *A View of the Internal Evidence of the Christian Religion*. London 1776.

Kennedy, John. *Presbyterian Authority and Discipline*. Edinburgh 1960.
Kennedy, John. *The Days of the Fathers in Ross-shire*. Inverness 1927.
Kerr, T. Angus. "Life and Ministry of the Rev. Hugh Cunningham of Tranent", *SCHS*, xv. Edinburgh 1966.
Killen, W. D. *Ecclesiastical History of Ireland*. London 1875.
Kyd, J. G. *Scottish Population Statistics*. SHS, Edinburgh 1952.

Lang, Sir Peter R. Scott. *Duncan Dewar's Accounts*. Glasgow 1926.
Latimer, W. T. *History of the Irish Presbyterians*. Belfast 1893.
Latourette, K. S. *History of the Expansion of Christianity*. London 1938–1945. 7 vols.
Lehmann, W. C. *Adam Ferguson and the Beginnings of Modern Sociology*. New York 1930.
Leishman, James Fleming. *Matthew Leishman of Govan*. Paisley 1921.
Lewis, George. *Scotland, a Half Educated Nation*. Dundee 1834.
Lindsay, Ian G. *The Scottish Parish Church*. Edinburgh 1960.
Lockhart, J. G. *Life of Sir Walter Scott*. Edinburgh 1845.
Peter's Letters to His Kinsfolk. Edinburgh 1819. 3 vols.
Some Passages in the Life of Mr Adam Blair. Edinburgh 1963.

Macaulay, Lord. *History of England*. Everyman edition. London 1953. 4 vols.
Speeches.
MacInnes, John. *The Evangelical Movement in the Highlands of Scotland, 1688–1800*. Edinburgh 1960.
"Baptism in the Highlands", *SCHS*, xiii. Edinburgh 1959.
MacIntyre, John. "John McLeod Campbell; Heretic and Saint", *SCHS*, xiv. Edinburgh 1963.
McKelvie, William. *Annals and Statistics of the United Presbyterian Church*. Edinburgh 1873.
MacKenzie, Henry. *Anecdotes and Egotisms*. Edinburgh 1808.
MacKenzie, Robert. *John Brown of Haddington*. London 1918.
McKerrow, John. *History of the Secession Church*. Edinburgh 1848.
Mackintosh, H. R. *The Person of Jesus Christ*. Edinburgh 1937.
Mackintosh, John. *The History of Civilization in Scotland*. Paisley 1892–6. 4 vols.
MacLean, Donald. *The Counter-Reformation in Scotland: 1560-1930*. London 1931.
MacLeod, Donald. *Memoir of Norman MacLeod*. London 1882.
McLeod, John. *Scottish Theology*. Edinburgh 1943.
MacLeod, Norman. *Reminiscences of a Highland Parish*. London 1891.
MacMillan, W. "The Baptismal Register of John MacMillan", *SCHS*, x. Edinburgh 1950.
McNair, Alexander. *Scots Theology in the Eighteenth Century*. London 1928.
McNeill, John T. *History and Character of Calvinism*. New York 1967.
MacWhirter, A. "Unitarianism in Scotland", *SCHS*, xiii. Edinburgh 1959.
Major, John. *A History of Greater Britain*. SHS, Edinburgh 1892.
Marwick, W. A. "Social Heretics in the Scottish Churches", *SCHS*, xi. Edinburgh 1955.

Mathieson, W. Law. *The Awakening of Scotland*. Glasgow 1910.
  Church and Reform in Scotland, 1797–1843. Glasgow 1916.
Maxwell, Thomas. "William III and the Scots Presbyterians", *SCHS*, xv. Edinburgh 1966.
  "Presbyterian and Episcopalian in 1688", *SCHS*, xiii. Edinburgh 1959.
Mechie, Stewart. *The Church and Scottish Social Development, 1780–1870*. Oxford 1960.
Miller, Hugh. *My Schools and Schoolmasters*. London 1860.
Monymusk Papers. SHS, Edinburgh 1945.
Morison, James. *The Extent of the Propitiation*. Glasgow 1841.
Morren, Nathaniel. *Annals of the General Assembly of the Church of Scotland*. Edinburgh 1838–40. 2 vols.

Neill, Stephen. *A History of Christian Missions*. London 1964. (*The Pelican History of the Church*, vi.)
Niebuhr, H. Richard. *The Social Sources of Denominationalism*. New York 1960.

Owen, Robert. *A New View of Society and Report to the County of Lanark*, ed. V. A. C. Catrell. London 1970.
  Life of Robert Owen. London 1971.

Perry, W. *The Scottish Prayer Book; Its Value and History*. London 1918.
Pope, Alexander. *Collected Poems*.
Primrose, J. B. *The Mother Anti-Burgher Church of Glasgow*. Glasgow 1896.

Rae, John. *Life of Adam Smith*. New York 1965.
Reid, H. M. B. *A Cameronian Apostle, being some account of John Macmillan of Balmaghie*. Paisley 1896.
  The Divinity Professors in the University of Glasgow. Glasgow 1923.
Riley, James F. *The Hammer and the Anvil*. Clapham, Yorks 1954.
Royal Commission on Ancient Monuments. *Report on the City of Edinburgh*. Edinburgh 1951.
Russell, Bertrand. *History of Western Philosophy*. London 1965.

Sage, Donald. *Memorabilia Domestica*. Edinburgh 1889.
Saunders, Laurance J. *Scottish Democracy, 1815–1840*. Edinburgh 1950.
Schmitz, Robert Morell. *Hugh Blair*. New York 1948.
Scott, Hew. *Fasti Ecclesiae Scoticanae*. 1st edition, Edinburgh 1866–71. 3 vols.
Sefton, H. R. "Robert Wallace; An Early Moderate", *SCHS*, xvi. Edinburgh 1969.
  The Early Moderates. MS. Ph.D. thesis, Glasgow University Library.
Shaw, Duncan. *The General Assemblies of the Church of Scotland, 1560–1600*. Edinburgh 1963.
Sheriff, Robert. *Diary*.
Small, Robert. *Congregations of the United Presbyterian Church from 1733 to 1900*. Edinburgh 1904. 2 vols.
Smith, Adam. *The Wealth of Nations*. Edinburgh 1838.
  Theory of Moral Sentiments. Glasgow 1809.

Smout, T. C. *A History of the Scottish People, 1560–1830*. London 1969.

Somerville, Alexander. *Autobiography of a Working Man*. London 1951.

Steven, W. *History of the High School of Edinburgh*. Edinburgh 1849.

Stewart, David. *The Seceders in Ireland*. Belfast 1950.

Story, R. H. *The Church of Scotland*. London 1890. 5 vols.

Struthers, Gavin. *The History of the Rise, Progress and Principles of the Relief Church*. Edinburgh 1848.

Tawnay, R. H. *Religion and the Rise of Capitalism*. London 1938.

Thomson, Andrew. *The Origin of the Secession Church*. Edinburgh 1848.

Thomson, James. *Poetical Works*, ed. G. Gilfillan, London 1853.

Turnbull, George. Diary of, SHS, i, Edinburgh 1893.

Turner, Alexander. *The Scottish Secession of 1843*. Edinburgh 1846.

Ulster, Records of the General Synod of. Belfast 1825.

Walker, William. *John Skinner*. Aberdeen 1887.

Warrick, John. *The Moderators of the Church of Scotland from 1690–1740*. Edinburgh 1913.

Watson, J. Steven. *The Reign of George III*. Oxford 1960.

Watt, Hugh. *Thomas Chalmers and the Disruption*. London 1943.

"Rax Me That Bible", *SCHS*, x. Edinburgh 1950.

"Robert Walker of the High Church", *SCHS*, xii. Edinburgh 1958.

"Thomas Gillespie", *SCHS*, xv. Edinburgh 1966.

Weber, Max. *The Protestant Ethic and the Spirit of Capitalism*. London 1968.

Whiteford, David H. "Jacobitism as a Factor in Presbyterian and Episcopalian Relationships", *SCHS*, xvi. Edinburgh 1969.

Willey, Basil. *The Eighteenth Century Background*. London 1957.

Wilson, W. *Memorials of R. S. Candlish*. Edinburgh 1880.

Witherow, T. *Historical and Literary Memorials of Presbyterianism in Ireland*. London 1879.

Wodrow, Robert. *Correspondence*. Edinburgh 1842–43. 3 vols.

The History of the Sufferings of the Church of Scotland. Glasgow 1828–30. 4 vols.

Analecta. Edinburgh 1842–43. 4 vols.

Woodside, David. *The Soul of a Scottish Church*. Edinburgh. 1918.

Woodward, E. L. *The Age of Reform*. Oxford 1958.

Index

Leechman, Principal, 22, 57
Leibniz, 88, 122, 159
Leishman, Matthew, 161, 246
Lennoxtown, 140
Leslie, John, 154–6, 212, 216
Leyden, 166–7
Lindsay, Dugald, 8
Lining, Thomas, 25
Linlithgow, 83
Liturgy, 17–18, 27–9, 37, 49, 55, 61, 72
Lochgoilhead 8
Locke, John, 31
Lockhart, J. G., 157, 212, 216
Logan, George, 33
Logie-Almond, 190
Loth, 13, 86
Lundie, Archibald, 6
Lyell, Sir Charles, 167

Macaulay, Lord, 1, 183
McCheyne, R. M., 215
MacConnell, James, 106
McCrie, Thomas, 151, 213, 220
McCulloch, William, 54–7
Macdonald, James and George, 199
MacDonald, Dr John, 244
McGill, Dr William, 106–7, 204
McKay, General, 2 4
Mackintosh, H. R., 205, 207
Mackintosh, John, 101
McKnight, Thomas, 154, 155
McLaine, Archibald, 8
MacLaurin, Colin, 154
MacLean, Donald, 137
MacLean, Hugh Baillie, 202–3
MacMillan, John, 26, 43
MacPherson, James, 101
Mair, Thomas, 42, 62
Major, John, 9
Malcolm, John, 111
Mallet, David, 125
Manses, 74–5
Mar, Earl of, 114
Marischal College, 99
Marischal, Earl of, 114
Marnoch, 237–8
Marrow of Modern Divinity, 35–9, 45, 215
Marshall, Andrew, 221
Mathieson, W. L., 226
Maule, Fox, 243
Maurice, F. D., 208

Maxton, 181
Maybole, 214
Mearns, Dr, 227
Melbourne, Lord, 239, 259
Melville, Andrew, 258
Methven, 253
Millenarianism, 201
Miller, Hugh, 145, 166
Miracles, 92, 95, 99–100
Mitchell, Donald, 182–3
Mitchell, John, 115
Moderates, 10, 21–3, 37–40, 50, 56–59, 62–81, 84, 98, 103–8, 154–156, 163, 198, 212, 221–6, 228, 259–265
Moderator, 1, 16, 20, 22, 38, 41–2, 58, 79, 214, 223, 237, 238, 248, 255
Moffat, Robert, 182
Moir, James, 106
Moncrieff, Sir Henry, 60, 152, 160, 211–12, 225
Moncrieff, Lord, 225, 227, 230
Monro, John, 8
Monteith, James, 142
Montgomery, Henry, 193
Monymusk, 115
Morison, James, 180, 219
Morison, Robert, 219
Mortlach, 134
Muir, Thomas, 148
Monro, General Robert, 3

Napier, Robert, 131
Nature of the Atonement, 31, 88, 90, 169
Neilson, J. B., 131
New Lanark, 178
New Machar, 40
Newton, Sir Isaac, 31, 88, 90, 169
Nonsubscribing Presbyterians, 34

Old Monkland, 229
Oldhamstocks, 6
Orbiston, 179
Ormiston, 74
Orwell, 62
Owen, Robert, 133, 177, 179
Oxford, 121, 189
Oyne, 252

Paip, Hector, 86
Paisley, 13, 80, 143, 255
Paley, William, 171